CIM
STUDY TEXT

Diploma

Integrated Marketing Communications

In this June 2003 edition

- Updated to reflect latest exams
- Updated Marketing at Work examples

BPP Professional Education
June 2003

First edition 1999
Fifth edition 2003

ISBN 0 7517 1110 1 (previous edition 0 7517 4133 7)

British Library Cataloguing-in-Publication Data
A catalogue record for this book
is available from the British Library

Published by

BPP Professional Education
Aldine House, Aldine Place
London W12 8AW

www.bpp.com

Printed in Great Britain by W M Print
45-47 Frederick Street
Walsall, West Midlands
WS2 9NE

We are grateful to the Chartered Institute of Marketing for permission to reproduce in this text the syllabus, tutor's guidance notes and past examination questions.

Page

BPP PROFESSIONAL EDUCATION

How to use this study text

Aims of this Study Text

To provide you with the knowledge and understanding, skills and applied techniques required for passing the exam

The Study Text has been written around the new CIM Syllabus and the CIM's Tutor's Guidance notes (reproduced below).

- It is **comprehensive**. We do not omit sections of the syllabus as the examiner is liable to examine any angle of any part of the syllabus - and you do not want to be left high and dry.

- It is **on-target** - we do not include any material which is not examinable. You can therefore rely on the BPP Study Text as the stand-alone source of all your information for the exam, without worrying that any of the material is irrelevant.

To allow you to study in the way that best suits your learning style and the time you have available, by following your personal Study Plan (see below)

You may be studying at home on your own until the date of the exam, or you may be attending a full-time course. You may like to (and have time to) read every word, or you may prefer to (or only have time to) skim-read and devote the remainder of your time to question practice. Wherever you fall in the spectrum, you will find the BPP Study Text meets your needs in designing and following your personal Study Plan.

To tie in with the other components of the BPP Effective Study Package to ensure you have the best possible chance of passing the exam

Recommended period of use	Elements of BPP Effective Study Package
3 - 12 months before exam	**Study Text** Acquisition of knowledge, understanding, skills and applied techniques
1-6 months before exam	**Practice and Revision Kit (9/2003)** Tutorial questions and helpful checklists of the key points lead you into each area. There are then numerous examination questions to try, graded by topic area along with realistic suggested solutions prepared by marketing professionals in the light of the Examiner's Reports. The September 2003 edition will include the December 2002 and June 2003 papers.
1 –6 months before exam	**Success Tapes** Audio cassettes covering the vital elements of your syllabus in less than 90 minutes per subject. Each tape also contains exam hints to help you fine tune your strategy.

Settling down to study

By this stage in your career you may be a very experienced learner and taker of exams. But have you ever thought about *how* you learn? Let's have a quick look at the key elements required for effective learning. You can then identify your learning style and go on to design your own approach to how you are going to study this text - your personal Study Plan.

Key element of learning	Using the BPP Study Text
Motivation	You can rely on the comprehensiveness and technical quality of BPP. You've chosen the right Study Text - so you're in pole position to pass your exam!
Clear objectives and standards	Do you want to be a prizewinner or simply achieve a moderate pass? Decide.
Feedback	Follow through the examples in this text and do the Action Programme and the Quick quizzes. Evaluate your efforts critically - how are you doing?
Study Plan	You need to be honest about your progress to yourself - do not be over-confident, but don't be negative either. Make your Study Plan (see below) and try to stick to it. Focus on the short-term objectives — completing two chapters a night, say - but beware of losing sight of your study objectives
Practice	Use the Quick quizzes and Chapter roundups to refresh your memory regularly after you have completed your initial study of each chapter

These introductory pages let you see exactly what you are up against. However you study, you should:

■ **read through the syllabus and guidance notes** - this will help you to identify areas you have already covered, perhaps at a lower level of detail, and areas that are totally new to you

■ **study the examination paper section**, where we show you the format of the exam (how many and what kind of questions and so on)

Key study steps

The following steps are, in our experience, the ideal way to study for professional exams. You can of course adapt it for your particular learning style (see below).

Tackle the chapters in the order you find them in the Study Text. Taking into account your individual learning style, follow these key study steps for each chapter.

Key study steps	Activity
Step 1 *Chapter topic list*	Study the list. Each numbered topic denotes a **numbered section** in the chapter.
Step 2 *Setting the scene*	Read it through. It is designed to show you **why the topics in the chapter need to be studied** - how they lead on from previous topics, and how they lead into subsequent ones.
Step 3 *Explanations*	Proceed **methodically** through the chapter, reading each section thoroughly and making sure you understand.
Step 4 *Key concepts*	**Key concepts** can often earn you **easy marks** if you state them clearly and correctly in an appropriate exam.
Step 5 *Exam tips*	These give you a good idea of how the examiner tends to examine certain topics – pinpointing **easy marks** and highlighting **pitfalls**.
Step 6 *Note taking*	Take **brief notes** if you wish, avoiding the temptation to copy out too much.
Step 7 *Marketing at Work*	Study each one, and try if you can to add flesh to them from your **own experience** - they are designed to show how the topics you are studying come alive (and often come unstuck) in the **real world**.
Step 8 *Action Programme*	Make a very good attempt at each one in each chapter. These are designed to put your **knowledge into practice** in much the same way as you will be required to do in the exam. Check the answer at the end of the chapter in the **Action Programme review**, and make sure you understand the reasons why yours may be different.
Step 9 *Chapter roundup*	Check through it very carefully, to make sure you have grasped the **major points** it is highlighting.
Step 10 *Quick quiz*	When you are happy that you have covered the chapter, use the **Quick quiz** to check your recall of the topics covered. The answers are in the paragraphs in the chapter that we refer you to.
Step 11 *Illustrative questions*	Either at this point, or later when you are thinking about revising, make a full attempt at the **illustrative questions**. You can find these at the end of the Study Text, along with the **Answers** so you can see how you did.

Developing your personal Study Plan

Preparing a Study Plan (and sticking closely to it) is one of the key elements in learning success.

First you need to be aware of your style of learning. There are four typical learning styles. Consider yourself in the light of the following descriptions. and work out which you fit most closely. You can then plan to follow the key study steps in the sequence suggested.

Learning styles	Characteristics	Sequence of key study steps in the BPP Study Text
Theorist	Seeks to understand principles before applying them in practice	1, 2, 3, 7, 4, 5, 8, 9, 10, 11 (6 continuous)
Reflector	Seeks to observe phenomena, thinks about them and then chooses to act	
Activist	Prefers to deal with practical, active problems; does not have much patience with theory	1, 2, 8 (read through), 7, 4, 5, 9, 3, 8 (full attempt), 10, 11 (6 continuous)
Pragmatist	Prefers to study only if a direct link to practical problems can be seen; not interested in theory for its own sake	8 (read through), 2, 4, 5, 7, 9, 1, 3, 8 (full attempt), 10, 11 (6 continuous)

Next you should complete the following checklist.

Am I motivated?   (a)

Do I have an objective and a standard that I want to achieve?   (b)

Am I a theorist, a reflector, an activist or a pragmatist?   (c)

- How much time do I have available per week, given: (d)
- the standard I have set myself
- the time I need to set aside later for work on the Practice and Revision Kit and Passcards
- the other exam(s) I am sitting, and (of course)
- practical matters such as work, travel, exercise, sleep and social life?

Now:

- take the time you have available per week for this Study Text (d), and multiply it by the number of weeks available to give (e).   (e)
- divide (e) by the number of chapters to give (f)   (f)
- set about studying each chapter in the time represented by (f), following the key study steps in the order suggested by your particular learning style.

This is your personal **Study Plan**.

Short of time?

Whatever your objectives, standards or style, you may find you simply do not have the time available to follow all the key study steps for each chapter, however you adapt them for your particular learning style. If this is the case, follow the Skim Study technique below (the icons in the Study Text will help you to do this).

Skim Study technique

Study the chapters in the order you find them in the Study Text. For each chapter, follow the key study steps 1-2, and then skim-read through step 3. Jump to step 9, and then go back to steps 4-5. Follow through step 7, and prepare outline Answers to the Action Programme (step 8). Try the Quick quiz (step 10), following up any items you can't answer, then do a plan for the Examination question (step 11), comparing it against our answers. You should probably still follow step 6 (note-taking), although you may decide simply to rely on the BPP Passcards for this.

Moving on...

However you study, when you are ready to embark on the practice and revision phase of the BPP Effective Study Package, you should still refer back to this Study Text:

■   as a source of **reference** (you should find the list of key concepts and the index particularly helpful for this)

■   as a **refresher** (the Chapter roundups and Quick quizzes help you here).

A note on pronouns

On occasions in this Study Text, 'he' is used for 'he or she', 'him' for 'him or her' and so forth. Whilst we try to avoid this practice it is sometimes necessary for reasons of style. No prejudice or stereotyping according to sex is intended or assumed.

Syllabus

Aims and objectives

■ To develop students understanding of the formulation and implementation of integrated marketing communication plans and associated activities

■ To enable students to appreciate and manage marketing communications within a variety of different contexts

■ To encourage students to recognise, appreciate and contribute to the totality of an organisation's system of communications with both internal and external audiences

■ To enable students to be aware of the processes, issues and vocabulary associated with integrated marketing communications in order that they can make an effective contribution within their working environment.

Learning outcomes

Students will be able to:

■ Determine the context in which marketing (and corporate) communications are to be implemented in order to improve effectiveness and efficiency, understand the key strategic communication issues arising from the contextual analysis and prepare (integrated) marketing communications plans

■ Determine promotional objectives, explain positioning and develop perceptual maps, and suggest ways in which offerings can be positioned in different markets

■ Formulate marketing communications strategies with particular regard to consumers, business-to-business markets, members of the marketing channel and wider stakeholder audiences such as employees, financial markets, environmental groups, competitors and local communities

■ Determine specific communication activities based upon knowledge of the key characteristics of the target audience. In particular, they will be able to suggest how knowledge of perception and attitude, levels of perceived risk and involvement can impact upon marketing and corporate communications

■ Select, integrate and justify appropriate promotional mixes to meet the needs of the marketing communication strategies

■ Determine appropriate levels of marketing communications expenditure/appropriation

■ Evaluate a variety of promotional campaigns drawn from different sectors

■ Be aware of the impact and contribution technology makes to marketing communications. Be appreciative and sensitive to issues associated with cross-border marketing communications

■ Advise on the impact corporate communications can have on both internal and external audiences and their role in the development of integrated marketing communications

Strategic marketing communications (20%)

1.1	A definition and appreciation of the scope and dimensions of marketing and corporate communications.
1.2	A contextual analysis understanding and justification for marketing and corporate communication strategies.
1.3	The strategic significance and impact of integrated marketing communications.
1.4	Identify key strategic communication issues that might influence an organisation's marketing communications.
1.5	The appreciation and recognition of the importance of ethical and technological influences on promotional activities and an awareness of the social responsibilities organisations have towards the way they communicate with their target audience.

Developing a theoretical understanding of marketing communications (20%)

2.1	Understanding the key drivers associated with information processing and buyer decision making processes.
2.2	Communication issues for internal and external audiences.
2.3	The role of personal influences on the communication process.

Managing the marketing communications process (40%)

3.1	The determination and appreciation of the prevailing and future contextual conditions as a means of deriving and developing promotional strategies and plans.
3.2	The target marketing process as a means of identifying significant promotional opportunities.
3.3	Determining promotional objectives and selecting positioning opportunities.
3.4	Identify, select and formulate promotional strategies, ensuring reference is made to: (i) push, pull and profile strategies (ii) any existing or proposed branding strategies (iii) the Internet and e-commerce activities relating to both consumer-to-business and business-to-business markets.
3.5	Selecting appropriate promotional mixes.
3.6	Determining message styles and key media goals.
3.7	Deciding upon the level and allocation of the promotional spend.
3.8	Managing internal and external resources necessary for successful promotional activities.
3.9	Managing and developing product and corporate brands.
3.10	Evaluating the outcomes of promotional activities.

Evaluation of different types of marketing communication campaigns (10%)

4.1	Knowledge and understanding of different campaigns from different context (including FMCG, business to business, services and public sectors, and not for profit organisations).
4.2	Consideration of the competitive conditions, available resources, stage in the product life cycle and any political, economic, social or technological factors that might be identified as influencing the development of a campaign.

Cross border marketing communications (10%)

5.1	Cultural, social and media influences.
5.2	Organisational type and communication approaches.
5.3	The adaptation/standardisation debate.
5.4	Agency structure and support

Note: The words 'promotional' and 'marketing communications' are used interchangeably.

Tutor's guidance notes

Below we summarise extracts from guidance notes issued to tutors. Here are some salient comments.

- The development of integrated marketing communications is the 'central pivot' of the paper. Students are expected to understand the linkages between each part.

- Students should appreciate the needs of a variety of stakeholders: 'co-ordination of the promotional tools alone is insufficient'. 'Integration refers to the totality of an organisation's communications. Therefore management of internal as well as external marketing communications is an essential part of the Unit'.

- 'An understanding of the overall context of the communication involves analysing a range of elements – delivered in the marketing plan, the needs of internal and external stakeholders.

- Although there is no single best teaching approach. Teaching can be focused on three areas.

  - Understanding the relevant conceptual issues and frameworks associated with marketing communications.

  - Analysing the contextual elements associated with marketing communications.

  - Developing a response to this analysis in the form of an integrated marketing communications plan.

- Focus on consumer markets remains important but more attention must be given to marketing communications within the marketing channels.

Following the launch of the revised Integrated Marketing Communications (IMC) syllabus in September 1999 and the examination in December 2000, a review of the syllabus was undertaken.

- The increasing influence of the Internet and related interactive communication facilities needs greater prominence in this syllabus. The strategic role of the Internet in terms of both business-to-consumer and business-to-business communications needs to be a clear part of the syllabus.

- Organisations have an increasing number of opportunities to communicate with their target audiences, partly due to the power of information technology. Consumers are becoming more discerning and vocal about the type and content of the communications they receive. There is also concern about the volume and accuracy of the information organisations hold about their customers. Therefore, issues concerning social responsibility as related to marketing communication activities need to be explicitly addressed in the syllabus.

- The syllabus review shows that while branding issues are represented in the syllabus they are subsumed within 3.4 'Identify, select and formulate promotional strategies' and 3.9 'Managing and developing product and corporate brands'. Branding is a major communication strategy at both the product and the corporate levels. It is necessary therefore to identify branding as a separate topic within the syllabus.

- Finally, examination performance indicates quite strongly that not all students understand the strategic issues associated with marketing communications. Therefore, the syllabus will be revised to make the identification of strategic issues more explicit.

List of websites

Integrated Marketing Communications Strategy – Syllabus 2000/2001 – CIM Tutor Manual

Websources

Syllabus section	Web address	Description
Strategic Marketing Communications	www.keynote.co.uk	Access to circulation data for UK newspapers and magazines provided by ABC (site registration required)
Developing a theoretical understanding of marketing communications	www.marcommwise.com	Useful articles on all aspects of marketing communications
	www.facetime.com	Good example of a site which overcomes the impersonal nature of the Internet by allowing the establishment of real time links with a customer service representative. Try the free demonstration!
Managing the marketing communications process	www.hotcoupons.com	Site visitors can key in their postcode to receive local promotions, and advertisers can post their offers on the site using a specially designed software package.
	www.nielsen-netratings.com	Details the current levels of banner advertising activity, including the creative content of the ten most popular banners each week
	www.doubleclick.net	DoubleClick offers advertisers the ability to target their advertisement on the web through sourcing of specific interest groups, ad display only at certain times of the day, or at particular geographic locations, or on certain types of hardware
Evaluating marketing communications campaigns	www.marcommwise.com	See the specialist section focused on measuring marketing communication effectiveness
	www.hitbox.com	Free software providing statistics on number of website visitors, paths taken through the website and other useful evaluation tools

Syllabus section	Web address	Description
Cross-border marketing communications	www.mckinseyquarterly.com (see 'economic performance' section)	Free full text articles on globalisation, economic development and cultural issues from one of the world's premier business journals
	www.oecd.org	The Organisation for Economic Co-operation and Development site links to articles, policy documents and other extensive resources on global trading issues, labour market deregulation and social policies
	www.eiu.com	The Economist Intelligence Unit provides detailed reports and other information about establishing and managing operations across national borders

Additional web addresses

Advertising Standards Authority	www.asa.org.uk
Data Protection	www.dataprotection.gov.uk
Direct Mail Information Service	www.dmis.co.uk
Direct Marketing Association	www.dma.org.uk
Independent Television Commission	www.itc.org.uk
Institute of Direct Marketing	www.theidm.com
Institute of Sales Promotion	www.isp.org.uk
Mail Order Protection Scheme	www.mops.org.uk
Market Research Society	www.mrs.org.uk
Radio Advertising Bureau	www.rab.co.uk
Royal Mail	www.royalmail.co.uk
The Advertising Association	www.adassoc.org.uk

Most of the companies discussed throughout the text, particularly in the Marketing at Work examples, have websites which students should be encouraged to seek out.

The exam paper

Format of the paper

	Marks
One compulsory case study, with two questions	40

Three questions from a choice of six (equal marks)	60
	100

Analysis of past papers

The analysis below shows the topics which have featured in papers set since December 1999.

December 2002

Part A (Compulsory case study: 40 marks)

1   Analysis of the luxury watches market.
    (a)   Use of push, pull and profile strategies
    (b)   Use of sports stars and celebrities in promotions
    (c)   Word of mouth communication

Part B (three questions from six, 20 marks each)

2   Advertising and online sales in the luxury goods market
3   Understanding consumer attitudes in the hair care market
4   Relationship marketing, customer retention and loyalty for a national lottery
5   Use of the marketing communications planning framework
6   Evaluating a pull-based marketing communications campaign for a children's clothes manufacturer
7   Provision of product and customer care information to the marketing channel

June 2002

Part A (compulsory, 40 marks)

1   Development of the 'coffee house' market in the UK, and the importance of positioning and branding activities.

    (a)   Positioning strategy for new entrant
    (b)   Tools of the promotional mix and media
    (c)   Role of marketing communications for the leading brands

Part B (three questions from six, 20 marks each)

2   Use of marketing communications to promote a new website
3   Changing customer attitudes
4   Communicating differentiating strategies in the low cost airline market
5   IMC and not for profit organisations
6   Advertising and brand building
7   Global advertising agencies and adapting communication messages for individual markets

December 2001

Part A (compulsory, 40 marks)

1   Civil engineering company seeking enhanced customer focus to add value and attract higher margins

(a)   Identification of communication strategy
(b)   Justification for the strategy
(c)   Tools in the promotional mix
(d)   Core message
(e)   Issues to consider before implementing an integrated marketing communications policy

Part B (three questions from six, 20 marks each)

2   Push and pull communications strategies; the marketing communications mix
3   Positioning concept
4   Online and offline communications
5   The business to business market
6   Perceived risk
7   Above-the-line versus sales promotion in branding strategy

June 2001

Part A (compulsory, 40 marks)

1   Analysis of three major breakfast cereal manufacturers and their products and brand marketing activity

(a)   Evaluation of each of the marketing communications strategies

(b)   Suggest how one of the competitors could use marketing communications to counter the promotional strategies of rivals

Part B (three questions from six, all 20 marks)

2   Effect of the Internet of channel communication and relationships
3   Objectives and their significance in a marketing communications plan
4   Marketing communication tools and branding
5   Methods for assessing success of direct marketing strategies
6   Significance of internal marketing communications
7   Differences in marketing communications for consumer and business to business markets

December 2000

Part A (compulsory, 40 marks)

1   Apollo Data Loggers: Report to directors identifying and prioritising key strategic issues concerning communications. Recommend and justify means by which technology might be used to develop communications strategy.

Part B (three questions from six, all 20 marks)

2   Developing integrated international marketing communications
3   Changing brand communications strategies over time
4   Developing and implementing integrated marketing communications strategy
5   Role of attitudes in buyer behaviour
6   Evaluation of FMCG marketing communications campaigns
7   Increasing role of direct marketing communications

June 2000

Part A (compulsory, 40 marks)

1   Woodstock Furniture: Prepare two year integrated marketing communications plan

Part B (three questions from six, all 20 marks)

2   Roles of opinion leaders and formers
3   Internet based marketing communications in business to business
4   Marketing communications contribution to business or consumer brands
5   Influence of external factors on marketing communications
6   Key media concepts in developing media strategy
7   Main theoretical elements of corporate identity/branding

December 1999

Part A (compulsory, 40 marks)

1   Dutton: Internal report on the key strategic issues facing the company

Part B (three questions from six, all 20 marks)

2   Perceived risk and risk reduction
3   Planned communication with channel members
4   The role of objectives in the communication planning process
5   Corporate identity and the use of ethical issues to differentiate OR external event's effects on corporate identity
6   Customer retention schemes
7   Internal marketing communications

Part A

Marketing communications and integration

What is 'Marketing Communications'?

Chapter Topic List	
1	Setting the scene: introduction to marketing communications
2	The strategy process
3	The link to business strategies
4	The link to marketing strategies
5	Integrated marketing communications
6	Defining integrated marketing communications
7	Strategic marketing communications issues

Learning Outcome

☑   Advise on the impact corporate communications can have on both internal and external audiences and their role in the development of integrated marketing communications

Syllabus References

☑   A definition and appreciation of the scope and dimensions of marketing and corporate communications

☑   A contextual analysis understanding and justification for marketing and corporate communication strategies

☑   The strategic significance and impact of integrated marketing communications

☑   Identify key strategic communication issues that might influence an organisation's marketing communications

Key Concepts Introduced

- Methods and media
- Exchange
- Strategy

- Integration
- Marketing communications
- Integrated marketing communications

1 Setting the scene: introduction to marketing communications

1.1 Most organisations, whether they operate in the private, public, not-for-profit or other sectors, all need to **communicate with their customers**. Communication through promotional activities is an integral and essential part of the marketing mix, part of an organisation's planned drive to satisfy customer needs. Marketing communications might therefore be understood to be **all forms of communication between an organisation and its customers and potential customers**.

Action Programme 1

Make a list of the range of audiences that all organisations, large and small, need to communicate with in order to survive, grow and meet their various goals.

1.2 Marketing communications also involves **all communications** by an organisation with its **environment** and the various **stakeholders** who might influence it, **not just its customers**.

Links with other papers

1.3 Marketing communications is one of the elements of the marketing mix and is responsible for the communication of the **marketing offer** to the **target market**. It is the task of a **planned** and **integrated** set of communication activities to communicate **effectively** with each of the target customer groups, wherever in the world they may be. Your studies of other Diploma level modules are therefore relevant. We must continually remind ourselves that we are not studying marketing communications strategies in isolation from the rest of the business or organisation. If they are to be successful, **marketing communications strategies must be integrated into the overall planning process**.

Exam Tip

The strategic role of marketing communications is extremely important.

Marketing communication methods

1.4 This is a very broad perspective and before we go any further we need to briefly consider the **tools and methods** of marketing communications.

The following diagram sets out the variety of promotional methods available to communicate with customers. These methods can be considered as a set of five, the **Marketing Communications Mix**.

Figure 1

1.5 These tools represent the deployment of **deliberate and intentional methods** calculated to bring about a favourable response in the customer's behaviour. The diagram represents the most obvious communication methods, though other parts of the marketing mix, including the product itself, pricing, policy and distribution channels, will also have decisive effects.

1.6 Choosing the correct tools for a particular promotions task is not an easy one. The process is becoming **more scientific** because of the access to consumer and media **databases**. Matching **consumer characteristics** with **media characteristics** can be rapidly carried out and promotional **budgets** evaluated for different mixes. In the final analysis however the expertise of the marketing manager is vital.

Key Concept

An obvious point, but remember that there are five principal **methods** of **marketing communication**. In addition there are a variety of **media** which are the means by which advertising can be used to reach target audiences.

Methods and media are different and should not be confused.

Economic justifications for marketing communications

1.7 Marketing communications can be considered in the context of the **exchange process**. Exchanges, or **transactions**, are central to much modern thinking in economics: all activity undertaken by individuals or organisations can be seen as a series of exchanges.

Key Concept

An **exchange** requires the participation of two or more parties, each offering something of value to the other. They enter freely into the exchange process. The relevance to marketing is obvious: buy something and you will have experienced an exchange.

1.8 **Communication is central to the exchange process**.

(a) **Differentiates** between competing offerings helping consumers to decide which exchanges to make, helping to prevent monopolies from developing, encouraging lower prices.

(b) **Reminds** customers of the benefits of past transactions and so convince them that they should enter into a similar exchange.

(c) **Informs** and makes potential customers aware of an organisation's offering.

(d) **Persuades** current and potential customers of the desirability of entering into an exchange relationship.

1.9 To reiterate this point (the DRIP model), marketing communications can work in the following ways.

- **D**ifferentiates
- **R**eminds/reassures
- **I**nforms
- **P**ersuades

Action Programme 2

Think of a product/service or brand and consider how the DRIP factors can be applied.

Creative and social justification

1.10 Communication can itself be the object of an exchange. In return for the consumer's interest and loyalty, communication is provided as **entertainment**, as **information** and as a vehicle for transferring **values and culture** to different groups. Thus 'ethical advertising' by, say, the **Co-op bank**, **Benetton's** controversial advertising or the Government's anti drink/drive campaigns, help to raise awareness of important social, political and environmental issues. Cadbury's Roses 'thank you very much' campaign instils values as well as selling the product.

Exam Tip

An exam question asked for a discussion of the comment 'Young people are threatened by the evil use of advertising techniques that stimulate the natural inclination to avoid hard work by promising the immediate satisfaction of every desire' (Pope John Paul II).

Arguments can be put forward that advertising is manipulative, that it encourages consumerism and wastes resources, that it creates an unfair barrier to entry and so hinders competition. Some people find it irritating and intrusive: they would say it spoils other forms of entertainment or that it trivialises serious issues.

2 The strategy process   examined 12/99

2.1 Whatever your perspective on marketing communications, it is apparent that to be effective organisations must adopt a **strategic perspective**. By using promotional activities over the longer term organisations are more likely to reach their **objectives** and build/sustain their **market position**.

2.2 What do you understand by the word **strategy**? Are you familiar with the marketing strategies of the organisation you work for? Are they written down and well articulated? Business and marketing strategies of organisations are often not well communicated. The companies that are excellent at the strategy process are very limited in number.

2.3 The word **strategy** has several meanings.

(a) At one level strategy follows on from the **defining of objectives**. Objectives answer the question of 'Where do we want to go?'. Strategies answer the question of '**How** do we get there?'.

(b) At another level the word 'strategic' has come to describe the more important process of **developing a complete long-term plan for the company**.

Marketing at Work

Under the headline 'New strategy helps Reckitt', the *Financial Times* carried an article that gave details of Reckitt & Colman's disposals and acquisitions programme ('How do we get there?'). Then it included a comment on the big picture from the company's chief executive, who said that the latest results 'bore the first fruits of the company's *strategy* of turning itself into a focused household goods and over-the-counter drugs supplier'.

Key Concept

Strategy is a natural follow-on from objective setting, and is a process of providing a framework for the *specific* actions of the business and marketing plans. It concerns the longer-term process involving major changes in a company's positioning, growth and profitability.

Mintzberg and strategy

2.4 Mintzberg argues that the word **strategy has long been used implicitly in different ways** and that recognition of multiple definitions is helpful. He suggests that there are **five definitions of strategy**: plan, ploy, pattern, position and perspective.

BPP
PROFESSIONAL EDUCATION

Definition	Comment
Plan	This definition indicates that strategy is a consciously intended course of action, a set of guidelines to deal with a given situation.
Ploy	A ploy is a manoeuvre intended to attack an opponent or competitor. A marketing company may threaten to enter a rival's market or to discount prices heavily as a way of threatening a rival's plan to enter the company's own established market.
Pattern	Strategy can be seen as the result of planning or as a stream of actions.
Position	Strategy can also be a position, that is, a means of locating an organisation in its environment. This may be thought of as a niche in a market place.
Perspective	It becomes an established way of perceiving the company and its markets. Employees become organisation minded.

2.5 There are **five types of strategies**.

(a) **Intended**: the result of a deliberate planning process.

(b) **Deliberate**: where the intended plans have been put into action.

(c) **Unrealised**: not all planned strategies are implemented.

(d) **Emergent**: sometimes strategies are created by force of circumstances.

(e) **Realised**: the final realised strategy results from a balance of forces of the other types of strategies.

These strategies are illustrated in the diagram below.

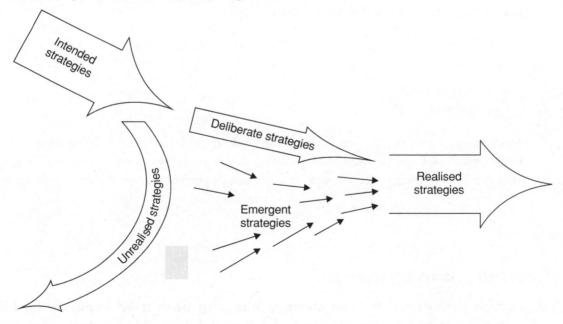

Deliberate and emergent strategies

From Mintzberg and Quinn *The Strategy Process (1997)*

2.6 Defining strategies in the ways described above still leaves the question of the **purpose of the strategies**. Definitions make it possible to classify strategies according to their various outcomes. The list below (again taken from the excellent Mintzberg and Quinn book, *The Strategy Process, 1997*) considers the variety of strategies.

Type of strategy	Comment
Planned strategy	Resulting from a formal planning process
Entrepreneurial strategy	Often associated with the personality of the owner/leader
Ideological strategy	Part of the value system or ethical stance of the organisation
Umbrella strategy	Imposed by senior management to provide a framework for middle and junior managers
Process strategy	The leader of a company may impose rules on the way the process of setting the strategy is carried out
Disconnected strategy	Smaller businesses or strategic business units may decide their own individual strategies
Consensus strategy	Strategy may emerge or converge in the absence of strong single leadership
Imposed strategy	A new owner or a strong customer may seek to impose a strategy on the organisation

Action Programme 3

What do you now understand by the word strategy?

Which organisations do you know that have clearly articulated strategies?

How would you articulate the strategies of the organisation that you work for or one that you know well?

3 The link to business strategies

3.1 It can be argued that it is almost impossible to generate marketing communication strategies in isolation. It may be possible to take individual communication actions, and these are frequently implemented successfully. However, **to produce a marketing communication strategy requires a full understanding of business strategy first.**

3.2 The link to business and marketing strategy can be seen as a **hierarchy**, best shown in a pyramid form.

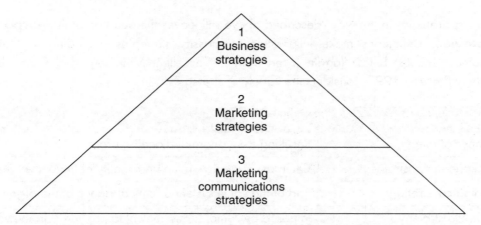

3.3 You should realise from the outset that studying for the CIM Diploma is in fact a form of management training. In other words, it is difficult to become an effective marketing manager without a good appreciation of the business context of the organisation.

Strategy and marketing communications

3.4 At a very general level marketing communications encompasses all forms of an organisation's communications with its **external** and **internal audiences**.

Action Programme 4

Define marketing communications within the context of your own organisation or an organisation of your choice.

Explore the boundaries between the external communications usually covered by marketing communications and the internal communications often associated with the accounting and personnel functions.

Look in particular at the customer care operations. How are they carried out and who is responsible for them?

3.5 Example: strategy and communications

Practically every day the business pages of a newspaper will report a significant strategic move by a major company. Here is a report of such a move by *Scottish & Newcastle* when it acquired brands such as Courage, John Smith's and Webster's to add to its own brands, which included Newcastle Brown, Theakston's and Younger's. Consider this news in terms of the ideas you have encountered in the opening pages of this Study Text (Mintzberg's five definitions, overall results and primary and supporting results, and so on). Then see if you can suggest how communications strategy will be affected.

'Scottish & Newcastle yesterday achieved its 20-year ambition to become a national UK brewer with the £425m agreed purchase of Courage from Foster's Brewing of Australia.

The combined business will be Britain's biggest brewer, with about 25 per cent of the market counting the production it controls directly. Bass, the traditional leader, has about 23 per cent.

Mr Brian Stewart, S & N's chief executive, said Courage made an "excellent fit" with his company. Courage breweries and sales concentrated in southern England would complement S & N's in Scotland and northern England.

The deal is likely to herald further restructuring and intensified competition in an industry beset by over-capacity and thin profit margins. "It's going to be a man's game out there," said Mr Mike Foster, chairman of Courage.

The deal is subject to scrutiny by the Office of Fair Trading, which has six weeks to consider the implications for competition. If it feels Courage's loss of independence will reduce competition it could ask S & N to sell some brands or brewing assets. More drastically, it could refer the deal to the Monopolies and Mergers Commission for a full review.

S & N said it was confident the creation of a stronger group with 25 per cent of the UK market would be acceptable to the OFT. It would continue with the bid even if it was referred.

S & N is likely to face strong opposition, however. The Campaign for Real Ale, which calculates S & N's new share at more than 30 per cent of the market, urged the MMC to study the purchase. "This merger is grossly anti-competitive," it said. It accused S & N of hypocrisy for arguing in 1986 when Courage abortively bid for it that the deal would be against the public interest.

To help fund the purchase, S & N will raise £354m in a one-for-seven rights issue at 475p a share, in two instalments of 190p and 285p. Its shares closed down 7p at 539p yesterday.'

Financial Times

3.6 Solution

Points you may have made include the following. This is not a comprehensive analysis.

(a) **Strategy**

    (i)   S & N's 20-year ambition is an example of strategy as a **plan** and a **pattern**.

    (ii)   It is an **intended** strategy that has been put into action. However, it is not a **realised** strategy because of the involvement of the Office of Fair Trading. **Emergent** strategies may be required to deal with this.

    (iii)   To competitors, the acquisition is a **ploy**; to the markets served it is a **position**. S & N become the overall market leader and achieved national coverage of the beer market.

    (iv)   From the point of view of Courage it is an **imposed strategy**.

    (v)   In terms of key business areas, **profitability** is a major issue ('thin profit margins') as is **management of operations** (reducing overcapacity).

(b) **Communications**

    (i)   S&N is going to have to get used to managing a significant number of **new brands**, communicating to a **new target market** (Southern England).

    (ii)   **Public relations** (PR) was crucial while the deal was being scrutinised by the OFT.

    (iii)   There is also a vociferous and influential **consumer group** - CAMRA - to cope with through PR.

    (iv)   The move would be unsettling for S & N employees and particularly for Courage employees. Effective reassuring **internal communications** are vital.

    (v)   **Shareholders** would need to be persuaded to accept the rights issue. PR is important ('S & N said it was confident ...'). Shareholders would be directly targeted with reassuring messages.

3.7   Try to conduct the exercise above whenever you are reading reports of companies' activities.

4 The link to marketing strategies

4.1 It is impossible to have an effective **marketing communications strategy** without a full understanding of **marketing strategy**. To be really effective the two levels of **marketing objectives** and **marketing communications objectives** must be **explicitly linked**. Considering the linkage between the two, marketing activities represent the answer to the question **'why'** and marketing communications activities represent the answer to the question **'how'**. To understand the difference tackle Action Programme 5.

Action Programme 5

For an organisation of your choice, ask the questions 'why' and 'how' in relation to its promotional activities. The question 'why' should lead you to the underlying reason (a marketing or business objective) and the 'how' question to the means (the marketing communication activities).

The extended marketing mix

4.2 Your answers to the last exercise will start to indicate the wide range of ends or objectives to which marketing communications can contribute. To understand this further it is useful to **define all the areas in which marketing activity and decisions take place**. All students will be familiar with the traditional 4Ps. But it is possible to extend this to 7Ps by including service elements (people, processes and physical evidence) or even to the 12Ps described below.

THE EXTENDED MARKETING MIX

The planning mix
- Profitability and effectiveness
- Positioning in the market
- Planning systems
- Performance of the organisation

The marketing mix
- Product decisions
- Price decisions
- Promotion decisions
- Place decisions

The service mix
- People resources
- Processes employed
- Physical evidence of service
- Periodicity and seasonality

4.3 You may not be immediately familiar with these 12Ps but you will quickly find that they are invaluable in both **analysing an organisation's marketing operations** and in subsequently **setting marketing objectives**. The point to be stressed is that all these 12 elements can be linked directly to marketing communications. Promotion only appears as one P in the marketing mix and this gives a misleading impression.

4.4 The **positioning** of a company within a market segment is increasingly recognised as of major importance. **Positioning is most visible through a company's overall identity and image**. This identity and image is directly featured through a planned communications programme.

The target market

4.5 You should have assimilated the idea of **market segmentation** thoroughly in the course of your earlier studies, and you will appreciate its importance in overall strategic marketing decisions about product mix, distribution policy and so on. Quite obviously, in the present context, **'how'** you communicate depends upon **'who'** you are trying to communicate with.

4.6 The relationship between segmentation and communications can be understood by considering segmentation on the basis of **'enduring'** variables and **'dynamic'** variables.

(a) **Media plans** (what media are used for communication) depend on **enduring variables** identified by segmentation according to geography, demographics and psychographics. These factors are relatively **constant** and do not change quickly.

(b) **Message design and positioning** (what is said and how it is said) depend upon **dynamic variables**, which are identified by segmentation according to such factors as level of usage, time of adoption, loyalty level or benefit sought. These factors tend **to vary** within individuals across product categories.

The marketing mix communicates

4.7 In a similar way the **product**, **price** and **place** elements of the marketing mix contribute to **promoting** a company.

4.8 Many retailers and products are very similar in character and quality. Companies have had to **distinguish** themselves in some other way, and, apart from competing on price, it is possible to promote other differences, such as in customer service. The **service mix** then becomes part of the marketing communications process.

Action Programme 6

Use the 12Ps of the extended marketing mix to explore the marketing communications activities of well known organisations. Use the form below and write in the linking of marketing communications to each element.

	Company A Name	Company B Name

Marketing mix element

1   Profitability
2   Positioning
3   Planning
4   Performance
5   Product
6   Price
7   Promotion
8   Place
9   People
10 Processes
11 Physical
12 Period

5   Integrated marketing communications

5.1   Strategy must be communicated in such a way that the messages are **consistent** through time and **targeted accurately** at **appropriate stakeholder audiences**. Each organisation must constantly guard against the transmission of **confusing messages,** whether this is through the way in which the telephone is answered, the impact of sales literature, the way sales persons approach prospective clients or the transparency of an organisation's overall corporate activities.

5.2   Marketing communications is about the promotion of both **the organisation** and its **products and services**. An increasing number of managers recognise the growing role the organisation plays in the marketing process (as part of a **profile strategy** – see Chapter 8) and the impact that organisational factors can have on the minds of consumers.

5.3   It appears logical to conclude that, if there are different audiences, they exist both inside and outside the organisation, and some of them actively contribute to the source of some communications (eg marketing communication agencies). It is important to bring corporate and business strategy together with marketing strategy so that all these elements can be integrated and marketing communication is effective.

5.4   A dictionary definition says that integration is 'combining parts into a whole'.

Key Concept

Immediately it can be seen that **integration of marketing communications** is possible at three levels.

- Integration with business strategy
- Integration with marketing strategy
- Integration of the promotional tools

5.5 Example

Thus a manufacturer of an exclusive and expensive perfume would have to take into account the **public relations aspects** of manufacturing using Third World labour or testing on animals; its **distribution policy** would support the image by selling through Harrods rather than Boots; its leaflets would fall out of *Vogue* and there would not be a 'win a body spray' competition in *Woman's Own*. Where would this company locate its main office? What would be the criteria for the recruitment of staff? Every aspect of the operation tells you something about the organisation and its product. **Integrated marketing communications is communication that delivers an utterly consistent message**.

6 Defining integrated marketing communications

6.1 Integrated marketing communications (IMC) means different things to different people, but is more likely to occur when organisations attempt to enter into a **co-ordinated dialogue with their various internal and external audiences**.

Key Concept

Marketing communications is a management process through which an organisation enters into a dialogue with its various audiences. To accomplish this the organisation develops, presents and evaluates a series of co-ordinated messages to identified stakeholder groups.

The objective of the process is to (re)position the organisation and/or their offerings, in the mind of each member of the target audience in a **consistent and likeable** way.

6.2 The word **dialogue** is used deliberately. Communication theory tells us that **feedback** is important. Of course, it is important to use feedback constructively and good marketing communications allows for the development of a **circle of information** between an organisation, its customers and interested stakeholders. Promotional messages should encourage target audiences to **respond** to organisations (or products/brands). This response can be immediate through, for example, **purchase behaviour**, registering on a **website**, using **customer care lines** or even through **storing information** in memory (or a file or desk) for future use.

6.3 The communication tools used in this dialogue and the messages conveyed should be **internally consistent with an organisation's strategies**. The target audiences should perceive the communication and associated cues as **co-ordinated, likeable and timely**. In addition, members of the target audience(s) should, at some time, be sufficiently motivated to want to respond to the communication and encourage future messages.

6.4 The word **positioning** is used in the definition as well. The manner in which an organisation (product or brand) is **perceived** relative to other competing products can be important to the level of success an organisation might enjoy.

6.5 Management pursuit and development of IMC involves the totality of an **organisation**, its **strategy** and all those with whom it **interacts**. IMC is too often depicted as just the co-ordinated impacts of the tools of the promotional mix, but it involves much more.

■ **A range of activities**

- **Customer/audience focus**
- **The breadth of the organisation**
- **Cultural factors**

The development of IMC

6.6 There are a number of reasons why organisations are seeking to establish IMC. The following table sets out some of the drivers behind this growth (Fill, 1999).

Organisational Drivers for IMC
- Increasing profits through improved **efficiency**
- Increasing need for greater levels of **accountability**
- Rapid move towards **cross-border marketing** and the need for changing structures and communications
- Co-ordinated **brand development** and **competitive advantage**
- Opportunities to utilise **management time** more productively
- Provide **direction and purpose**

Market Based Drivers for IMC
- Greater levels of **audience communications literacy**
- **Media cost** inflation
- Media and audience **fragmentation**
- **Stakeholders** need for increasing amounts and diversity of information
- Greater amounts of message **clutter**
- **Competitor activity** and low levels of brand differentiation
- Move towards **relationship marketing** from transaction based marketing
- Development of **networks, collaboration and alliances**

Communication Based Drivers for IMC
- **Technological advances** (Internet, databases, segmentation techniques)
- Increased **message effectiveness** through **consistency** and reinforcement of core messages
- More effective **triggers** for brand and message recall
- More **consistent** and less confusing brand images
- Need to build **brand reputations** and to provide clear identity cues

6.7 IMC is resisted for many reasons. Failure to establish IMC as a total concept may be for one or other of the following reasons.

- Financial structures and frameworks
- Reluctance to change
- Traditional hierarchical management and brand structures
- Attitudes and structure of suppliers and agencies
- Perceived complexity of planning and co-ordination
- Lack of experience

6.8 Overcoming these different forms of resistance can be tricky and partly because of the enormity of the task, especially in global organisations, there are few examples of truly rooted IMC. Here are some of the ways in which the restraints can be overcome.

- Adopting a customer focused philosophy
- Using training and development programmes
- Appointing change agents
- Planning to achieve competitive advantage
- Developing an incremental approach

6.9 The diagram below sets out a model of IMC and demonstrates the way in which the different elements of an organisation's activities need to be brought together if IMC is to flourish (Fill, 1999).

Integrated marketing communications is a strategic approach to the management of an organisation's marketing communication activities.

7 Strategic marketing communications issues

7.1 Marketing communications is a fast moving discipline, not least due to the rapidly developing use of **newer technologies** such as the **Internet**. Organisations increasingly need to be aware of changes taking place and how these will affect their communications strategies. Lead times are short and competitors catch up quickly so anticipation of significant factors and their effects is vital.

7.2 Issues that might be considered to be currently affecting marketing communication strategy development are outlined below.

Integration

7.3 Not only must firms ensure that there is consistency in the delivery of messages to customers and other stakeholders, their **communications planning** needs to be an **integral part of their overall business and marketing planning**.

(a) **Objectives** at all levels (business, marketing and communications) need to relate to each other.

(b) **Strategies** have to relate to the objectives set.

(c) Creative strategy and execution will ensure consumers and stakeholders receive **consistent messages** across all media.

(d) This includes consistency between **strategic approaches**, push, pull and profile and the respective **communications mixes** selected.

Media fragmentation

7.4 The **increasing availability of different media** can to some extent make successful integration difficult to achieve, particularly on an international scale.

(a) Cable, satellite and digital TV all provide media buyers with an increasing and complex **range of opportunities**.

(b) Newsagent shelves are packed with new magazines and other products aimed at consumers with **differing and changing lifestyles**.

(c) New media, including the Internet, present challenges for all communicators as **consumers look for new ways to gather information and make purchases**.

Audience fragmentation

7.5 Markets are also fragmenting. The process of segmentation becomes more difficult, with **smaller target groups** seeking product benefits to more closely match their individual needs.

(a) This has led to developments in **relationship marketing**, with communications taking place on a one to one basis, even in fmcg sectors.

(b) Companies are recognising the **lifetime value of customers**, with **retention** more effective than the constant demand for new business.

(c) **Direct marketing**, led by sophisticated **database developments**, is taking over from traditional mass communication techniques.

Ethical issues

7.6 Marketing has long been criticised in some consumer quarters for creating unnecessary demand for products which consumers cannot afford to buy. The advent of the so-called 'sophisticated consumer' suggests that consumers are no longer so gullible. They will make choices based on information that they consider believable from companies that they trust.

Measuring response

7.7 In addition to the media fragmentation discussed above, marketers are seeking **measurable effectiveness from their communications budgets**. Agencies who have grown on the creation of expensive campaigns, which have been difficult to evaluate the success of, are now seeking new ways of demonstrating effectiveness. This has included a shift toward **direct response** advertising and the use of **TV programme sponsorship** where target audiences can be more closely identified with brands.

Chapter Roundup

- Marketing communications fulfils a variety of roles within organisations. Principally it is used to **inform, remind, persuade and differentiate** an organisation and its products/services

- **Strategy** is concerned with the long-term plans for an organisation's **positioning**, its **growth** and the achievement of its **profit targets**, and for rewarding its **shareholders**. It is helpful to accept that there are multiple definitions.

- Marketing communications strategies **cannot be formulated and analysed in isolation** from the strategies of the organisation as a whole or from its marketing strategies. Marketing activities can be defined in terms of the **12Ps of the extended marketing mix** and each of the 12 elements can be linked directly to marketing communications.

- Integrated marketing communications encompasses all forms of communication between an organisation and its customers and potential customers. More broadly, it is **all forms of communication by an organisation with its environment, including internal communication** with employees and managers.

Now try Question 1 at the end of the Study Text

Quick Quiz

1   What are the DRIP elements of marketing communications? (1.9)

2   What is a strategy? (see paras 2.2 and 2.3)

3   Name Mintzberg's 5Ps of strategy. (2.4)

4   Draw the diagram of deliberate and emergent strategies. (2.5)

5   Draw the diagram linking business and marketing communication strategies. (3.2)

6   What are the 12Ps? (4.2)

7   What is a definition of integrated marketing communications? (5.1 - 5.4)

8   What are some of the issues affecting the current development of marketing communication strategy? (section 7)

Action Programme Review

1   Your list may include any number of the following.

   (a)   **Customers**, users (of competitor products/services).

   (b)   **Non users**, suppliers, distributors (such as wholesalers, dealers and retailers).

   (c)   **Employees**, head office staff.

   (d)   **Financial service organisations**, trade unions, the local community, the wider national or international community, trade and professional associations, local or national government bodies, the media .... to name a few.

2   You could try applying this to your own organisation or look to apply to a specific market sector and compare the way in which different competitors approach each aspect.

3   Many organisations publish their strategies as part of their Annual Report. Try obtaining some from a selection of companies and compare different approaches. The *Financial Times* offers a free service for obtaining these reports. Alternatively, check the company website.

4   What kind of strategies are being used: push, pull, profile? Talk to those responsible to determine the rationale for their development. Are mechanisms in place for assessing the success of any customer care programmes?

5   Again, company Annual Reports, websites and the general business media will be useful in finding information relating to these questions. The 'marketing press' – *Campaign*, *Marketing* or *Marketing Week* – may provide coverage of communications activities being employed.

6   You may find it easier to start this process by looking first at your own organisation. Once you become more familiar with the differing issues, extend to the kind of companies mentioned. It could be beneficial to compare the communications of your competitors using this method – are they doing anything significantly different?

Part B

Contextual Aspects

Understanding Communication and Contexts 2

Chapter Topic List	
1	Setting the scene
2	Understanding how communication works
3	Understanding the principles of context analysis
4	Integrated marketing communications plans

Learning Outcome

☑ Determine the context in which marketing (and corporate) communications are to be implemented in order to improve effectiveness and efficiency, understand the key strategic communication issues arising from the contextual analysis and prepare (integrated) marketing communications plans

Syllabus References

☑ A contextual analysis understanding and justification for marketing and corporate communication strategies

☑ Understanding the key drivers associated with information processing and buyer decision making processes

☑ The determination and appreciation of the prevailing and future contextual conditions as a means of deriving and developing promotional strategies and plans

Key Concepts Introduced

- Noise
- Opinion leaders/formers
- Innovation
- Diffusion
- Context

1 Setting the scene

1.1 Before looking at the issues that determine the nature and direction of particular communication activities it is important to appreciate **how communication is understood to work**. The prime aim of marketing communications is to **induce a dialogue and influence a customer's buying behaviour**.

2 Understanding how communication works

2.1 Kotler, *Marketing Management: Analysis, Planning, Implementation and Control* (1999), has put forward a simple **model of the communication process** to provide a framework for answering these questions. This is shown in the diagram below.

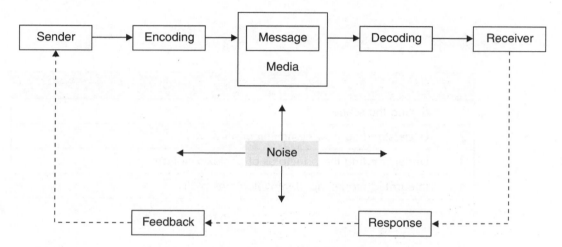

2.2 The elements of the model can be classified in the following way.

Element	Comment
Parties	
■ Sender	Sends the message to the other party; source; communicator
■ Receiver	Receives message; audience; destination
Communication tools	
■ Message	Content of communication
■ Media	Communication channels
Communication functions	
■ Encoding	Meaning is given in symbolic form (words etc) by sender
■ Decoding	Receiver translates and interprets message
■ Response	Receiver reacts to message
■ Feedback	Part of receiver's response is communicated back to sender

2.3 As Kotler states, this model underscores many of the factors in effective communication. Senders need to understand the **motivation of their audiences** in order to structure messages that the audience will **interpret correctly** through the **decoding** process. The sender also has to ascertain the most **effective communication media** through which to reach the audience and must also establish effective **feedback channels** in order to find out the receiver's response to the message.

Action Programme 1

(a)   Find some adverts - watch TV for half an hour or flick through a newspaper or a magazine.

(b)   Analyse each advertisement in the above terms. Consider who are the parties involved (*you* may not be the intended receiver), what communication tools are used, what sort of codes are used and how they will be decoded (for example, by people in different income brackets or with different tastes), what form feedback will take, and so on.

2.4   This communication process is **not carried out in isolation**. There are many senders competing with their messages for the attention of the receiver. As a result there is considerable **noise** in the environment, and an individual may be bombarded by several hundred commercial messages each day.

Key Concept

Noise can be defined as all those factors that prevent the decoding of a message by the receiver in the way intended by the sender. It could perhaps be called a communication dysfunction.

2.5   **Indeed, there is not just one receiver**, **but many**, and the receivers may communicate with each other regarding the sender's message. By virtue of experience or social standing one particular receiver may **influence** the opinions of others regarding the product that is the subject of the message. This is known as **opinion leadership** and may lead to a **two-step flow of communication**, whereby mass messages are filtered through opinion leaders to a mass audience. This can be represented diagrammatically below.

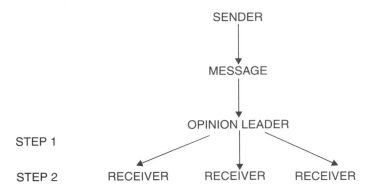

2.6   **One of the marketer's tasks is to identify the relevant opinion leaders**.

Key Concepts

- **Opinion leaders** are 'those individuals who reinforce the marketing messages sent and to whom other receivers look for information, advice and opinion' (Rice).

- **Opinion formers** are people who are designated as 'expert' and knowledgeable about a subject: their advice is credible (eg pharmacists provide advice about medicines).

In addition, **opinion leaders** may communicate a marketing message to those members of the group who may have missed the **original message**. The marketer's task in identifying opinion leaders is made more difficult by the fact that **opinion leadership is dynamic**. At one time it was believed that opinion leadership was confined to a few prominent members of society, but increased understanding of the concept has shown that a person may be an opinion leader in certain circumstances but an **opinion follower** in others.

Opinion leaser (eg hifi enthusiast)	Opinion former (eg pharmacists)
Interested in a topic	Part of job
Hobbyist	Objectivity valued
Enthusiastic (eg likes gadgets)	Easy to target, as often known (eg all pharmacists are registered)
Hard to target	

Exam Tip

A relatively straightforward question on this topic came up in June 2000. Note the two issues:

- Characteristics of opinion leader/former
- Different approaches to communicating with them.

This **'two-step'** approach contrasts to **Kotler's** simple model of communication identified earlier, which is a **'one-step'** model.

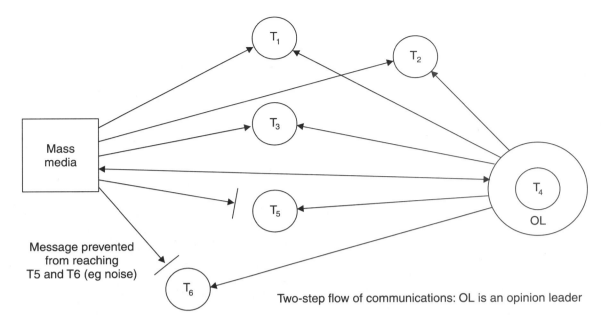

Two-step flow of communications: OL is an opinion leader

2.7 It is possible to conceive of communications as flowing in many directions, from a variety of people within **communication networks**. This is referred to as a '**multi-step**' approach.

The process of diffusion and adoption

2.8 An important contextual condition that affects marketing communication activity is the **launch of new products**, and the propensity of consumers to respond to communication about new products.

Key Concept

An **innovation** refers to any good, service or idea that is perceived by someone to be new.

2.9 This is a subjective view, as a new product idea may have a long history but be an innovation to the person concerned. **Innovations can be classified into three main groups**.

Innovation	
Continuous innovation	The **modification** of an existing product rather than the invention of a completely new one. This causes the least disruption to established patterns of consumer behaviour.
Dynamically continuous innovation	Either the **creation of a new product** or the alteration of an existing product, but not significantly altering existing patterns of consumer buying or product use.
Discontinuous innovation	The introduction of a **completely new product** that **alters existing consumer buying patterns** in a radical way.

Action Programme 2

Can you think of products that fit into each of these three categories?

Adoption

2.10 Kotler says that adopters of new products have been observed to move through the following five stages.

Stage of adoption	Comment
Stage 1: **Awareness**	The consumer becomes aware of the innovation but lacks information about it.
Stage 2: **Interest**	The consumer is stimulated to seek information about the innovation.
Stage 3: **Evaluation**	The consumer considers whether to try the innovation.
Stage 4: **Trial**	The consumer tries the innovation to improve his or her estimate of its value.
Stage 5: **Adoption**	The consumer decides to make full and regular use of the innovation.

2.11 The progression suggests that the **marketer of the innovative product should aim to facilitate consumer movement through these stages**. The process of adoption of innovation described here bears a remarkable similarity to the **'core' process of consumer buying behaviour**, which we will shall look at in the next chapter. Indeed, when considering the adoption process, all we are considering is the consumer buying behaviour process for a new rather than an existing product.

Diffusion

Key Concept

Diffusion has been defined as the process by which an innovation is communicated over time among the individuals within society who comprise the target market.

2.12 **Four key elements significant to the process of diffusion**

- The **innovation** itself
- The **communication processes** and channels used
- The **time** at which individuals decide to adopt the product
- The **social systems** involved

2.13 At the heart of the diffusion process is the decision by an individual to adopt the innovative product or service. This process of adoption focuses on **the processes through which** an individual passes from first hearing about the innovation to eventual adoption. Adoption is the decision of an individual to become a regular user of a product.

Categories of adopters

2.14 It is a fact, however, that people differ markedly in their readiness to try new products. There are five categories of adopters, which are often described diagrammatically in terms of a normal distribution curve (showing their relative numerical importance), as follows.

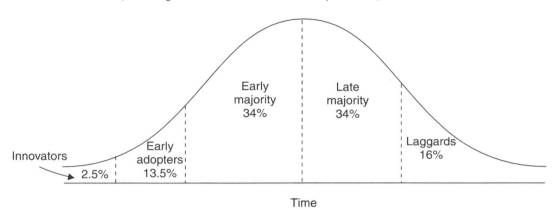

2.15 Characteristics of the various adopter groups

Measure	Comment
Innovators	■ Eager to try new ideas and products ■ Higher incomes ■ Self confident
Early adopters	■ Reliant on group norms ■ Oriented to the local community ■ Opinion leaders
Early majority	■ Deliberate more carefully ■ Process of adoption takes longer ■ Positioned between the earlier and later adopters
Late majority	■ Pressure to conform ■ Sceptical ■ Below average income and education
Laggards	■ Independent ■ Tradition-bound ■ Lowest socio-economic status

2.16 The **time dimension** to the process of diffusion and adoption is important. The diagram suggests that **each group learns by observing the previous group's behaviours** and then adopts the behaviour itself. If this is correct then the influence of the **innovators** and the **early adopters** cannot be overestimated: the innovators in terms of starting off the process by making the **first purchase**, and the early adopters by virtue of their role as **opinion leaders**. The marketer should therefore have as clear an understanding of the dynamics of this process for his own industry as possible.

Encouraging adoption

2.17 It is a common assertion that **90% of new products fail**. How, therefore, can a marketer ensure that his new product stands the best chance of success in the market? There are five **characteristics associated with the success of new products**.

Characteristics	Comment
Relative advantage	The extent to which the consumer perceives the product to have an advantage over the product it supersedes.
Compatibility	The degree to which the product is consistent with existing values and past experiences of the potential customers.
Complexity	The degree to which a new product is perceived to be complex and difficult to use.
Trialability	New products are more likely to be adopted when customers can try them out.
Observability	A measure of the degree to which adoption of the product, is visible to friends, neighbours and colleagues. This seems to affect the diffusion process by allowing potential customers to see the benefits of the product. This process can be given added impetus if the product is seen to be used by celebrities or other role models.

Action Programme 3

Apply this list of characteristics to the following innovations.

(a)   Mobile telephones
(b)   Banking by telephone or the Internet
(c)   Multimedia home entertainment (DVD)
(d)   Quorn (fungus based food products)

Communications and the product life cycle

2.18 The consumer adoption process describes the way in which new products and services become accepted by different 'types' of consumer over time. The **product life cycle concept** describes the rate at which this process takes place for different types of product.

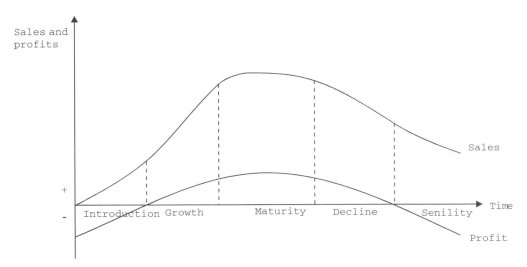

The diagram illustrates the different phases products and services pass through over time. The length of time products take to move through the stages will be dependent upon the type of product and a range of other marketing factors which determine how successful the product actually becomes.

2.19 Different kinds of communication will be appropriate at different stages.

(a)   Initially the objectives will be to **create awareness** and will involve **advertising**, particularly for fmcg products. **Sales promotion may also feature** to gain acceptance and encourage repeat purchase.

(b)   In **growth phases**, advertising will still be important but at a **reducing percentage** of sales.

(c)   At **maturity**, more active **segmentation and targeting** becomes significant as competition intensifies.

(d)   Although in many cases products do not 'decline', **sales may reduce** significantly, and **promotional activity will probably reduce**.

(e)   For products where sales continue to be healthy, promotion will still be a major element of the marketing mix as **brands** seek to maintain or improve their positions by encouraging brand switching.

2.20 Organisations have a number of strategies at their disposal to influence customers to adopt innovations and, among these, marketing communication is obviously very important. For example, in markets where **continuous innovation** is the norm, organisations can encourage trial through **free samples** and **price promotions**.

2.21 Encouraging adoption for a **discontinuous innovation** is more problematic because the product cannot be purchased on a trial basis. **Advertising** may have to be used to promote awareness and communicate product features. One advertising strategy used by organisations to promote innovative behaviour is to show 'astute' buyers purchasing the most advanced products.

3 Understanding the principles of context analysis

3.1 Such simple communications models are useful as a first base in helping us understand the communications process, but the marketing communications process must be placed in its wider context. The overall aim of marketing communication is to influence buyers in such a way that they are inclined to buy the product or service on offer.

Key Concept

Context. The behaviour of the participants and the overall conditions in which they receive, interpret and respond to communications affects further communication activities and behaviour.

3.2 Example: AUDI

(a)   Imagine yourself as a teenager and your possible/likely reaction to a television advertisement for an Audi.

(b)   Now imagine yourself as a successful middle-aged business person viewing the same advertisement, who has an Audi as part of their total remuneration package.

(c)   Will the reaction be the same? Will the take-out from the commercial be similar? Will there be the same level of effectiveness?

It is highly unlikely that the reactions will be similar and even if two business people see the same advertisement they will decode and interpret it differently if only because of their different experiences and the environments in which they see the Audi message.

3.3 In the example of the Audi advertisement, it was the **context of the two receivers** that was considered. Now think about the organisation, Audi, and the **context in which it developed the advertisement**.

(a)   Yes, they had to consider the two business people (or the relevant segment) but they also had to consider the market conditions, the stage of development the particular Audi model had reached, the economic conditions, the actions of their competitors and their own corporate and marketing strategies and the level of resources available to this particular campaign.

(b)   In other words, their own context had to influence their marketing communications activities and that advertisement/campaign in particular.

3.4 Marketing communications occur in particular contexts, we might say **unique** conditions.

(a)   It is very helpful when developing strategy and writing communication plans to understand the prevailing contextual conditions.

(b)   Imagine the different forces and restraints operating on manufacturers in the following circumstances.

- Launching new products
- Reviving a flagging brand
- Price competition
- Introducing a new variant
- A new competitor enters the market
- Regulations change
- Promotional budget is slashed

Action Programme 4

Consider yourself as the marketing communications manager for each of the following organisations. Make a list of the factors that might affect the marketing communications of the company.

British Airways	A high street hairdressing salon
BMW	Fiat
Marks & Spencer	A local council
Inland Revenue	Benetton

3.5 It should be clearer now that **each marketing communications programme is developed in unique circumstances**. It is vitally important that the **contextual conditions are analysed** in order that any factor that may influence the content, timing or the way the audience receives and interprets information, be identified and incorporated within the overall plan.

3.6 In order to help provide for a systematic appraisal of the prevailing and future conditions, a context analysis is recommended when formulating an Integrated Marketing Communications programme. This consists of a review of the various sub-contexts.

Main sub-contexts:

Exam Tip

This framework is not prescriptive and other frameworks and factors can be introduced, reflecting the organisation or brand and its particular conditions at any one moment, but you may wish to utilise this framework to help develop your understanding and familiarity with this concept.

A brief introduction to the elements of context analysis

The business context

3.7 This part of the analysis involves a consideration of the **markets and conditions** in which the organisation is operating, which are of prime concern for the integrated marketing communication programme.

3.8 **Competitors' communications**, general **trading conditions** and trends, the organisation's **corporate and marketing strategies**, a detailed analysis of the **target**

BPP
PROFESSIONAL EDUCATION

segment's characteristics and a **brand audit** are the primary activities associated with this context.

The customer context

3.9 Here the emphasis is upon understanding **buyer behaviour** and the decision-making processes that buyers in the market exhibit. The objective is to isolate any key factor in the process or any bond that customers might have with the product/brand. This can then be reflected in any communication.

The stakeholder context

3.10 Integrated marketing communications recognises that there are **audiences other than customers**, with whom organisations need to communicate. For example, members of the **marketing channel**, the **media**, the **financial community**, **local communities** and **shareholders** all seek a dialogue with the **focus organisation**. The strength and duration of the dialogue may vary, but messages need to be developed and communicated, and the responses need to be understood and acted upon wherever necessary.

The organisational context

3.11 The characteristics of the organisation can impact heavily on the nature and form of the communications they enter into. It is important, therefore, to consider the **culture and the strength of identity the workforce has with the organisation**. In order to appreciate the strength of this sub-context think about the way the staff of different companies communicate with you as a customer. Internal and external audiences communicate with each other and this is a significant part of Integrated Marketing Communications.

The external context

3.12 Integrated Marketing Communications is influenced by a number of factors in the **wider environment**. These political, economic, social and technological elements are largely uncontrollable by organisations. Nevertheless, they can shape and determine what, when and how messages are communicated to audiences.

4 Integrated marketing communication plans 12/02

4.1 Major tasks facing those responsible for marketing communications

- **Who** should receive messages
- **What** the messages should say
- What **image** of the organisation/brand receivers should retain
- How much is to be **invested** in this process
- How the messages are to be **delivered**
- What **actions** receivers should take
- How the whole process should be **controlled**
- **Determine** what was achieved

4.2 In order to manage effectively it is useful to work within a **planning framework**. The framework that follows is important for these reasons.

(a) It forms the overall **structure for the rest of this Study Text** and hence your understanding of this subject.

(b) It is the structure whereby **marketing communications plans can be developed for use in the examination, your other studies at Diploma level, and in the workplace**. Whether you work for a large multinational, a not-for-profit organisation, a medium-sized service sector organisation or a small independent trading company, the structure is equally applicable.

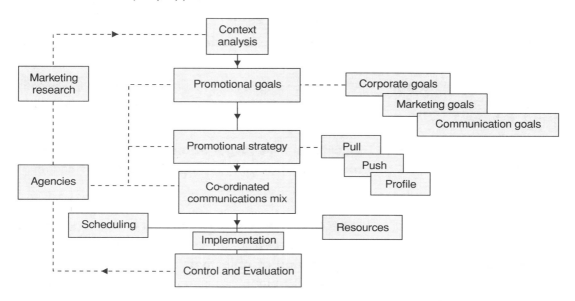

Marketing communications planning framework (Fill, 2002)

4.3 The marketing communications planning framework (MCPF) represents a **sequence of decisions** that should be made in order to achieve coherent marketing communications. In the real world many of the required actions and decisions may not be undertaken in this order and many ideas are implicit, in that they are not subject to formal articulation. However, it is helpful to develop our understanding of Integrated Marketing Communications by following this sequence. Indeed, many organisations have found that by employing such a formalised approach as the MCPF, they have been able to understand and develop more effective marketing communications.

Exam Tip

The examiner will test understanding of the planning process. This might be through the preparation of a marketing communication plan. However, you might be asked to explain the linkages between the various parts of the plan or asked to focus on the key strategic elements. Whatever the tasks required students are advised strongly to develop their understanding of this framework and to practise its application to mini-case questions. The December 2002 exam contained a Section B question which asked candidates to discuss how the use of a marketing communications planning framework might assist in the development of campaigns.

4.4   Linkages within the marketing communications planning framework (Fill, 2002)

	Derived from
Objectives	■ The marketing plan (including the competitor analysis) ■ The business context ■ The customer context ■ The stakeholder context ■ The internal context
Strategic balance (Push, pull and profile)	An understanding of the **brand**, the needs of the **target audiences** (including employees and other stakeholders) and the **marketing goals**.
Brand/product positioning	The **perception**, **attitudes and motivations** of users and non-users.
Message content and style	An understanding of the level of **involvement**, perceived **risk**, **DMU analysis**, **information processing** styles and **positioning** intentions.
Promotional tools and media	An analysis of the **target audience** and their **media habits**, **media compatibility**, **competitor analysis** and resource review.

4.5   The essence of the MCPF is that the process begins with an attempt to understand the **context** within which the communications are expected to work. This is referred to as the **context analysis**. This leads to the **determination of objectives** or the particular desired outcomes from the marketing communications activities: for example, an increase in the number of people who are aware of a new product offering.

4.6   From this point, a communication strategy is developed that is essentially a **determination** of the **overall focus** of the marketing communication activities. This is then supported by the development of suitable **messages** and the formulation of suitable **promotional mixes**.

4.7   **Human and financial resources** need to be assessed before a **schedule** is determined and the plan **implemented**. The final part of the process is to **investigate what has been achieved** in the campaign and to use the knowledge as an input into the next context analysis, as the cycle is repeated for the next promotional exercise.

 Exam Tip

As stated previously, this planning framework forms the structural basis for the rest of this Study Text and serves as the anchor for your learning sequence. You are advised to refer back to this framework at frequent intervals and to practise using it on cases and examples as necessary.

Chapter Roundup

- An **understanding of the way communication works** is an important part of building skills and knowledge about marketing communications.

- The **one-step model of communication** depicts communication as a linear process, but **feedback and interaction** are important parts of practical communications.

- The **two-step** and **multi-step models** reflect the influence of other people on the communication process. **Opinion leaders** play important roles in bringing credibility, and hence conviction and belief, to the way people understand the communications they receive.

- Communications are delivered and interpreted in **contexts**, the unique conditions in which each set of communication messages are designed and received.

- There are **five main contextual areas** that need to be considered when developing marketing communication campaigns. These are the **business, customer, stakeholder, organisational** and **external contexts**.

Now try Question 2 at the end of the Study Text

Quick Quiz

1   Why is it important to understand the theory of marketing communications? (see para 1.1)

2   Draw the communication process diagram. (2.1)

3   Describe the difference between an opinion leader and opinion former. (2.6)

4   What is the difference between a one-step flow of communication and a multi-step flow? (2.6 – 2.7)

5   Draw the two-step model of communication. (2.5)

6   What are the three main groups of innovations? (2.9)

7   What are the five categories of adopter? (2.14)

8   What marketing communications may be appropriate in the mature phase of the PLC? (2.19)

9   Why is a context analysis important? (3.5)

10   Name five main areas that a context analysis should review. (3.6)

Action Programme Review

1   As you develop your studies and examine more closely the use of different promotional tools, come back to this exercise and see how it applies to them eg direct mail or PR.

2   **Three suggestions**

(a)   *Continuous innovation*: software packages such as Windows XP; these have to be similar enough to previous versions not to require extensive retraining by the user

(b)   *Dynamically continuous innovation*: cheap electronic typewriters and PCs

(c) *Discontinuous innovation*: strictly speaking, this is more rare; the photocopier, or the fax machine or the video recorder are good examples

3   You might want to consider the role marketing communications could play in overcoming any perceived problem areas.

4   **Points to consider**

(a) British Airways has a strong national identity. Moves to change the aircraft livery from the Union flag design met a high level of resistance.

(b) BMW positions itself at the luxury end of the market, but has developed sports cars and 4X4 vehicles.

(c) Marks & Spencer have lost market share in recent times.

(d) The Inland Revenue have undergone a number of changes, but members of the public will always have negative association with 'tax collectors'.

(e) This is a young person's industry. Fashion is a key factor.

(f) Italian car producers once had a reputation for great engines but rust-prone bodywork. Fiat has helped dispel the negative images. Their small cars (Punto, Seicento) sell well and the Multipla was car of the year. But what of their larger models?

(g) A local council is accountable to the community and so this should be a major focus.

(h) Benetton are known for their controversial and high-profile adverts.

The Customer Context 3

Chapter Topic List	
1	Setting the scene
2	Consumer buyer behaviour
3	Factors influencing consumer buying behaviour
4	The consumer decision-making process
5	Involvement
6	Perceived risk
7	Organisational buying behaviour
8	The process of organisational buying behaviour
9	Influences on organisational buying behaviour
Knowledge brought forward from earlier stages	

Learning Outcome

☑ Determine specific communication activities based upon knowledge of the key characteristics of the target audience. In particular, they will be able to suggest how knowledge of perception and attitude, levels of perceived risk and involvement can impact upon marketing and corporate communications

Syllabus References

☑ Understanding the key drivers associated with information processing and buyer decision making processes

☑ Communication issues for internal and external audiences

☑ The role of personal influences on the communication process

Key Concepts Introduced

- Consumer buying behaviour
- Belief
- Culture
- Attitude
- Lifestyle
- Word of mouth
- Motivation
- Risk
- Perception
- Decision making unit

1 Setting the scene

1.1 The main aim of this chapter is to **develop an understanding of the various elements that influence the way individuals use information and make purchase decisions**. From this understanding it is possible to see how marketing communications can impact on customers and help them in the various decisions they need to make.

Links to other papers

1.2 You should have studied buyer behaviour in depth in your earlier studies. Please refer to the material below (and the 'Knowledge Brought Forward' section at the end of this chapter). Should the material on these pages be unfamiliar then it is recommended that you spend some time revising this area.

2 Consumer buying behaviour

Key Concept

Consumer buying behaviour can be defined as, 'the decision processes and acts of individuals involved in buying and using products or services.' (Dibb *et al, Marketing: Concepts and Strategies* (1994)).

2.1 As Dibb *et al* say, the study of consumer buying behaviour by an organisation is important for a number of reasons.

(a) The **buyer's reaction** to the organisation's marketing strategy has a major impact on the success of the organisation.

(b) If organisations are truly to implement the marketing concept, they must examine the main influences on **what, where, when and how customers buy**. Only in this way will they be able to devise a marketing mix that satisfies the needs of the customers.

(c) By gaining a better understanding of the factors influencing their customers and how their customers will respond, organisations will be better able to predict the **effectiveness of their marketing activities**.

2.2 However, not all consumers behave in the same way. Decision making and purchase patterns of behaviour vary considerably within individuals and across product categories. This **complexity must be recognised** and **marketing communications adapted** to meet the needs of different customers.

Marketing at Work

From the unabashed artificiality of Mr Whippy to the erotic promise of Haagen-Dazs, ice cream – so we are led to believe – varies dramatically.

Now, however, that belief has been exposed as a fallacy by an academic's claim that commercial ice creams are much the same.

'There's a limit to which they can differ from each other,' said Peter Barham, a physicist at Bristol University. 'Yes, there is a variation in terms of quality due to the range of ingredients – top ice creams use fresh cream and eggs and the cheaper ones use milk powder – and of course there are differences in flavours. But they all have a problem of storage which means that there's a limit to how different their texture can be.'

His claim that there is little to choose between mass-produced ice creams will be reiterated by a consumer psychologist, who will argue that it is image rather than taste that determines which ice cream we buy.

'At its most basic, ice cream is little more than frozen emulsified fat with a flavour in it. There will be a difference in flavour but the real difference in quality for the price differential is relatively minimal,' said consultant psychologist Paul Buckley.

But these claims were dismissed last night by representatives of the UK's £1bn-a-year ice cream industry.

'We totally reject the idea that all ice creams are the same,' said Annette Low, a spokeswoman for Ben and Jerry's. 'Premium ice-creams like Ben and Jerry's or Haagen-Dazs are partly defined by the amount of air in the ice cream and partly by the amount of butterfat. The less air, the more dense and rich it is. We also use premium ingredients, so our chocolate comes from Belgium rather than from the States, and our milk and creams from community farmed cows from Vermont.'

(*Guardian*, 4 June 2001)

3 Factors influencing consumer buying behaviour
6/02, 12/02

3.1 The 'core' process of consumer buying behaviour will be influenced by a number of outside variables. These variables have been classified by Wilson *et al*, *Strategic Marketing Management: Planning, Implementation and Control* (1999), as follows, with the focus progressively narrowing.

- Cultural
- Social
- Personal
- Psychological

3.2 Each factor will be considered in more detail separately, but it is essential to remember that they are not **mutually exclusive**. Marketers must have a clear understanding of how the various factors interact and how they influence buyer behaviour, both separately and in their totality.

Cultural factors

3.3 These are the most fundamental of the influencing factors, and include culture, subculture and social class.

Key Concept

Culture comprises the values, attitudes and beliefs in the pattern of life adopted by people that help them interpret and communicate as members of society.

3.4 **Culture** is largely the result of a learning process. As we grow up we learn a set of values, perceptions, preferences and behaviour patterns through socialisation in the family and other institutions such as school and work.

3.5 This broad set of values is then influenced by the **subcultures** in which we develop. Subcultural groups can be defined in terms of religion, ethnic characteristics, racial characteristics and geographical areas, all of which further influence attitudes, tastes, taboos and lifestyle.

3.6 A third cultural influence is that of **social stratification**, that is social class. The key characteristics of social class have been highlighted as follows.

(a) People within a particular social class resemble each other more than they resemble those from other social classes.

(b) Social class is determined by a series of variables such as occupation, income, education and values, rather than by a single variable.

(c) Individuals can move from one social class to another.

Social factors

3.7 Within the context of culture, an individual is also influenced by a series of social factors, such as **reference groups**, family, social role and status, all of which can have a direct effect on buying behaviour.

3.8 Reference groups are groups 'with which an individual identifies so much that he or she takes on many of the values, attitudes or behaviours of group members' (Dibb *et al*). Four types have been identified.

(a) **Primary membership groups**, which are generally informal and to which individuals belong and within which they interact (family, friends, neighbours, work colleagues and so on).

(b) **Secondary membership groups**, which tend to be more formal than primary groups and within which less interaction takes place (trade unions, religious groups and professional societies are examples).

(c)   **Aspirational groups**, to which an individual would like to belong.

(d)   **Dissociative groups**, whose values and behaviour the individual rejects.

Action Programme 1

The CIM is, presumably, one of your own aspirational groups. What other reference groups do you have? Divide them according to the above classifications.

The family

3.9   Another major social influence is the family, particularly with regard to the roles and relative influence exerted by different family members. Research has indicated three patterns of decision making within the family.

(a)   **Husband dominated**: life insurance, cars and television.

(b)   **Wife dominated**: washing machines, carpets, kitchenware and non living room furniture.

(c)   **Equal**: living room furniture, holidays, housing, furnishings and entertainment.

Marketing at Work

Changing behaviour

Not so long ago, a maternal seal of approval would have been the kiss of death for a product marketed at teenagers. However, unpublished research by advertising agency Ogilvy & Mather suggests that British teenage girls have open relationships with their mothers, share interests with them and admire what they have achieved.

The findings paint a picture of 13 to 18 year olds who want to be in control of their destinies and who are hard to shock.

They are independent and confident, though this confidence may sometimes be misplaced. Shopping is a frequent and social event, and they want access to brands even though they are on limited budgets.

At a more detailed level, the study highlights differences in how the younger and older girls related to brands and advertising.

Where younger girls seek security from brands that give them a sense of belonging and are a sign that they know what is fashionable, older teenage girls are more concerned with the 'integrity' of brands, looking for a sign of quality and a means of self-expression.

For advertising aimed at young girls to be effective, the most important elements are its final form and its display in magazines read by the target audience. For the older girls, however, the key to effectiveness seems more a matter of brand relevance.

Marketing at Work

The Advertising Association has produced a leaflet called Parent Power, which takes parents through the rigours of saying no to children's repeated requests for new purchases. It also describes how to explain the process of advertising to children, has guidelines for advertising to children and describes how to lodge a complaint.

Personal factors

3.10 Influencing factors that can be classified as **personal** include such things as age and life cycle, occupation, economic circumstances and lifestyle.

3.11 Individuals will buy different types of product depending on their **age**. This is particularly relevant to such products as clothes, furniture and recreation. However, consumption may also be shaped by the stage of the **family life cycle** within which an individual falls.

3.12 A person's **occupation** will influence consumption and the task for marketers is to identify the occupational groups that have an above average interest in their products and services.

3.13 Buying patterns are also heavily influenced by an individual's **economic circumstances**. Kotler states that an individual's economic circumstances consist of:

- Spendable income: its level, stability and time pattern
- Savings and assets, including the percentage that is liquid
- Borrowing power
- Attitude toward spending versus saving

However, people coming from the same subculture, social class and occupation may lead completely different **lifestyles**.

Key Concept

A **lifestyle** is an individual's mode of living as identified by activities, interests and opinions.'

Marketers will search for relationships between their products and lifestyle groups. There are many different lifestyle classifications; two examples, from McCann-Erikson and Taylor Nelson, are given in the table in Action Programme 2.

Marketing at Work

Advertisers are failing to notice the growing population of over 50 year olds, according to research by Datamonitor. By 2025 there are expected to be 177 million in this age group in Western Europe.

Three groups of over 50 year old consumers have emerged:

- 'Woofs': well off older folk
- 'Youthfully spirited': less financially secure then 'woofs', but willing to experiment

■   'Self preservationists': older, more conservative than the other groups.

Companies are obsessed with youth, and the staff in advertising agencies are predominantly under 30.

Psychological factors

3.14 The process of buyer behaviour is also influenced by **four major psychological factors**:

- ■   Motivation
- ■   Perception
- ■   Learning
- ■   Beliefs and attitudes

Motivation

Key Concept

Motivation has been defined as, an inner state that directs or channels behaviour.

3.15 Motivation arises from perceived needs. These needs can be of two main types - **biogenic** and **psychogenic**.

(a)   Biogenic needs arise from **physiological states** of tension such as hunger, thirst and discomfort.

(b)   Psychogenic needs arise from **psychological states** of tension such as the need for recognition, esteem or belonging.

3.16 Most needs are not intense enough to motivate an individual to act immediately, but when aroused to a sufficient level of intensity the individual will be motivated to act in order to reduce the perceived tension.

Theories of human motivation

3.17 **Maslow's** theory of motivation seeks to explain why people are driven by particular needs at particular times. Maslow argues that human needs are arranged in **a hierarchy** comprising, in their order of importance: **physiological** needs, **safety** needs, **social** needs, **esteem** needs and **self-actualisation** needs.

3.18 Maslow states that a person will attempt to **satisfy the most important need first**. When that need is satisfied it ceases to be a motivator and the person will attempt to satisfy the next most important need. For example, if you are hungry (a physiological need) you will venture out to get a sandwich.

3.19 **Herzberg** developed a 'two factor theory' of motivation that distinguishes between **factors that cause dissatisfaction and factors that cause satisfaction**. The task for the marketer is, therefore, to avoid 'dissatisfiers' such as, for example, poor after-sales service, as these things will not sell the product, and may well unsell it. In addition the marketer should identify the major satisfiers or motivators of purchase and make sure that they are supplied to the customer.

Action Programme 2

(a) Look at the two tables below. Have you moved, or are you about to move, from one category to another? What about the members of your family and your friends and colleagues at work?

(b) See if you can think of five products or services that it would be easy to sell to a person in each of the lifestyle categories described.

(c) For each product or service identified in (b), devise a communications strategy that would encourage the person in question to try your company's brand.

Life-style categories		
McCann-Erikson Men	**McCann-Erikson Women**	**Taylor Nelson**
Avant Guardians. *Concerned with change and well-being of others, rather than possessions. Well educated, prone to self righteousness.*	Avant Guardians. *'Liberal left' opinions, trendy attitudes. But out-going, active, sociable.*	Self-explorers. *Motivated by self-expression and self-realisation. Less materialistic than other groups, and showing high tolerance levels.*
Pontificators. *Strongly held, traditional opinions. Very British, and concerned about keeping others on the right path.*	Lady Righteous. *Traditional, 'right-minded' opinions. Happy, complacent, with strong family orientation.*	Social resisters. *The caring group, concerned with fairness and social values, but often appearing intolerant and moralistic.*
Chameleons. *Want to be contemporary to win approval. Act like barometers of social change, but copiers not leaders.*	Hopeful seekers. *Need to be liked, want to do 'right'. Like new things, want to be trendy.*	Experimentalists. *Highly individualistic, motivated by fast-moving enjoyment. They are materialistic, pro-technology but anti traditional.*
Self-admirers. *At the young end of the spectrum. Intolerant of others and strongly motivated by success. Concerned about self-image.*	Lively ladies. *Younger than above, sensual, materialistic, ambitious and competitive.*	Conspicuous consumers. *They are materialistic and pushy, motivated by acquisition, competition, and getting ahead. Pro-authority, law and order.*
Self-exploiters. *The 'doers' and 'self-starters', competitive but always under pressure and often pessimistic. Possessions are important.*	New unromantics. *Generally young and single, adopting a hard-headed and unsentimental approach to life. Independent, self-centred.*	Belongers. *What they seek is a quiet, undisturbed family life. They are conservative, conventional rule-followers.*

Token triers. *Always willing to try new things to 'improve their luck', but apparently on a permanent try-and-fail cycle. Includes an above average proportion of unemployed.*

Sleepwalkers. *Contented under-achievers. Do not care about most things, and actively opt out. Traditional macho views.*

Passive endurers. *Biased towards the elderly, they are often economically and socially disfranchised. Expect little of life, and give little.*

Lack-a-daisy. *Unassertive and easy-going. Try to cope but often fail. Not very interested in the new.*

Blinkered. *Negative, do not want to be disturbed. Uninterested in conventional success - in fact, few interests except TV and radio.*

Down-trodden. *This group is shy, introverted, but put upon. Would like to do better. Often unhappy and pressurised in personal relationships.*

Survivors. *Strongly class-conscious, and community spirited, their motivation is to 'get by'.*

Aimless. *Comprises two groups, (a) the young unemployed, who are often anti-authority, and (b) the old, whose motivation is day-to-day existence.*

Perception

Perception is defined as the process by which people organise and interpret stimuli into a meaningful picture.

3.20 The way consumers view an object (for example, their mental picture of a brand or the traits they attribute to it) will affect how they act towards it, and this possible difference in perception can be explained by the three perceptual processes, **selective attention**, **selective distortion** and **selection retention** (leading to eventual recall).

Selective attention

3.21 A receiver will not notice all the commercial messages that he comes into contact with, so the sender must design the message so that it **wins attention** in spite of the surrounding noise. Repetition, size, contour, music and sexual attraction are features used to attract attention.

Selective distortion

3.22 In many cases receivers distort or change the information they receive if that information does not fit in with their existing attitudes, beliefs and opinions. In other words, **people hear what they want to hear**. Selective distortion may take a variety of forms.

    (a)   **Amplification** (where receivers may add things to the message that are not there)

    (b)   **Levelling** (where receivers do not notice other things that are there).

The task of the sender is to produce a message that is clear, simple and interesting, what many refer to as **likeable**.

Selective recall and message rehearsal

3.23 A receiver will retain in memory **a small fraction of the messages** that are perceived and processed. The sender's aim is to get the message into the receiver's **long-term memory**, because once in the long-term memory the message can modify the receiver's beliefs and attitudes. However, to reach the long-term memory the message has to enter the **short-term memory**, which has only a limited capacity to process information. The factor influencing the passage of the message from the short-term to the long-term memory is the amount and type of **message rehearsal** given by the receiver.

3.24 In message rehearsal the receiver **elaborates on the meaning of the message** in a way that brings related thoughts from the long-term memory into his short-term memory.

(a) If the receiver's initial attitude to the object of the message is **positive** and he rehearses **support arguments** then the message is likely to be accepted and have **high recall**.

(b) If the receiver's initial attitude is **negative** and the person rehearses **counter arguments** against the object of the message then the message is likely to be **rejected**.

Learning

3.25 Learning concerns the process whereby an individual's **behaviour changes as a result of their experience**. Theories about learning state that it is the result of the interplay of five factors.

- Drives
- Stimuli
- Cues
- Responses
- Reinforcement

3.26 (a) A **drive is a strong internal force impelling action**, which will become a motive when it is directed to a particular drive-reducing **stimulus** object (the product).

(b) **Cues are minor stimuli** (such as seeing the product in action, favourable reactions to the product by family and friends, communicated by **word-of-mouth**) that determine when, where and how the person responds.

(c) Once the product is bought, if the experience is rewarding then the **response** to the product will be **reinforced**, making a repeat purchase the next time the situation arises more likely.

Beliefs and attitudes

Key Concept

A **belief** is 'a descriptive thought that a person holds about something' (Kotler).

3.27 Beliefs are important to marketers as the beliefs that people have about products make up the **brand images** of those products.

Key Concept

An **attitude** describes a person's 'enduring favourable or unfavourable cognitive evaluations, emotional feelings, and action tendencies toward some object or idea' (Kotler).

Exam Tip

Consumer attitudes in the hair care market featured in the December 2002 exam. The examiner noted that the L'Oreal slogan "Because I'm worth it" was an excellent example, quoted in many answers.

3.28 **Attitudes lead people to behave in a fairly consistent way towards similar objects**. Attitudes can be regarded as a short-cut in the thought process by ensuring that people do not have to interpret and react to every object in a fresh way. Attitudes settle into a consistent pattern and to change one attitude may entail major changes to other attitudes.

Action Programme 3

How might these ideas be applied to the marketing communications strategy of Jaguar?

4 The consumer decision-making process

4.1 As the main aim of marketing communications is to influence consumers with regard to a specific product or service offered, it is essential that the marketing communications practitioner has some understanding of the process by which consumers reach decisions to buy or not buy.

4.2 Steps in **the buying process**:

Step 1. **Need recognition**

Step 2. **Information search**

Step 3. **Evaluation of alternatives**

Step 4. **Purchase decision**

Step 5. **Post purchase evaluation**

Action Programme 4

Before reading on, think about a recent purchase of a fairly major item that you have made. Did you go through the stages listed above? Explain what the *need* was, how you searched for *information* and so on.

Step 1: Need recognition

4.3 The process begins when the buyer recognises a need or problem. This can be triggered by **internal stimuli**, such as hunger or thirst, or **external stimuli**, such as social esteem. If the need rises to a threshold level it will become a **drive** and from previous experience the buyer will know how to satisfy this drive through the purchase of a particular product. The task for the marketer is to identify the circumstances and/or stimuli that trigger a particular need, and use this knowledge to develop marketing strategies that trigger **consumer interest**.

Step 2: Information search

4.4 Once aroused, the customer will search for more information about the products that will satisfy the need. The information search stage can be divided into two levels.

(a) '**Heightened attention**', where the customer simply becomes more receptive to information about the particular product category.

(b) '**Active information search**'. The extent of active search will depend on the strength of the drive, the amount of information initially available, the ease of obtaining additional information and the satisfaction obtained from the search.

4.5 The task for the marketer is to decide which are the major information sources that the customer will use and to analyse their relative importance. According to Kotler **consumer information sources fall into four groups**.

- **Personal sources**: family, friends, neighbours, work colleagues
- **Commercial sources**: advertising, salespeople, packaging, displays
- **Public sources**: mass media, consumer rating organisations
- **Experiential sources**: handling, examining, using the product

4.6 A consumer will generally receive the most information exposure from commercial sources, but the **most effective information exposure comes from personal sources**. Each information source performs a somewhat different function, with consumers being informed by commercial sources and this information being legitimised (or not) by personal sources.

Key Concept

Word of mouth is the operating of communication by human interaction.

4.7 Through this information-gathering process the consumer will learn about **competing brands and their relative pros and cons**. This will enable the consumer to narrow down the range of alternatives to those brands that will best meet his or her particular needs and maybe confer prestige, in the case of luxury goods. What has been called the '**choice or evoked set**'.

Exam Tip

Word of mouth communication featured in the December 2002 exam.

Step 3: Evaluation of alternatives

4.8 Trying to describe the process of evaluation of alternatives is not easy as there is no generally accepted single evaluation process. Most current models of evaluation are **cognitively oriented: in other words they take the view that the customer forms judgements largely on a conscious and rational basis**.

4.9 Kotler states that, as the consumer is trying to satisfy some need with the buying process, he will be looking for certain benefits from the product chosen and each product will be seen as a '**bundle of attributes**' with varying capabilities of delivering the benefits sought and hence satisfying the need. The composition and the relative importance of the components of this bundle of attributes will differ between customers, and therefore the marketer should determine what importance the customer attaches to each attribute.

4.10 The consumer is likely to build up a set of **brand beliefs** about the position of each brand with regard to each attribute. The sum of these brand beliefs will make up the **brand image**. The consumer will most likely choose the brand that holds the optimum balance between those attributes that are perceived to be the most important.

5 Involvement

5.1 The length and duration of each of these stages of the buying process will vary with each individual and with each purchase decision. **Consumers do not care to the same degree about all their purchase decisions**. Their **level of involvement** is said to vary and two types of involvement can be identified: **high** and **low**.

5.2 **High involvement decisions** are those that are **important** to the customer in some way. For example, they may be related to luxury purchases, closely tied to the customer's ego or self image. Therefore a greater amount of **care and attention** is given to these decisions, and marketing communications has an important role to play in assisting consumers make such decisions. For this reason online communications and purchasing may be less significant in the market for luxury goods, where customers like to 'feel' and test a product.

5.3 **Low involvement decisions are not so important**, so the level of care is much lower. Consequently individuals do not spend much time searching for information and the role of marketing communications messages is different.

BPP
PROFESSIONAL EDUCATION

6   Perceived risk

12/99, 12/01

6.1   Allied to the concept of involvement is **perceived risk**.

Key Concept

Risk is hard to define as it has precise meanings in different contexts. In marketing, risk relates to the possibility that the outcome of a decision will not have the desired affect or may make the situation worse. The amount of risk perceived in purchases varies from individual to individual and across product categories. By identifying the dominant forms of risk present at any one time it is possible to design messages that can help to reduce levels of perceived risk.

Risk	Comment	Dealing with it
Performance	Will the product function properly?	Guarantees money back
Financial	Can I afford it, is it good value?	Emphasise value for money, quality
Physical	Will the product harm me or other people?	Emphasise safety
Ego	Will the product satisfy my needs for self esteem and self image?	Aspiration groups
Social	Will significant others disapprove?	Suggest psychological rewards
Time	Have I the time to go shopping to buy this product?	Importance or convenience of product

6.2   Most individuals will experience a number of these risks when making purchase decisions. It is unlikely that all these risks will present at any one time. Once the **dominant risks** are identified, marketing communications can be used to transmit messages that seek to reduce these risks.

(a)   Should **finance** be an important factor, then interest free credit may help reduce this risk.

(b)   If **social risk** is high then pictures of people smiling and giving approval to the person using the product (eg children in Sunny Delight advertisements) will be effective.

Exam Tip

This topic featured in the Specimen paper and both December 1999 and December 2001. Note that risk is more than 'danger': It can include psychological factors – a sense of discomfort.

Of course a product may reduce certain sorts of risk, and so risk-reduction (eg safety-shields in cars) can be an explicit message.

6.3 Celebrity **endorsement**, the **approval** of opinion formers and **visual demonstrations** of the product/service in action are all important communication methods. Of course, one of the main methods is **branding**. Branding is a particularly powerful form of marketing communication as it allows individuals to assimilate product **information** quickly, identify levels of **product quality** and so reduce their levels of felt risk.

7 Organisational buying behaviour

7.1 **Organisational (or industrial) buying** has been defined as 'the decision-making process by which formal organisations establish the need for purchased products and services and identify, evaluate and choose among alternative brands and suppliers' (Webster & Wind, *Organisational Buying Behaviour,* 1972).

7.2 Kotler identifies a number of **differences between organisational and consumer markets** that mean that a modified approach needs to be taken when considering the process of buying behaviour.

(a) Organisational markets normally comprise **fewer buyers**, with those buyers often being very **concentrated** (a few buyers are responsible for the majority of sales).

(b) Because of this smaller customer base and the importance and power of larger customers there is generally a **close relationship between buyer and seller** in organisational markets, with a great degree of customisation and co-operation on product specification and other requirements. Organisational buyers are often geographically concentrated.

7.3 A number of **demand factors** also influence the nature of organisational markets. Demand for industrial goods is ultimately **derived** from the demand for consumer goods. If the demand for these consumer goods slackens then the demand for the industrial products that contribute to their production will also fall. In addition, the total demand for many industrial products is **inelastic**, (not much affected by price changes). Demand for industrial products may also be quite **seasonal** and more **volatile** than that for consumer products.

7.4 The specific characteristics of organisational markets may vary according to the **types of organisations** that comprise the market. Dibb *et al* identify four types of organisational markets: producers, resellers, governments and institutions.

Market	Comment
Producer	Organisations that purchase products for the purpose of making a profit by using them to produce other products or by using them in their own operations.
Reseller	Intermediaries such as retailers and wholesalers who buy the finished goods in order to resell them to make a profit.
Government	National and local governments who buy a variety of goods and services to support their internal operations and to provide public services.
Institutional	Organisations that seek to achieve charitable, educational, community or other non-business goals.

8 The process of organisational buying behaviour

8.1 Process of organisational buying behaviour

Stage 1. **Recognise the problem**: the stimulus may come from within or outside the firm

Stage 2. **Develop product specifications to solve the problem**. People participating in the buying decision assess the problem and determine what will be required to resolve or satisfy it.

Stage 3. **Search for products and suppliers**. The third stage of the process is similar to that of **information search**, utilising trade shows, trade publications, supplier catalogues, and soliciting proposals from known suppliers.

Stage 4. **Evaluate products and suppliers relative to specifications**. These are evaluated in order to ascertain whether they meet the product specifications developed in the second stage.

Stage 5. **Select and order the most appropriate product**. In some cases an organisational buyer may select a number of suppliers in order to reduce the possibility of disruption. The order will then be made, often with specific details regarding terms, credit arrangements, delivery dates and technical assistance or after-sales service.

Stage 6. **Evaluate the product and supplier performance** by comparing with specifications regarding product quality and the performance of the supplier over the terms of the contract.

8.2 Again, as with consumer buying behaviour, the full buying process may not be applicable in all cases. **Three main types of organisational purchase can be identified**. The **number of individuals** involved in the process, and the **length of the buying process** will be influenced by the type of purchase.

(a) **New task purchase**

The organisation is facing a need or a problem for the first time and the full organisational buying process will probably occur, with detailed specifications of both product and ordering routines for this and future purchases. Much information will generally be needed in order to make the purchase. These new task purchases can be important to sellers as they might be the start of a long and profitable relationship in which they sell large amounts of their products.

(b) **Modified re-buy**

Something about the buying situation has changed. Such situations may include circumstances where a buyer requires faster delivery, different prices or a slightly different product specification.

(c) **Straight re-buy**

The buyer routinely purchases the same products under the same terms of sale. In such situations the buying process will be truncated.

The Decision Making Unit (DMU)

8.3 One of the major differences between consumer and organisational buying behaviour is the fact that **organisational purchase decisions are rarely made by a single individual**. This has a significant influence on the buying process in the organisational context. Normally, purchasing decisions are made by a number of people from **different functional areas**. This complicates the process of marketing and selling the product and it is important that the marketer is fully aware of the **composition of the buying group**.

8.4 A framework for considering these issues was provided by Webster and Wind, *Organisational Buying Behaviour* (1972), with the concept of the Decision Making Unit (DMU).

Key Concept

The **Decision Making Unit** is defined as 'all those individuals and groups who participate in the purchasing decision process, who share some common goals and the risks arising from the decisions'.

8.5 Webster and Wind suggested six **groups within the Decision Making Unit**.

(a) **Users**, who may initiate the buying process and help define purchase specifications

(b) **Influencers**, who help define the specification and also provide an input into the process of evaluating the available alternatives

(c) **Deciders**, who have the responsibility for deciding on product requirements and suppliers

(d) **Approvers**, who authorise the proposals of deciders and buyers

(e) **Buyers**, who have the formal authority for the selection of suppliers and negotiating purchase terms

(f) **Gatekeepers** who, by controlling the flow of information, may be able to stop sellers from reaching individuals within the buying centre

8.6 The size, structure and formality of the DMU will vary depending on the specific situation. The marketer has to consider five questions.

(a) **Who** are the principal participants in the buying process?

(b) In what areas do they exert the **greatest influence**?

(c) What is their **level of influence**?

(d) What **evaluative criteria** do each of the participants make use of and how professional is the buying process?

(e) To what extent is **buying centralised**?

9 Influences on organisational buying behaviour

9.1 Kotler identifies four main forces influencing the organisational buyer, shown below in order of progressively narrowing focus.

- **Environmental**
- **Organisational**
- **Interpersonal**
- **Individual**

9.2 **Environmental forces** include such factors as the level of primary demand, economic outlook, the cost of money, the rate of technological change, political and regulatory developments and competitive developments.

9.3 Each organisation has its own objectives, policies, procedures, organisational structures and systems, which may constrain the freedom of action of organisational buyers. For example, an organisation may insist on long-term contracts or may require special credit arrangements.

9.4 **Interpersonal factors** are important where the buying decision may involve a number of people. Within the buying group, the use of **power** and the level of **conflict** could significantly influence organisational buying decisions.

9.5 **Individual factors** are the personal characteristics of the individuals in the buying group such as age, education, personality and position. These will affect the decision-making process, and the seller must be aware of their potential influence.

Organisational buyer behaviour matrix

9.6 An alternative framework for explaining the main **influences and participants in the process of organisational buying behaviour** has been put forward by the American Marketing Association, as shown below.

Departmental influences

Within the organisation

	Within the organisation	In other departments
Within the buying department	*Cell 1* Purchasing agent	*Cell 2* Buying centre
	Cell 3 Professionalism	*Cell 4* Organisational environment

In other organisations

9.7 **Cell 1: the purchasing agent**. This represents the buyer within the organisation and within the buying department. Various factors will influence the buyer, including social factors, price and cost factors, supply continuity and risk avoidance.

(a) **Social factors** include the relationships, friendships and antipathies that exist between buyer and suppliers and the extent to which these impinge on purchasing decisions.

While in an ideal world such social factors should not influence decision making, they are, in reality, an important factor in the equation.

(b) **Price and cost factors** are obviously important and can include such things as the economic state of the buying organisation, the level of competition among suppliers, any cost/benefit analyses that might have been conducted, the purchasing budget and the personality and background of the purchasing agent (for example, an agent with an accountancy background may be more cost conscious).

(c) **Supply continuity** is a function of the number of suppliers that are available and the importance of the purchased item to the organisation.

(d) **Risk** avoidance is a common motivation for organisational buyers.

9.8 **Buyers can typically cope with risk in a number of ways**

(i) **Exchanging information** with their customers and prospects

(ii) Dealing only with those suppliers with which the company has previously had **favourable experiences**

(iii) Applying strict **rules**

(iv) Dealing only with suppliers who have a long established and favourable **reputation**

(v) Introducing **penalty clauses**, for example for late delivery

(vi) **Multiple sourcing** to reduce the degree of dependence on a single supplier

9.9 **Cell 2: the buying centre**. This cell equates to the Decision Making Unit, where the focus is within the firm but between departments. Some of the influencing factors in this cell include organisation structure and policy, power, status and conflict procedures, and gatekeeping.

(a) With regard to **organisational structure and policy**, the place of the purchasing department within the organisation is very important as it will determine such matters as the level of influence and the reporting relationships.

(b) **Power, status and conflict procedures** relate to the degree to which the buyer or purchasing department wishes to change or maintain the status quo. For example, decentralisation and divisionalisation of the organisation may motivate outside departments to initiate their own buying decisions.

(c) **Gatekeeping** controls the flow of information in the organisation and the person who acts as the gatekeeper can exert considerable influence.

9.10 **Cell 3: professionalism**. This cell examines the influence of professional standards and practice in other organisations, the main factors being specialist journals, conferences and trade shows, word of mouth communication and supply-purchase reciprocity.

(a) **Specialist journals**, conferences and trade shows are likely to be the source of much professional knowledge.

(b) **Word of mouth communication**, or the professional 'grapevine', can act as a potent force within the profession.

(c) **Supply-purchase reciprocity** refers to arrangements whereby two organisations reach an agreement to supply each other.

9.11 Cell 4: the organisational environment. This cell is concerned with factors outside both the purchasing department and the organisation.

- Economic, commercial and competitive forces
- Political, social and legal environment
- Technological change
- Co-operative buying (through, for example, the formation of consortia)
- Nature of the supplier

Selection criteria

9.12 The consideration of this area so far has concentrated on the factors influencing the organisational buying decision. The issue of precisely **how** organisational buyers make the purchase decision, in terms of the selection criteria determining the choice of supplier, has been the subject of various pieces of research. For example, in a survey of purchasing managers it was found that the most important selection criteria were as follows.

- Delivery capability
- Quality
- Price
- Repair and after sales service
- Technical capability
- Performance history
- Production facilities
- Help and advice
- Control systems
- Reputation

- Financial position
- Attitude toward the buyer
- Compliance with bidding procedures
- Training support
- Communications on the progress of the order
- Management and organisation
- Packaging
- Moral/legal issues
- Location
- Labour relations

9.13 Others have introduced an additional level of analysis into their research in the form of the **type of buying situation**, leading them to suggest the following influences as important.

(a) **Routine order products**

- Delivery
- Reliability
- Price
- Reputation

(b) **Procedural problem products** (for example, computers and other types of office machinery)

- Technical service
- Supplier flexibility
- Product reliability

(c) **Political problem products capable of creating organisational rivalries**

- Price
- Reputation of supplier
- Product reliability
- Service reliability
- Supplier flexibility

Knowledge brought forward from earlier stages

WHAT DO WE MEAN BY THE CUSTOMER?

Central to the principle of marketing-led organisations is the process of **getting to know our customers**. They need first to be identified before they are understood.

Customers may be within an organisation as well as external to it.

Because the Decision-Making Unit comprises a number of individuals, and the decision-making process is often a lengthy and complex one, there is an important distinction to be made between **customers**, who buy the product/service, and **users**, who make use of its provision. The **Decision Making Unit** is the group of people who come together to influence, positively or negatively, a purchase decision. They usually comprise gatekeepers, initiators, influencers, deciders, buyers, users and financiers. Reaching the key figures in the DMU is a crucial role of the marketer.

The **Decision-Making Process** describes the steps that are taken over time in order to make a purchase decision.

THE COMPONENTS OF THE DECISION MAKING UNIT

Individuals are important in all buying decisions, either for themselves or on behalf of an organisation. Marketers need to understand their **motives, psychology and influences**, and how these combine to form a motivation mix.

Group membership and dynamics are of particular significance, as individuals can be highly influenced by their primary groups, that is family and work. **Reference group theory** investigates how individuals use the norms of groups to provide a reference point or benchmark for their own activity.

The **family** is of critical importance to individuals, as a network of relationships, reference group and social unit. The Decision-Making Unit operates most often in a family context, with different family members adopting different roles.

Organisational decision making is based on the same DMU model but is generally more **rational**. The interaction of DMU members is influenced by a great many variables.

PSYCHOLOGICAL INFLUENCES ON BEHAVIOUR

A consumer's **self-image** may lead him to choose brands which support him and help him towards his expected self-concept.

An **attitude** is a relatively consistent, learned predisposition to behave in a certain way in response to a given object.

Attribution theory states that attitudes are formed by people's interpretations of their own behaviour and experiences.

Consistency theories state that individuals seek cognitive consistency, experiencing tension if this is not achieved.

Marketers often seek to change attitudes. Factors affecting attitude change are existing attitudes, source factors (who is telling us), message features, the communication channel, receiver attributes and product characteristics.

A person's **need** for something becomes a **want** to satisfy that need, which then sets a **goal** for how to achieve **satisfaction** of the need.

Needs are **biogenic** (innate), **psychogenic** (innate) or **secondary** (learned). Innate needs are activated by deprivation: they must then either be satisfied or avoided. Secondary needs are activated by stimuli.

Motives may be aroused **physiologically** (hunger pangs), **emotionally** (fantasy), **cognitively** (recognition) or **environmentally** (external stimuli).

Motives can be **rational** or **emotional**.

Maslow's hierarchy of needs theory classifies needs into five types and arranges them as a pyramid.

Vroom's expectancy theory relates the desire for a potential outcome to the strength of expectation that a certain action will actually result in that outcome.

SOCIAL INFLUENCES ON BEHAVIOUR

Socialisation is the process by which each individual learns the social expectations, goals, beliefs, values and attitudes that enable him to exist in society.

Socialisation is a **learning process** that may come about through classical conditioning, cognitive learning, imitation, identification, or role play/experimentation.

The groups that play the greatest part in **consumer socialisation** are the family, school, peer groups and the mass media.

Role theory is concerned with the roles that individuals act out in their lives and how the assumption of various roles affects their attitudes to other people.

SOCIOLOGICAL INFLUENCES ON BEHAVIOUR

The term '**culture**' encompasses the sum total of learned beliefs, values, customs, rituals, languages, symbols, artefacts and technology of a society or group.

Products can be invested with cultural meaning by marketing efforts; that meaning is transferred to a buyer who uses the product in a cultural context and hence imbues it with further cultural meaning. This is called **transfer of cultural meaning**.

Marketing cross-culturally has many advantages for marketers but brings with it a number of new challenges. Two approaches can be used: **localised markets** (marketing a product so that it fits into the existing culture) or **global marketing** (capitalising on the fact that culture changes and develops, so a 'foreign' product can gain acceptance into different cultures in the same form worldwide).

THE INFLUENCE OF ECONOMIC FACTORS

Four models of consumer decision making define the **economic motivation of consumers**.

- The **economic man** is perfectly rational and has perfect information.
- The **passive man** is wholly impulsive.
- The **cognitive man** is a problem solver who is as well informed as he needs to be.
- The **emotional man** aims primarily to satisfy his emotional needs rather than his purely economic ones.

Consumers make choices because their resources are scarce. The cost of an item measured in terms of the alternatives forgone is called its **opportunity cost**.

Price elasticity of demand measures how far a change in price will cause a change in demand. Income elasticity of demand measures the same thing for a change in income levels.

The **trade or business cycle** typically goes through boom, recession, depression and recovery. At each stage, income levels and hence demand will be changing.

SOURCES OF CHANGE

More sophisticated communication systems have made the world smaller but cultures around the world are just as likely to reject an encroaching cultural change as embrace it. The decision either to go for a global brand, standardised in all its markets, or a local marketing strategy is a finely balanced one.

Technology affects the marketer in three ways: it is **included** in new products, it enables new **products** to be produced, and it allows new products to be **delivered**. It also allows older products to become **obsolescent** more quickly, and changes the ways in which work is performed.

Green issues have a significant impact on the marketer.

Behaving **ethically** has become a key strategy for many organisations. The choice is between being merely **compliant** with the law, or having a **corporate image** of being an **ethical organisation**, which to many customers is a very appealing thing.

Chapter Roundup

- In order to reach and influence members of the target audience it crucial to understand the

- Analysis of this contextual element revolves around the way in which marketing communication messages are **processed**, **interpreted and acted upon**.

- Therefore, perception, motivation, learning and attitudes are **key pyschological factors** that need to be appreciated.

- It is vital for marketers to have an understanding of the processes that customers go through when buying a product, whether this product is being bought by a consumer for individual consumption or by an organisation. **The buying process**, both organisational and consumer, can be simply summarised as follows:

  o Recognition of problem/need
  o Information search
  o Evaluation of alternatives
  o Purchase decision
  o Post purchase evaluation

- The extent to which a consumer engages in all these stages will depend on the size, complexity and specific circumstances of the buying situation. A **range of influencing factors** can be identified that could possibly affect the process. Such factors need to be recognised by marketers so that they are taken into account in marketing and promotional activity.

Now try Question 3 at the end of the Study Text

Quick Quiz

1   What factors influence consumer buying behaviour? (see para 3.1)

2   What are the key characteristics of social class? (3.6)

3   What psychological factors influence buyer behaviour? (3.14)

4   What are selective attention, distortion and recall? (3.21 - 3.23)

5   What is the difference between a belief and an attitude? (3.27 – 3.28)

6   What are the six forms of perceived risk? (6.1)

7   What are the features of organisational markets? (7.2 - 7.4)

8   What six groups make up the Decision Making Unit? (8.5)

9   What factors influence organisational buying? (9.1)

10 How does 'professionalism' influence organisational buying? (9.10)

11 List some possible organisational selection criteria. (9.12, 9.13)

Action Programme Review

1   This list is likely to include groups which might be classified into business and personal categories. Can you identify any situations where these groups may have influenced your purchasing behaviour in either a business or personal context?

2   This exercise normally provides for an interesting discussion within a group situation. Try this with other members of your study group or some work colleagues.

3   *Perception*

Jaguar want customers to perceive its vehicles as having the traditional values of style, distinctiveness and performance but it also wants to add modern qualities of technology, reliability and excellent services. All marketing communications should reflect and reinforce these perceptions. The recent ads starring Sting are helping to do this. (More importantly, Jaguars' entry into formula One with British drivers, especially the fun-loving Eddie Irvine, is helping to establish Jaguar as a sporty, up-to-date marque.)

Learning

Customers learn about Jaguar cars by a number of means. An awareness campaign of an ongoing nature is necessary to keep reminding people of the nature of Jaguar. The company used Classic FM commercial radio to do this and also sponsored radio programmes likely to be listened to (probably in their current car) by the target market. The company also used newspaper advertisements in the quality press with coupons to enable potential customers to send for details. Jaguar replied with high quality literature and also passed names on to local dealers who could then make telephone contact. In this way potential Jaguar customers were able to learn about the products in a systematic and progressive manner.

Buyers' motivation

Jaguar cars meet higher levels of needs for a status symbol (esteem), and marketing communications must reflect this. It is also possible to encourage customers to feel part of the Jaguar 'club', meeting their social needs. Some customers will feel fulfilled by achieving a lifetime's dream of owning a Jaguar.

There may be different motivations for different segments, and the products themselves may be used to communicate in different ways. Older customers prefer larger, maybe Daimler-badged cars from the range. The smaller, sporty models appeal to the younger customer.

Values, attitudes and lifestyles (VALS)

Attitudes can be broken down into cognitive, affective and conative elements.

(a)   Cognitive represents awareness of Jaguar
(b)   Affective is the positive (or negative feeling) towards Jaguar
(c)   Conative is the intention to purchase

Jaguar scores highly on the first, reasonably well on the second, but has scored insufficiently on the third 'buying' level. Products and advertising have been put in place to correct this, for example by developing smaller, more economical models to appeal to a wider audience.

Much buyer behaviour is shaped by group influence. Groups can develop their own norms. Marketing communications need to promote the idea of a successful lifestyle. Senior managers *deserve* the reward and enjoyment of a car of distinction: a Jaguar. Other groups are being targeted too: younger managers who want to demonstrate their success by the ownership of a Jaguar.

4   When you have completed this, consider what were the major influencing factors on the purchase decision. Did reference group membership play a part?

The Business Context

4

Learning Outcome

☑ Determine the context in which marketing (and corporate) communications are to be implemented in order to improve effectiveness and efficiency, understand the key strategic communication issues arising from the contextual analysis and prepare (integrated) marketing communications plans

Syllabus References

☑ A contextual analysis understanding and justification for marketing and corporate communication strategies

☑ The strategic significance and impact of integrated marketing communications

☑ The determination and appreciation of the prevailing and future contextual conditions as a means of deriving and developing promotional strategies and plans

☑ The target marketing process as a means of identifying significant promotional opportunities

Key Concepts Introduced

- Corporate strategy
- Target marketing process
- Market segmentation
- Lifestyle
- Positioning

1 Setting the scene

1.1 The **nature of the prevailing market conditions** is an important context that needs to be considered when developing marketing communications activities. The focus of this chapter is on the influence of an organisation's **corporate and marketing strategies** and the way they link to promotional approaches. The **target market process** and the influence of **segmentation** on the communications that follow are essential to this perspective.

Links to other papers

1.2 The content of this chapter is relevant to your *Planning and Control* studies, as it places marketing communications firmly within the context of the organisation and its marketing plan. The business context is also a key factor in the *Analysis and Decision* case study.

2 The business context

2.1 An organisation's interaction with the various **markets in which it operates** is, of course, crucial. In order that its marketing communications be effective it is necessary to understand the conditions and elements that prevail in specific markets.

- Is the market **expanding or contracting**?

- What are the **values and beliefs** held by the target audience towards its products and those of competitors?

- What are the attitudes of **intermediaries**?

- What is the nature of **competitive communications**?

3 Hierarchies of strategies and objectives 12/99

3.1 As we have already emphasised, the nature of marketing communications strategy has to be viewed within the context of an **overall marketing strategy**, since a promotional strategy cannot exist in isolation. Prior to the promotional strategy being decided, the company will make a series of **corporate** and/or **business unit** decisions that will determine the nature of the overall marketing strategy.

3.2 Each level of the organisation has a hierarchy of:

- **Objectives**
- **Strategy**
- **Tactics**

3.3 **The tactics of the upper level then become the objectives of the next level** down in the organisation. The levels we can usually consider are:

- **Corporate** (and then business unit, if separately managed)
- **Functional** (including marketing)
- **Activity** (including marketing communications)

These relationships are shown in diagram below, Simon Majaro's Planning Hierarchy.

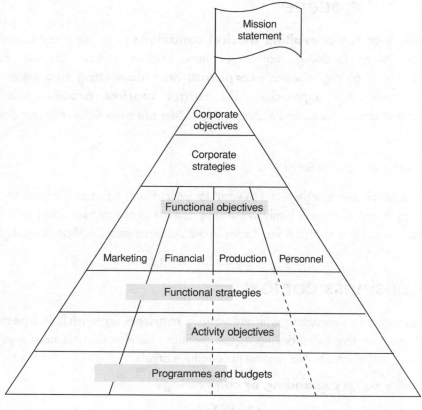

The planning hierarchy by Simon Majaro

3.4 An organisation's **mission statement** is a **description of long-term vision and values**. Mission statements have become increasingly common because they can provide **clear guidance** to managers and employees on the future direction of the organisation, and can be used to develop a **hierarchy of objectives** that link the long-term vision and values with specific objectives at each level of the organisation.

4 Corporate strategy and business strategy

Key Concept

Corporate strategy is concerned with identifying the scope of activities and markets with which the company wishes to be associated.

4.1 The direction in which a company will move forward will be dependent upon a number of factors.

- The nature of the **changing environment**
- The existing and future **resource capabilities** of the organisation
- The strategies adopted by **competitors**
- The expectations and values of the **management and workforce**
- The maintenance of a **competitive position** within the market

The strategic triangle

4.2 One way of looking at this is from the perspective of the three main players, as in the '**strategic triangle**', so called by Japanese management consultant Kenichi Ohmae.

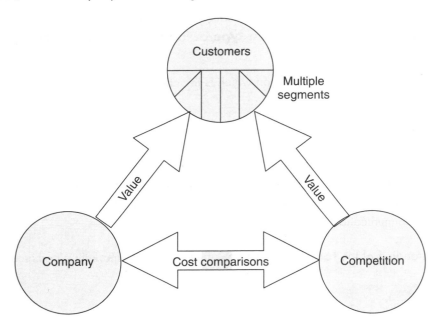

The strategic triangle

4.3 Once the corporate strategy has been decided, this may then be translated into a **business unit strategy**. Business unit strategy is concerned with how individual strategic business units will **compete within their chosen market**. This might involve **repositioning** of the business unit within the market in order to compete more effectively or the **creation of new business units** to take advantage of new market opportunities.

4.4 **Functional strategies (or operational strategies)** encompassing marketing, finance, production and personnel will then be created to support the corporate or individual business unit strategy. As part of the marketing mix, a **promotional strategy** will be devised that will integrate into the strategic marketing plan.

4.5 The framework within which the promotional strategy operates is built upon prior decisions regarding **product policy, segmentation and targeting**. As a consequence, should any of these decisions be flawed, then the promotional strategy is somewhat restricted.

4.6 This example highlights the contribution that a promotional strategy makes within the overall corporate strategy. It also shows how **corporate level or business level decisions provide the framework within which the promotional plan can function**.

Competitive strategy

4.7 In your studies of *Planning and Control*, you will cover the **competitive forces** in detail, and the various competitive strategies firms adopt.

4.8 In **Porter's model** there are three broad strategies.

	Marketing communications impact
Cost leadership	Still needs to offer a clear identity for the product or service
Differentiation	Communicate differentiated benefits and brand benefits. Branding is tied up with differentiation
Focus	Direct communications at target audience

4.9 In the short term, marketing communications are directed against competitors because **marketing communications are a type of 'noise'**. Two examples are:

- Repositioning
- 'Knocking copy' (eg disputes on which is the cheapest air fare)

5 The marketing plan

5.1 Marketing communication strategies are intended to support and deliver the marketing objectives. **Marketing objectives are prepared and articulated through a marketing plan**. This document acts as a cornerstone for the development of effective marketing communications.

5.2 An understanding of the **target audience** is fundamental to marketing communications.

Key Concept

The **target marketing process** (TMP) consists of segmenting the market, targeting particular segments and then positioning the offer in the selected segment in order to achieve the marketing goals.

5.3 We have included information about **segmentation** here as it is an important part of the promotional plan, although you will be familiar with much of it already.

Market segmentation

Key Concept

Market segmentation is the process of breaking down the total market into segments that share common properties, that is, customers who behave in a similar way and who can be reached by similar strategies.

5.4 The overriding requirement for modern marketing is **better targeting** at **specific segments**. This applies to a range of activities including the location of a new retail superstore, the stocking of a range of products, the placement of an advertisement in a newspaper or the launching of a new product into the market. The key aim is to communicate effectively with as many people as possible within a given market, while minimising the waste in communicating with those people in whom the organisation is not interested.

Bases for segmentation

5.5 The major issue surrounding the debate on market segmentation is the **criteria upon which markets are segmented**. There are five main bases upon which markets can be segmented.

- **Geographics**
- **Demographics** (including socio-economics, age, race, religion)
- **Geodemographics**
- **Psychographics** (including attitudes, interests, opinions and lifestyle)
- **Behaviour** (including benefits sought, brand loyalty/usage rates, situation specifics).

Geographic segmentation

5.6 **Geographic segmentation** is possibly one of the easiest forms of dividing markets into individual segments. This form of segmentation depends upon there being discernible disparities in consumer buying behaviour between one region and the next. Among other things, geographic segmentation may require a different stocking policy in-store and different promotional techniques for the separate regions.

Demographic segmentation

5.7 **Demographics** encompass age, sex, education, income, occupation and family composition. Consumption of holidays and of clothing provide good examples of segmentation based upon age. Saga holidays cater for the older age groups. Mothercare provide clothing and related products for babies and young children. An important element within this form of segmentation is the **family life cycle**. Wells and Gubar established the nine stage family life cycle outlined below.

Stage of life cycle		Characteristics
1	**Bachelor stage**: young single people living at home	Have limited or no financial commitments. Buy stereos, cars and fashion conscious.
2	**Newly married couples**. Dual incomes, no children	Financially well off, tend to buy consumer durables.
3	**Full nest 1**: youngest child under 6	Cash position is low, savings are minimal. Purchase toys, clothes, baby foods and some white goods.
4	**Full nest 2**: oldest child over 6	Returning to dual incomes, savings improving; purchasing bicycles, computers, holidays.
5	**Full nest 3**: older married couples with dependent children	Financially more secure, some children working, increased ability to purchase desirables and luxury goods.

Stage of life cycle	Characteristics
6 **Empty nest 1**: children left home and head of household still in work	House ownership at a peak, savings at a maximum; purchase holidays and spend more on recreation and home improvements.
7 **Empty nest 2**: older married, no children at home, husband and wife retired	Reduction in income, dependent upon pension, savings and investments. Health conscious and buy medical products.
8 **Solitary survivor** in the workforce	Income high.
9 **Solitary survivor**, retired, dependent	Income at its lowest, may sell home, may require attention.

5.8 In the UK, however, the **changing political and social environment** is impinging upon this analysis. The need for increased financial awareness and planning at a younger age will affect disposable income in earlier years (ie stages 2 and 3), while improving financial spending power in later years (stages 6 and 7). This has been brought about because of the prospect of cutbacks in state pensions so that many more people have taken out their own pensions policies. This has provided the opportunity for financial institutions to promote a wide range of products, particularly to the younger age groups.

5.9 While the **family life cycle** chronicles the age and income attributes, it ignores some other more fundamental matters. As we move through the above stages, not only does income vary, but attitudes and expectations also change and this can have significant impact upon the consumption process.

5.10 For example, more women are having children later in life while older people, rather than winding down, are now more likely to engage in leisure and sports pursuits later in their lives, as well as embarking upon new challenges, such as education. The traditional associations between age and life styles are changing, requiring a new marketing focus.

5.11 One of the more common means of demographic segmentation is by **socio-economic grading**. This involves characterising a market by occupational status, related specifically to the head of the household. Commonly referred to as the AB/C1/C2/DE classification, it is based upon JICNARS (Joint Industry Committee for National Readership Surveys) and assumes that buying behaviour is related to occupational types.

A: Upper middle class
B: Middle class
C1: Lower middle class
C2 Skilled working class
D: Manual workers
E: Those at the lowest level of subsistence

5.12 This approach has some major weaknesses.

(a) It **tends to ignore income**, especially dual incomes where both the husband and wife are in employment.

(b) Concentration on the **head of household** occupation wrongly assumes that buying behaviour by other family members will be related to this.

(c)   While comparisons between the highest and lowest categories may afford some benefits, comparisons between the **middle groups** are somewhat less useful.

5.13 Nonetheless, this basis is still widely used because the main newspapers present their readership profiles in this manner, and the information that supports this system is relatively easily obtained. Despite its limitations, socio-economic segmentation, when combined with income levels and other segmentation criteria, still plays a valuable role in identifying customer groups.

Geodemographics

5.14 **Geodemographics** can be defined as the analysis of people according to where they live. It relies on the concept that people live in relatively homogenous neighbourhoods, and that these neighbourhoods are capable of classification. Another way of describing geodemographics is as 'locality marketing', because one of the features of geodemographics is the facility to locate the neighbourhoods in question.

Widely-used geodemographic systems

5.15 (a)   *ACORN* (A Classification Of Residential Neighbourhoods) divides up the entire UK population in terms of the type of housing in which they live. For each of these areas, a wide range of demographic information is generated and the system affords the opportunity to assess product usage patterns, dependent upon the research conducted within national surveys. There are 54 separate groupings, including the following examples.

  - Wealthy suburbs, large detached houses
  - Private flats, elderly people
  - Gentrified multi-ethnic areas
  - Rural areas, mixed occupations
  - Council areas, residents with health problems

(b)   *PINPOINT*. The Pinpoint Identified Neighbourhoods system utilises information from disparate sources in conjunction with the Ordnance Survey to target individual houses within the 150 houses denoted by an enumeration district.

(c)   *MOSAIC*. This system also analyses information from various sources including the census, which is used to give housing, socio-economic, household and age data; the electoral roll, to give household composition and population movement data; post code address files to give information on post 1991 housing and special address types such as farms and flats.

Marketing at Work

Circular Distributors claims to be the leader in Britain in delivering advertising leaflets and free samples door to door: it claims to deliver to 19.5m of the UK's 22m households.

The company uses Mosaic, which splits UK residents into a number of consumer types, categorised by income levels, addresses (grouped into postcode areas) and tastes as indicated by certain products and services.

As a general rule, for instance, people in Merseyside spend 20 per cent more per head on toys and other products for children (such as prams) than people elsewhere in the UK. In Surrey, people are 20 per cent less likely to visit pubs regularly and only half as likely to go to wine bars as the average British citizen.

Using this type of data, split up into much smaller areas, comprising around 700 or so households, Circular Distributors can decide on which areas of Britain are most likely to be receptive to the specific promotional offers or adverts that one of its clients wants dropped through people's letterboxes on a targeted basis.

In this way, for example, literature related to special deals in a cut-price supermarket would find its way to poorer households in a run-down inner city area, while wealthier families in the suburbs might receive leaflets asking them to take expensive holidays.

Source: Financial Times

Behavioural segmentation: benefits sought

5.16 **Benefit segmentation** relates to the different benefits being sought from a product or service by customer groups. Individuals are segmented directly according to their needs.

5.17 Individuals can be categorised by **usage patterns** (whether they are light, medium or heavy users of a product or service). The TGI (Target Group Index) helps to identify these groups for a wide range of products and services. This form of segmentation assists the marketer in developing distinct and personalised strategies aimed at specific users. For example, banks and other financial institutions have introduced incentive schemes for customers when using their credit cards. This allows heavy users of the service to amass points and convert them into gifts.

Behavioural segmentation: situation specific

5.18 **Situation specific segmentation** refers to the actual situation in which consumption of the product takes place. Dependent upon the situation, it would appear that a different form of the product may be appropriate, or even an alternative brand. For example, the purchase of ice cream may vary in relation to the following situations:

- A special occasion
- Everyday consumption by the family
- An outdoor picnic
- In a restaurant

5.19 In each of these situations the consumer will **evaluate alternative product types and brands**. Where the evaluation of brands takes place, the attributes of each brand will also vary in importance depending upon the situation in which consumption takes place. Part of the communication process is to keep the brand at the forefront of the consumer's **evoked set**, and to **emphasise the situation specific benefits** of the product.

Action Programme 1

Nestlé manufacture a range of confectionery products that fit with this situation specific typology, these include Quality Street, After Eights and Kit Kat. For each of these products:

- Identify the situation for which they are purchased
- Identify the target groups
- Evaluate the communication techniques used for each product

Psychographics

A **lifestyle** is a pattern in an individual's pursuit of life's goals, reflected in how a person wishes to spend both their time and money, and therefore in their activities, interests, opinions and values.

5.20 Quantitative measures of lifestyle are known as **psychographics**. Psychographic segmentation provides a richer analysis of the consumer than is provided by simple demographic segmentation. It does not replace demographic segmentation but enhances it, and in so doing provides the opportunity to target individual consumers more precisely within a specific geographic area.

5.21 A major tour operator in the UK recognised the difference between demographics and psychographics and the implications for developing a promotional strategy. Two families living next door to one another, with similar family life cycles and income profiles, demonstrated different attitudes to spending their holidays. One family was keen on package holidays abroad, while the other family preferred camping and walking holidays. **The two families have similar demographic profiles but contrasting psychographic lifestyles.** The consequence is a need for alternative communication strategies.

5.22 **Lifestyle segmentation** groups people in relation to how they spend their time and money. Traditional socio-economic groupings aggregate individuals in terms of their occupation. Recent lifestyle analysis deals with **how people spend their money** rather than how much they earn. Young and Rubicam, the international advertising agency, developed an alternative segmentation system, the Four Cs (**Cross-Cultural Consumer Classification**), which identified the following groups.

Group	Characteristics
Mainstreamers	■ Brand conscious ■ Seek security/reliability ■ Risk averse ■ Buy British
Aspirers	■ Image conscious ■ Seek individual recognition ■ Conspicuous consumption ■ Fashion oriented
Achievers	■ Career oriented ■ Achieved personal success ■ Like to be in control ■ Personal wealth
Reformers	■ Value of life ■ Highly educated ■ Independent ■ Family oriented

5.23 The major problem with psychographics is that, unlike other segmentation approaches, it is difficult to assign any form of **specific measures**. Although it is possible to identify the number of males aged 24-35 in a given area earning £25,000 per annum, it is almost impossible to estimate how many are fun-loving, carefree and fashion-oriented. Nonetheless, this does not prevent advertising agencies portraying these and other characters as part of the communications message. Psychographics is inextricably tied in with other demographic and economic descriptions.

Action Programme 2

With reference to Young and Rubicam's Four Cs, identify recent advertisements on television that refer to each of the groups specified. For each one, evaluate to what extent the characteristics portrayed are similar and identify other factors that are indicated.

Nesting

5.24 The diagram on the next page shows how major bases for segmentation can be combined together in a way that can be described as 'nesting'. This entails starting with broadly observable, or **macro**, factors and progressing to more specific and subtle **micro** factors.

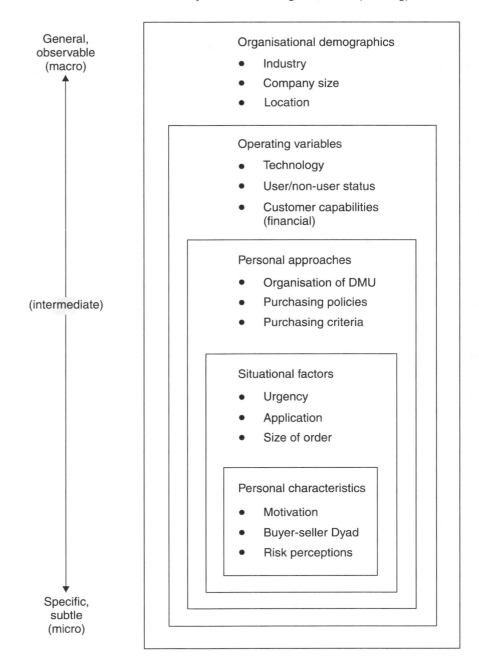

Major bases for segmentation (nesting)

General,
observable
(macro)

Organisational demographics
- Industry
- Company size
- Location

Operating variables
- Technology
- User/non-user status
- Customer capabilities (financial)

(intermediate)

Personal approaches
- Organisation of DMU
- Purchasing policies
- Purchasing criteria

Situational factors
- Urgency
- Application
- Size of order

Personal characteristics
- Motivation
- Buyer-seller Dyad
- Risk perceptions

Specific,
subtle
(micro)

Criteria for effective segmentation

5.25 One of the **problems** of market segmentation is determining **to what extent definable market segments are worth pursuing**, especially when considering developing an individual promotional campaign. There are a number of criteria that need to be satisfied in order for a market segment to be deemed **commercially viable**.

5.26 Size **or substantiality**. One of the first questions to be asked concerns whether the market is of sufficient **size** to justify attention. Will the segment generate sufficient **demand** and hence sales to help create the required return from the sector? This will depend to some extent on the resources at the disposal of the company. Many small segments can be identified but they are not seen as being worthy of further attention. Morgan, the family run car manufacturer, which produces fewer than 10 cars a year, finds the segment in which it competes lucrative, while Ford and GM would undoubtedly find this market unprofitable.

5.27 Measurability. The market segment needs to have characteristics that will assist in measuring the **market potential** both for the producer and the consumer. It is necessary to establish whether there are discrete groups of people with relatively homogeneous buying habits.

5.28 Access. A necessary prerequisite is that the market is capable of being accessed both from the point of distribution and promotion. A fairly scattered market segment in terms of geographic penetration would lead to wasted promotional expenditure if it appealed to only 10% of the market. Modern **direct marketing techniques**, however, reduce the potential waste.

5.29 Uniqueness in response. The market segment identified must exhibit similar behavioural characteristics and respond in a similar way to a targeted marketing strategy.

5.30 Stability. For any company to **divert resources** to a particular market segment that has been identified, it must reassure itself that the segment will remain fairly **stable over a long enough time period** to warrant specific marketing attention.

5.31 Actionability. This is the degree to which **marketing programmes can be formulated** for attracting and servicing segments. To take a rather extreme example, a marketing programme to expand the volume of sales for existing Rolls Royce models by attracting people on only average incomes is not actionable. If Rolls Royce chose to expand its targets in this way, a new product would need to be developed.

Marketing at Work

Establishing the Marmite brand: 1902-1975

Marmite's strange appearance, smell and ingredients had limited its appeal to adult non-users. Therefore new users were gained by persuading mothers to feed their babies Marmite .These children then acquired a taste for Marmite and when they in turn had children they tended to pass on the Marmite 'habit'. A unique mother and baby lifecycle was thus created.

Continuing the growth of the brand: 1975-1998

Two crucial decisions were taken in 1975.

- The advertising budget was doubled and has remained at higher levels ever since
- New advertising was introduced to emphasise Marmite's relevance to adults as well as children

Advertising successfully broadened out the lifecycle to create higher levels of adult consumption of Marmite, while maintaining the core mother and baby lifecycle.

These two decisions contributed to increases in volume sales of Marmite of over 50% from 1975 to 1998 and succeeded in producing an average annual return on investment in Marmite advertising of 27%

Current developments

Marmite's TV advertising is firmly targeted at adults and plays on the acquired taste of the product: 'you either love it or hate it'.

Source: Reproduced with kind permission of IPA.

6 Market targeting

6.1 Once the market has been segmented along the relevant bases, the marketing manager must decide which market to target with the promotional effort. The firm has four options:

- **Undifferentiated** marketing
- **Differentiated** marketing
- **Concentrated** marketing
- **Customised** marketing

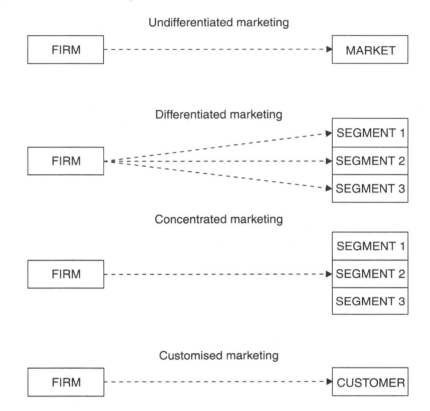

6.2 **Undifferentiated or mass marketing** occurs where an organisation tends **to ignore the differences that exist within a market, and aims to provide a standard product or service to a wide variety of customers**. McDonald's, the fast food chain, provide a standardised product range and service environment to a wide audience although they actively employ a number of distinct promotional campaigns that appeal to the widest possible audience, irrespective of income, age, sex and occupation.

6.3 **Differentiated marketing** acknowledges the differences that exist in customer tastes and a **separate marketing mix is developed for each identifiable market segment**. This strategy is quite **common in large companies**, as is reflected in a trend towards **multiple product offerings**. It offers the advantage of recognising the demand variations that exist and capitalising on them, in contrast to undifferentiated marketing. Kellogg's, the breakfast cereal manufacturer, adopts multiple marketing strategies to accommodate the requirements of a diverse market, including children, adults, families, the health conscious, and weight watchers.

6.4 **Concentrated marketing focuses attention solely upon a distinct customer group** to the exclusion of all others. The aim is to concentrate on one segment and focus resources on **excellence in a more limited market**. Examples include Ferrari (car manufacturer), Saga holidays (tour operator), and Steinway (piano manufacturer), where the company targets individuals and/or groups on one or a combination of characteristics, such as income or age.

6.5 **Customised marketing** refers to the extent to which organisations will move towards **individually-tailored products** to meet individual customer needs. Both Nissan and General Motors are working towards computer-generated cars which will reflect the personal whims desires of the customer. **Financial products** offered by the banking and financial sector are increasingly reflecting the need for tailoring to individual financial circumstances.

6.6 The fundamental basis on which the marketer selects one of these approaches to the segments available is a **cost/benefit analysis**. The marketer **expects to generate additional revenue** from a segment by satisfying the needs of that group, and by developing effective promotional activities that better match that segment. In doing so, the marketer **incurs additional costs** for new advertisements, promotions, sales force activities, public relations campaigns and so on. The marketer will only choose to develop a new segment if the **incremental revenues generated exceed the incremental costs** of serving that segment.

Positioning

6.7 **Positioning** is a natural outcome of this analysis and selection process. Having selected a market the next important step is to be positioned in the market in such a way that **customers can understand and differentiate your product** from your competitors' offerings. Positioning is about both the **tangible** and **intangible elements** of a product, however, and Integrated Marketing Communications has an important role to play in presenting the total product/brand to the target market.

Marketing at Work

The I.T. giant Oracle, previously linked firmly with big database technology, is keen to have its name at the forefront of the development of "web services" whereby the Internet becomes the back to bone of a company's IT set-up by connecting all of its disparate systems, from finance to customers supply chain. Oracle communicates to a large section of its target market through techniques like e-mail and web-based seminars. Customers can be taken through a process online, from initial interest through to final sale.

Key Concept

Positioning is about how the target market perceives the presentation of the product/service relative to competing products. It is what is in the minds of the target audience.

6.8 The principal goal at this stage is **to determine how the product/brand is perceived by the target audience and to make a managerial judgement about whether**

the current position is strategically suitable and sustainable or whether it needs to be changed. From here positioning goals can be determined.

6.9 The **target marketing process** is important for the development of effective marketing communications. Through the development of a **profile** of members of the target market, it becomes easier to **design messages** and to **select media** that will enable those messages to **reach** the target audience, be **understood** and **acted upon** as intended.

Chapter Roundup

- In order to be effective the development of marketing communications must take place within the

- This involves an understanding of **corporate mission**, **objectives and strategy**, with the marketing strategy built upon prior decisions regarding product policy, segmentation and targeting.

- The overriding requirement for marketing in today's modern markets is **better targeting**, and this means aiming at the proper segment of the market. Common criteria for **market segmentation** are geography, demographics, geodemographics, behaviour and psychographics.

- To determine **whether a segment is worth pursuing**, the market needs to consider the size, measurability, access, uniqueness of response, stability and actionability of the segment.

- The basic options in targeting are **undifferentiated** or mass marketing, **differentiated** marketing, **concentrated** marketing and **customised** marketing. The approach is selected on the basis of **cost/benefit analysis**.

- **Positioning** of a product is concerned with how it creates and establishes an **image** in the minds of consumers and how it is evaluated against competing products. Positioning may be according to attribute, price and quality, use or application, product user, product class or competition.

Now try Question 4 at the end of the Study Text

Quick Quiz

1   What areas might be explored when analysing the business context? (see para 2.1)

2   Outline the concepts of segmentation, targeting and positioning.(5.4, 6.1, 6.8)

3   What might be covered in a demographic segmentation analysis? (5.7)

4   What is geodemographics? What are the widely-used systems? (5.14, 5.15)

5   Identify possible usage patterns for a product and a service of your choice. (5.18)

6   Which groups are identified in Young and Rubicam's Cross-Cultural Consumer Classification? (5.22)

7   What is nesting? (5.24)

8   Explain four possible target market decisions. (6.1 - 6.5)

9   What is positioning concerned with? (6.7)

10 How might the target marketing process help marketing communications? (6.9)

Action Programme Review

1   Another example you could have considered is Cadbury's *Roses*, where the buying situation in the advertisement involves a sense of guilt on the part of the giver for not appreciating the receiver. Many products in this category are purchased as gifts for differing reasons rather than for individual personal consumption. You may also consider here the role of point of sale displays as an influencing factor in the purchasing decision process.

2   Try undertaking this task by examining advertisements for products in the same category eg alcoholic drinks or motor cars. You can identify which brands are being promoted to the different classifications.

The Organisational Context

Chapter Topic List	
1	Setting the scene
2	Internal marketing communications
3	Corporate branding and communications
4	How much is to be invested in integrated marketing communications?

Learning Outcomes

☑ Determine the context in which marketing (and corporate) communications are to be implemented in order to improve effectiveness and efficiency, understand the key strategic communication issues arising from the contextual analysis and prepare (integrated) marketing communications plans

☑ Determine appropriate levels of marketing communications expenditure/ appropriation

☑ Advise on the impact corporate communications can have on both internal and external audiences and their role in the development of integrated marketing communications

Syllabus References

☑ Communication issues for internal and external audiences

☑ Deciding upon the level and allocation of the promotional spend

☑ Managing internal and external resources necessary for successful promotional activities

☑ Managing and developing product and corporate brands

Key Concepts Introduced

- Internal marketing
- Organisational culture
- Corporate personality
- Corporate image
- Corporate identity

1 Setting the scene

1.1 This chapter focuses on the various **internal aspects of an organisation** that can influence the effectiveness of Integrated Marketing Communications. Management has a higher degree of influence over these variables than over some of the others. Analysis of these factors can therefore lead to actions that may have considerable impact on the effectiveness of Integrated Marketing Communications plans. The importance of proper planning and control in this context should be obvious to you, and provides a link to your other studies at Diploma level.

2 Internal marketing communications   12/99, 6/01

 Key Concept

Internal marketing is the direction of marketing activities to groups within the organisation. Internal marketing communications can enhance the efficiency and effectiveness of transactions within the organisation and finally provide for greater levels of affiliation or bonding within the organisation.

2.1 Recognition that **employees are an important market segment** in their own right is increasing. As mentioned earlier, employees not only have needs of their own which require satisfaction but they also represent an important interface between an organisation and its customers and other stakeholders. If IMC is to be achieved then **internal communications must be consistent with external communications**.

2.2 Part of the overall task facing those preparing marketing communications strategies is to determine the quality and effectiveness of the current internal communications in order that:

- Any shortfall between actual and expected **effectiveness** of the current communication programme can be corrected as soon as possible

- It is **consistent** with the aims and objectives of the business and marketing strategies

- The needs of the **corporate brand** are supported by a suitable internal programme

2.3 Internal Marketing Communications plays three roles.

Role	Content
DRIP factors	**D**ifferentiate **R**emind/reassure **I**nform **P**ersuade
Transactional	Co-ordinate actions Use resources efficiently Direct developments
Affiliation	Motivate employees Encourage identification with the company Promote and co-ordinate activities with non-members

2.4 The number and variety of **internal audiences** will vary from organisation to organisation. The word employees is a general term often applied to describe this audience. This can be misleading as employees are a very varied group, all of whom perform different functions and contribute to the company's goals is different ways.

2.5 The **tools used for internal marketing communications** are many and varied. Traditional tools include memoranda, reports, notice boards, meetings, conferences, videos and house magazines and bulletins. Increasingly, organisations are employing **new technology** to supplement and replace these forms of communication. The use of e-mail, intranets and the Internet, video conferencing and the rapidly advancing use of e-commerce enable faster, more informative communications.

Organisational culture

2.6 All organisations consist of **people who work together to achieve agreed goals**. These people can be referred to as **members**. Those people who do not necessarily work for the organisation and who are external to the organisation are referred to as **non-members**. The relationship between members and non-members is partly a function of the quality of communications that exist between both parties.

Key Concept

Organisational culture refers to the collective beliefs and values that are shared among members of an organisation.

2.7 There are many different types of culture ranging from the hierarchical to the organic, from the innovative to the traditional. One of the more frequently observed cultures is the **production orientation, where members perceive their products and the associated technologies as the most important aspect of their work**. The opposing view is the **customer focus**, whereby meeting customer needs is seen as paramount for the achievement of business performance success.

Action Programme 1

Think about your employer's organisation (or one with which you are familiar) and consider the dominant culture and how it might influence internal and external communications?

What should be done to improve the current situation?

2.8 **Culture change** is one of management's most persistent challenges, with many organisations attempting to move to a culture that has a strong customer focus. Encouraging members to look and think about non-members when they have been orientated to an introspective view of the world is a necessary but difficult task to accomplish.

Marketing at Work

United Friendly

When United Friendly (a financial services organisation) purchased a financial planning company from American Express it was clear that the profiles of the two organisations were radically different.

United Friendly targeted policy holders in the lower income brackets while the American Express organisation aimed their fee-based financial planning services at a more affluent and sophisticated audience.

The context analysis revealed, unsurprisingly, that there was a need to bring together the two differing cultures and unify them behind a single brand.

To accomplish this, a new corporate identity was commissioned and an advertising agency and a public relations agency were appointed. It was soon established that the objectives of the new programme were to:

- Communicate the rationale behind the initiatives to all staff
- Stimulate feelings of common bonding among all internal audiences
- Unite the workforce behind a single brand
- Motivate the sales forces at a time of deep recession in the industry

The principal form of external communication was a corporate advertising campaign called 'Person to Person' and featured employees instead of actors. The campaign was to burst on 4 September and there was a series of events leading up to the Launch day, many of which were designed to involve staff and encourage participation.

A schedule of internal communication was developed which involved:

Internal newsletters, the staff magazine, a launch day pack for each of the 4,200 employees, a 20 minute video, a competition and various merchandising items (mugs, T shirts etc). Excluding the advertising, the programme cost just £135,000.

The results of the programme were impressive. A questionnaire sent to 2,506 staff a month after the launch revealed satisfaction levels with regard to the packs, the run-up to the launch, the launch day meetings and the overall provision of timely useful information, to be in excess of 80% on one item and over 90% on all others.

Source : adapted from the IPR - Sword of Excellence Awards

2.9 **An organisation's culture is often reflected in the style and form of its internal and external communications**. Procter & Gamble's culture is built on a traditional hierarchy, they tend to appoint staff from within and they are seen to be risk averse. Their advertising tends to be product performance orientated whereas their principal rival, Lever Brothers are said to be less formal and the tone and form of their advertising is more image based and more emotional in content.

Exam Tip

In December 1999, internal communications was combined with the use of technology. Candidates had to state why internal communications are important, and suggest how technology might be used.

Of course, it could be easy to cite examples such as 'e-mail' and 'intranets'. However, people have to be persuaded to use them in an appropriate way, and perhaps must even be discouraged from doing so. In short, there may need to be a communications campaign to promote the use of technology.

Corporate codes and corporate culture

2.10 British Airways were once accused of waging a 'dirty tricks' campaign against its competitor Virgin Atlantic. British Airways maintained that the offending actions (essentially, the poaching of Virgin's customers) were those of a small group of employees who had overstepped the bounds of 'proper' behaviour in their eagerness to foster the interests of their employer.

2.11 An alternative view digs a little deeper. Some observers believed that the real villain of the piece was British Airways' abrasive corporate culture.

2.12 One of BA's responses to its defeat in the courts against Virgin and the bad publicity arising from the case was to introduce a **code of ethics**. Many commentators would argue that this is inadequate on its own. To be effective a code needs to be accompanied by positive attempts to foster guiding values, aspirations and patterns of thinking that support ethically sound behaviour - in short a **change of culture**.

2.13 Increasingly, organisations are responding to this challenge by devising ethics training programmes for the entire workforce, instituting comprehensive procedures for reporting and investigating ethical concerns within the company, or even setting up an ethics office or department to supervise the new measures. Marketing communications in the form of internal marketing of the organisation's values has a key role to play.

2.14 The development of suitable integrated marketing communication messages requires that all **corporate communications are consistent**. The task of analysing and understanding the organisational context should not be overlooked if IMC is sought.

3 Corporate branding and communications 6/00

3.1 Some of the analysis undertaken at this point in the development of integrated marketing communication plans has a direct impact upon the corporate communication strategies and in particular the form and nature of the **corporate identity** that may be part of the strategies determined later in the plan. Corporate identity is increasingly referred to as **corporate branding**. Both terms will be used here interchangeably.

3.2 Corporate identity consists of various elements and it is important to understand the nature of these elements and the way in which they interact.

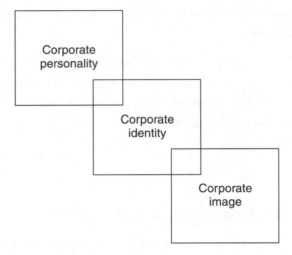

Key Concepts

- **Corporate personality** is about organisational culture, values and strategy. It is about the real organisation and what it stands for.

- **Corporate identity** is about what the organisation projects to its various audiences.

- **Corporate image** is concerned with the perception audiences have of an organisation as a result of both planned and unplanned cues that people pick up: what people really think about the organisation.

3.3 **Corporate branding** is about the visual and behavioural elements of an organisation. This means that in addition to the logos, signage, letterheads and architecture, **corporate identity** incorporates the **outsider's perceptions** of the behaviour, attitudes and actions an organisation exhibits.

3.4 The **corporate identity** projected by an organisation to its **various stakeholders** is partly a reflection of the **personality** of the organisation. The personality is made up of the **strategy**, **culture** and prevailing **philosophy**. Understanding these elements is important if the correct visual and behavioural signals are to be communicated externally. It is from these signals that stakeholders form impressions (an **image**) of the organisation. Corporate image therefore, is formed from the planned signals in addition to all those unplanned signals that organisations inevitably communicate. Cues of corporate identity are:

Cue	Comment
Behaviour	What an organisation actually does – 'actions speak louder than words'
Communication	Visual and verbal messages
Symbolic	Logo, letterheads etc

Marketing at Work

Beyond petroleum

BP Amoco launched a 'beyond petroleum' campaign to highlight its concern to become 'greener'. The BP logo (a shield) was replaced with a green and yellow flower.

3.5 Analysis of the organisational context is required to determine the perceptions and attitudes priority stakeholders have towards the organisation. The **size of the gap** between the way the organisation **is perceived** and the **desired or intended image determines** the objectives of the **communication programme**.

3.6 A **Corporate Perception Gap Grid** (Fill, 2002) helps reveal the nature and size of the task to be undertaken.

Large gap (perceived)

Targeted adjustment   Information provision and correction

Few stakeholders   Many stakeholders

Monitoring   Incremental

Small gap (perceived)

3.7 **Measurement of corporate image** is a complex and often lengthy procedure.

(a) One approach is to measure the **strength of a number of key dimensions or attributes** which stakeholders determine as important. For example, these might be perceptions of customer service, reliability, integrity, product quality and research and development.

(b) The same process can be used to measure **perceptions of competitors**, and hence it is possible to see where any competitive advantage might lie.

(c)   **Communication programmes** can then be used internally to help correct any deficiency, and externally to inform stakeholders of the organisation's new or enhanced ability.

3.8   **Corporate reputation** refers to the deep seated feelings people have towards an organisation. Developing a strong reputation is important and can be one of the most significant assets an organisation can possess. Understanding, protecting and enhancing a reputation is an important aspect of a marketing communications plan.

Exam Tip

Corporate communications are a key aspect of the syllabus, and corporate identity can be seen as an internal and external projection. It is an important underpinning to the profile strategies covered later in this Study Text.

4   How much is to be invested in integrated marketing communications?

4.1   In order that marketing communications be implemented successfully, **financial resources** are inevitably consumed. Some organisations spend very large sums each year on advertising alone.

4.2   At this stage in the development of an integrated marketing communications plan, a broad understanding is necessary to determine the **financial constraints** that are to be applied to any agreed marketing communication activity. In other words, the financial context needs to be determined so that inappropriate strategies are not developed. Pinpoint accuracy is not expected as further detailed financial work is undertaken at a later stage.

4.3   It is important to understand the general level of financial resources that are available, as this **influences the breadth and depth of the communication strategies** that are to follow. For example, if a broad figure of £300,000 is discussed, then a television campaign will not be possible. Very often the vast bulk of the communication spend is directed at the media so it is not surprising that new media and more cost effective media are being supported.

4.4   In reality, the general level of available financial resources within organisations and product categories is known. Budgets tend not to swing violently from year to year. Regrettably this is one of the key budget areas that is often axed or severely pruned when trading takes a downward turn. A check needs to be undertaken to determine the broad approach the organisation intends taking.

Action Programme 2

Find out the amount spent on communications (or perhaps just advertising) for a number of different brands, across different sectors. (This information can often be found in *Marketing* magazine)

How have these amounts changed over recent years ?

What might be the reason for these variations? Find out the real reason.

Chapter Roundup

- The development of integrated marketing communications requires that **those working for** organisation but that this support is **communicated to all relevant external audiences**.

- **Good internal marketing communication** is of paramount importance and a review in the form of an organisational contextual analysis enables understanding of what employees value and believe.

- Internal communication programmes can be implemented to **inform, remind and persuade** different internal audiences about issues concerning the organisation's goals and processes. Through this communication process **cultural changes** can be assisted and the **corporate brand** developed, so that external audiences can identify and understand the **focus organisation**.

- The development and maintenance of a strong **corporate reputation**, through the use of a range of identity cues, is an integral and necessary part of these types of communication programmes.

- Checking on the overall amount of money that is likely to be assigned to the **promotional budget** is a useful activity at this stage. Any significant variations on previous periods need to be made clear as the financial restrictions may have a major impact on the strategies that are to follow.

Now try Question 5 at the end of the Study Text

Quick Quiz

1   Why is internal marketing communications an important part of integrated marketing communications? (see para 2.1)

2   What are the roles of internal marketing communications? (2.3)

3   Make a list of possible internal audiences and the tools used to communicate with them. (2.4)

4   What is organisational culture? (2.7)

5   How might corporate culture affect communication? (2.9)

6   What is corporate identity? (3.2)

7   What is corporate branding? (3.3)

8   How is image different to identity? (3.8)

9   What is corporate reputation? (3.9)

10   Why is it important to understand how much money is likely to be assigned to an integrated marketing communication plan at this stage? (4.3)

Action Programme Review

1   If you have identified some significant problem areas, what role can communications play in addressing them – staff training, intranets, newsletters, social events?

2   If most of the data you have been able to find relates to advertising and the trends appear downwards, this may be due to the fact that alternative communications activities are being utilised such as direct mail or sponsorship.

Other Contextual Elements

6

Chapter Topic List	
1	Setting the scene: the external context
2	Political, legal and regulatory influences
3	Economic influences
4	Social influences
5	Technological influences
6	The ethical context

Learning Outcome

☑ Determine the context in which marketing (and corporate) communications are to be implemented in order to improve effectiveness and efficiency, understand the key strategic communication issues arising from the contextual analysis and prepare (integrated) marketing communications plans

Syllabus References

☑ The appreciation and recognition of the importance of ethical and technological influences on promotional activities and an awareness of the social responsibilities organisations have towards the way they communicate with their target audience

☑ Communication issues for internal and external audiences

☑ The determination and appreciation of the prevailing and future contextual conditions as a means of deriving and developing promotional strategies and plans

☑ Consideration of the competitive conditions, available resources, stage in the product life cycle and any political, economic, social or technological factors that might be identified as influencing the development of a campaign

BPP
PROFESSIONAL EDUCATION

Key Concept Introduced

■ Interactive marketing

1 Setting the scene: the external context 12/99, 6/00

1.1 The completion of a contextual analysis requires consideration of some of the **wider issues and influences** that might affect an organisation's promotional activities. The full range of potential influences cannot be considered here because of a lack of time, space and, to a certain extent, necessity.

Links with other papers

1.2 In essence the development of effective marketing communications programmes is dependent upon, and an incorporation of, some of the influences from the external environment and the **ethical and cultural context** in which organisations operate. This may include an **international aspect** if the communications programme crosses borders.

Exam Tip

The June 2000 exam had a section B question on the impact of general environmental factors on communication campaigns. Rather than listing generalities, try to focus them on the marketing communications impact.

The external context

1.3 The context for the development and implementation of marketing communication activities is influenced by events in the wider **external environment**. The best course of action is very often to **accommodate these influences rather then ignore or resist them.**

1.4 Examples

 (a) A government body may change the regulations concerning labelling requirements

 (b) A person or organisation that was being sponsored or endorsed has fallen from public acceptance

 (c) Because of adverse weather conditions, the price of an essential raw ingredient has risen astronomically

 (d) An industry-wide malpractice (eg pension mis-selling) may reflect on all organisations in that industry.

1.5 The development of the **Internet** has helped transform the **communication expectations** of many organisations, both internally and externally.

1.6 Use of the PEST (Political, Economic, Social and Technological) framework can help reveal some of these external events. But remember that it is the **communication impact** of the PEST related events that is important to us when developing our marketing communications plans.

2 Political, legal and regulatory influences

2.1 An organisation's marketing communication activities are constrained by **legal and regulatory processes**.

2.2 In the UK, no one Act of Parliament provides a comprehensive framework for the regulation of promotional activity. Over 150 Acts of Parliament and Statutory Instruments (quite apart from case law) form the **legal framework** within which advertising and sales promotion operate.

2.3 Compliance with all legal provisions is no guarantee against repercussions because, in addition to this **statutory regulation** (indeed, because of its piecemeal nature), there is a structure of **self regulating codes of practice** and standards that is often more restrictive than the law itself.

The nature of regulation

2.4 The rules governing the acceptability of communication can be summed up in a phrase that is widely recognised by advertising practitioners and general public alike: communication must be **'legal, decent, honest and truthful'**. We will look at each aspect in turn.

Legal

2.5 Advertisements should not contain anything which is in breach of the law or omit anything required by law. For example, adverts should not show discrimination on the grounds of colour, race or ethnic origin (Race Relations Act, 1976) or on the grounds of sex and marital status (Sex Discrimination Act, 1975).

Decent

2.6 The Obscene Publications Acts 1959 and 1964 state that it is an offence to publish an obscene article, 'whether to gain or not.' An article is defined as obscene if 'the effect is likely to deprave or corrupt persons who are likely to see, read or hear the matter embodied in it'.

2.7 In a business context, more specific examples include the Indecent Advertisements (Amendment) Act 1970, which states that is an offence to exhibit any picture or printed or written matter of an indecent or obscene nature. The Unsolicited Goods and Services Act 1971 states that it is an offence to send unsolicited material (or advertising material) that describes or illustrates human sexual techniques.

Honest and truthful

2.8 These last two elements can be combined as the legal provision in this area does not make a clear distinction between the two. The main statute covering this area is the **Trade Descriptions Act 1968**, which prohibits any person, in the course of a trade or business, from applying a false description to goods, or from supplying or offering to supply any goods with a false trade description. The Act defines a trade description as an indication, either direct or indirect, regarding such issues as quantity, size, composition, method of manufacture, fitness for purpose, approval or endorsement by any individual or organisation and the past history of the product. The scope of this legislation applies to **all areas of promotion**, including packaging, illustrations, advertisements, demonstrations and oral statements.

2.9 Under this heading of honesty and truthful presentation a number of issues arise. A retailer may be liable for criminal proceedings if legal provisions are contravened with respect to endorsement (for example, suggesting that Madonna uses your brand of hair-spray if she does not), defamation, slander of goods and 'passing off' (for example, giving the impression that your corner shop is a branch of Sainsbury's).

Marketing at Work

Legislation and advertising – not such strange bedfellows

Governments in many parts of the world have attempted to stop people smoking tobacco by taking legislative steps to prevent advertising and sponsorship of tobacco products and compel manufacturers to place 'health warnings' on packaging. Tobacco products are also heavily taxed to dissuade current and potential consumers on the grounds of price. There is an increasing recognition that legislation alone cannot win the battle.

The debate on the effects of promotion has been intense with anti and pro lobbies attempting to counter each other's arguments. The anti-smoking campaigns have largely focused on shock tactics, highlighting dangers to health. Whilst this strategy has met with some success, alternative approaches are also proving their worth, particularly in reaching what might be called 'hard core' audiences, low income and ethnic groups.

The Department of Health in the UK is working with Abbott Mead Vickers – BBDO, the advertising agency, with the aim of devising campaigns that are aimed at persuading 1.7 million smokers in these groups to give up by 2010. The agency has been looking at the efforts of agencies in other parts of the world. This has included the work of a Florida based agency, Crispin Porter and Bogusky, who have been successful in reducing youth smoking with an anti-smoking brand called 'truth'. This focuses on demonising sleazy practices of the multinational tobacco companies. The aim is to empower the target audience to make their own decisions rather than lecture them on health dangers.

Financial Times 13/10/2000 by John Thornhill

Self-regulatory codes of practice

2.10 **Self-regulatory codes of practice** are usually issued by trade associations in order to establish standards for members to follow. Prime examples are the British Codes of Advertising and Sales Promotion, which are administered by the Advertising Standards Authority (ASA). Revised versions of these codes came into force in 1999.

2.11 The rationale for self regulation is that restraints that are **self imposed** are, for that very reason, **more likely to be readily accepted** than restraints imposed from outside. The aim of self regulation is to complement statutory control by offering more **flexibility and informality**. The provisions of such codes of practice can be more easily and quickly adapted to changing circumstances than can statutory provisions and, in addition, their interpretation is more flexible, giving appropriate weight to the intentions of the authors of the code as opposed to the strict interpretation of statute that the courts must adhere to.

2.12 Marketing communications practitioners must be aware of changes and **adapt campaigns and activities** accordingly. Pharmaceutical companies must provide, on the label, certain drug related information. The recent discussion about genetically modified foods and labelling is an issue about which food manufacturers must be aware. Regulations emanating from the **European Union (EU)** can have an impact on promotional practices.

2.13 The main political and legal issues in the near future are likely to emanate from the European Union, where future legislation and the establishment of regulatory bodies will affect marketing communications. One area that is currently under close scrutiny by the EU is the **direct marketing industry**, as there is little harmony within the Union.

2.14 While the UK has a rather liberal attitude to the activities that may be engaged in under the **sales promotion** umbrella, countries such as Luxembourg, Switzerland and West Germany have a far more sober approach. Here, activities such as branded offers, in-pack premiums and money off next purchase are all prohibited.

2.15 A further problem which affects the direct marketing industry is the **postal system** which currently contrives to thwart best practice within the EU. Europe's bureaucratic postal authorities, most of them monopolies, are analysing the prospects of new EU legislation, which will require them to provide a harmonised and efficient postal system at a competitive price.

Cross-border advertising

2.16 The current position is that there must be **overriding reasons relating to the public interest for imposing additional national rules on communications**, and these rules must be 'proportionate' to the public interest objectives, and therefore not go further than is needed to achieve these desired objectives. However, to test the validity of current national restrictions on commercial communications through the courts takes several years for each case. Many regard national advertising restrictions as thinly veiled protectionism.

2.17 The threat of legislative pressure from the EU has also contributed to the introduction of **greener products and packaging**. A number of European countries already have in place packaging controls far more stringent than exist in the UK. The EU Directive on Packaging and Packaging Waste attempts to harmonise the different policies of the member states. Once implemented, existing packaging will need to be modified to meet new requirements.

2.18 The effects of both **consumer and legislative pressures** are likely to include the following.

- Increased use of **recyclable** materials
- Increased use of **refillable** containers
- **Replacement of some materials** used with less harmful ones.

Marketing at Work

EC initiative on unfair marketing practices

It has been reported that a new EC directorate, DG SANCO (Health and Consumer Protection), is looking at issues such as misleading advertising, viral marketing, advertising to kids, competition claims, free offers and sponsorship. This work is believed to be at an early stage and may not necessarily end in legislation but properly enforced codes of practice. SANCO may encourage member states to coordinate activities in these areas with agencies responsible for enforcement to ensure consistency.

From an article in *Marketing Business* April 2001

3 Economic influences

3.1 The economic trading conditions can also affect marketing communication strategies. **Consumers are taking more care in their purchase decisions** and erring on the side of caution when it comes to the big items such as the home and car. This actually leaves more to be spent on luxuries and those items that contribute to the quality of life.

3.2 At the same time, greater amounts of personal disposable income will have to be set aside for items such as pensions, health care, dental charges and education, especially as children reach higher education. This type of planning is starting at a much younger age as people face the prospect of a much shorter working life and extended retirement.

3.3 Higher levels of unemployment and downsizing in what were traditionally perceived as safe industries (banking and the financial services industry) have forced people to realise that job security no longer exists and that career changes are likely to be more frequent.

Trading down?

3.4 There has also been a certain amount of trading down in the shopping habits of the affluent, particularly when it comes to grocery shopping. Abbot Mead Vickers in their own research studies have discovered that up to 20% of the ABC1's have switched towards the discount retailers, in order to release money for other, luxury purchases. This appears to reflect a need for closer management of financial resources of the individual and the family.

The impact on advertisers

3.5 **Values**, **attitudes and lifestyles** change when there is a recession, and advertisers need to respond to these changes by altering their advertising strategies to match the changed needs of their customers.

3.6 Marketers are well aware of the characteristics of the needs and wants of consumers. **Needs** are those products and services that are purchased because they must be, while **wants** are those products that people enjoy buying but may not have the spending power to buy, in practice.

3.7 During the 1980s, the difference between these purchases became blurred, but in the 1990s a clear dividing line was drawn between the two. Consumers are much more aware of what they want, and will not be easily or readily fooled by today's advertiser.

3.8 **Advertisers have to display greater openness and honesty** within their communications. There is an argument that they need to include more factual information about the product and be more sensitive to the need to communicate value for money with products that deliver real benefits and excellent performance. Advertisements for cars in the 1990s seem tedious and tame to the car buff of the 1980s. Air bags, anti-lock braking systems, side impact protection, built-in child seats, front and rear head restraints and improved fuel consumption are all very worthy - and very dull.

Marketing at Work

Ronseal, the manufacturers of wood preservatives adopted an advertising campaign that employed the services of a member of the general public to deliver the message that Ronseal wood preservatives 'do exactly what they say on the tin'. The advertisements attempt to project a sense of honesty and reality by employing such a theme.

3.9 The '**needs and wants**' approach provides a useful framework around which organisations will develop their communication strategies in the future.

3.10 Within the needs sector, products that do not attempt to compete on a **price** basis will have to work much harder to promote their **perceived value** to the consumer, both in terms of the product benefits and the communication strategy that supports it.

3.11 Brands that fail to **reinvest and maintain a premium position** in the minds of the consumer will suffer at the expense of own brand and generic products.

3.12 Advertisers have typically found it more challenging to communicate the **wants** than the **needs**, since they have to appeal more to **emotion and imagination** as opposed to **intellect and reason**.

3.13 By the nature of the purchase, **a luxury item requires more shopping time and effort**, and ultimately more money. Therefore, consumers are more willing to shop around and are well able to resist the advertising trick of promoting style without substance.

3.14 Advertisers are therefore having to explore the **motives for purchase** more deeply, and take full account of the anxieties a consumer experiences when purchasing such products.

4 Social influences

4.1 Inextricably entwined within the changes that have manifested themselves in the economy are the **social shifts** that have occurred and that are likely to remain for a considerable time.

4.2 The number of older people will increase over the next 40-50 years, while the number of younger people will show some decline towards the end of this period. This observation is based on a prediction that the average number of children per family will decline from its current level of 2.1 towards around 1.8.

4.3 In the meantime, organisations are having to reassess their marketing strategies in the face of a **population restructuring**.

Cultivating the younger and older markets

4.4 More and more companies are beginning to target the **younger markets** as the next generation of big spenders. The British youth market is becoming big business, but advertisers have to be constantly on their feet to maintain the momentum.

4.5 However, it is the 15-24 age group which is potentially the most lucrative, as companies realise that by catching them young, they can convert these individuals into the consumers of the future.

4.6 This age group is currently the largest market for the consumption of confectionery, crisps, snack-foods and soft and carbonated drinks. The development and growth of bottled water in the UK is attributed solely to this group.

4.7 This group are also the highest spenders on sportswear and the most likely to use newsagents and after-hours convenience stores. They also spend heavily on CDs, videos and sound systems.

4.8 Other firms are beginning to realise that the more **elderly segment** is likely to become increasingly important as it expands and also, because of the more adequate provisions people are currently making for their pensionable years.

Marketing at Work

Targeting the over 50s

People in many parts of the world are living longer and the so-called 'grey market' is the fastest growing demographic sector in Europe. The sector is as complex as any other and requires a detailed approach to market segmentation. Three age bands have been identified.

Thrivers, 50-59, teenagers in the 1960s are now affluent, active and healthy. *Seniors*, 60-69, coped with rationing during the second world war and after and are generally not interested in self gratification but concerned with health issues and personal comfort. *Elders*, 70 plus, grew up in times of significant hardship, are now largely free of debt. Further activity is required in order to segment on the basis of income, lifestyle and lifestages.

Communications activities need to account for failing eyesight, the suitability of imagery, choice of words and language and media selection. Direct mail is considered to be a particularly effective medium with older consumers welcoming personal attention as they may feel increasingly isolated due to their age. This may provide platforms for developing relationships via careful targeting. Opportunities exist in this sector for companies marketing cars, holidays, financial products and other 'luxury goods'.

From an article in *Marketing Business*, September 2000

The changing family unit

4.9 The UK has seen a rapid growth in **single parent families** over the past ten years and this trend is likely to grow. Advertisers will have to address this shift, since they have continuously focused attention on the traditional family unit: among the most famous of advertisements are those featuring the Oxo family.

4.10 Increasing numbers of working women and a trend towards **parental role reversals** (with the husband staying at home and looking after the home and children) will affect the way in which advertisers target the new decision makers. More and more advertisers (Volkswagen, Prudential Financial Services) portray the female as the independent and dominant partner.

4.11 As **women gain power in the job market**, they also gain financial power and become more aware of the purchases traditionally reserved for the male. Advertisers are now having to target them both in attempting to sell their products.

Home shopping

4.12 Individuals can shop from home and choose items from an armchair in the living room. Infomercials (combining information with a commercial) which the consumer has selected are relayed directly to the home. These may be recipes, DIY tips, car maintenance and so on. Consumers will be able to purchase the ingredients or parts they require simply by pointing a cursor on a computer screen at the desired goods.

Marketing at Work

It is estimated by Verdict Research that home shopping will become a £300m market in the UK. US operator QVC (Quality, Value and Convenience) launched television shopping in the UK through satellite, which is available to cable and Sky subscribers.

QVC, which offers everything from pet food products to hi-fi equipment, estimates that it receives between 3,000 and 4,000 callers a day, and that the current value of sales is £23m and expected to grow.

Freemans, the catalogue company, which currently has 10% of the home shopping market, is keen to make inroads into this sector. Over 5,000 of its agents are equipped with the necessary hardware and software to make instant buying decisions. Customers are able to view a full motion picture and then order via a modem.

4.13 It is, however, difficult to predict how successful and how big the market for **home shopping** will become in the UK. It appeals to consumers within the United States because many people live in remote parts, some distance away from a main shopping centre. Within the UK however, the vast majority of people live within easy reach of a shopping centre or out-of-town complex. The speed of adoption will depend upon how readily the British public accept and use the new technology and to what extent they will be deterred from actively browsing around the shops.

5 Technological influences

5.1 In some ways **interactive marketing** is simply computerised personal selling. However, its great advantage is that it can consistently deliver the same, very high quality, messages to anyone that makes an enquiry, unlike a conventional salesforce made up of a multitude of individual personalities. TV home shopping, where a product is advertised on TV and interested customers phone in to order it, is one example. A free CD-ROM carrying a computer program that gives appropriate multimedia (words, sound and pictures) responses to choices made by the person using it is another. A third is an interactive kiosk, used in banking and travel, to inform customers about financial services or potential holiday destinations.

Key Concept

Interactive marketing is a term used to describe any form of marketing in which the customer can respond instantly to the promoter and *vice versa*, rather than there being a time lag.

5.2 For many products and services the questions that customers ask and the responses they give when offered options are very limited in number, and a little experience allows the development of a computer program with images and data that give the ideal answer to queries, and which processes responses with 100% accuracy. The responses will also be stored for later analysis and identification of further marketing opportunities.

5.3 Interactive media are regarded as so important that articles on the marketing implications are rife in all newspapers and business journals.

5.4 The growth of interactive media has been driven by the **technological development** in computers, telecommunications and the Internet. Growth areas include **digital TV**, **e-mail** devices attached to 'traditional' land-line telephones and **Wireless Application Protocol** (WAP). WAP allows Internet access via mobile communications.

The Internet

5.5 The Internet is covered in detail in section 10 of Chapter 9, and you should scan through that chapter now if you want a more in-depth discussion.

5.6 The **Internet** is a growing phenomenon. There are a number of Internet related companies which have floated and achieved very high prices based on their potential to grow. The number of Internet users is increasing rapidly and, as the cost of Internet access falls, more Internet users are expected.

5.7 The **principles behind Internet sites** are simple. Visitors search for the sites they are interested in and go to the **home pages** of the relevant companies. The home pages provide general **information on the company** but, more importantly, the visitor is provided with a series of choices. Typically, this would be the **type of product** the company has to offer. The visitor then selects an option and 'drills down', that is, they click on options to reveal more **specific and detailed information** on the item in which they are interested.

5.8 More sophisticated sites allow the customer to leave their details with the company and there is a greater degree of **interaction**. The potential for **Internet commerce** (e-commerce) is huge. Customers should be able to find whatever they want quickly and easily and purchase it there and then.

Marketing at Work

Groceries online

Verdict, the retailing consultancy, predicts that online shopping will be worth some £12.5 billion by 2005. This represents a significant increase from the £581 million spent in 1999. This growth will come largely from the grocery market with supermarket shoppers switching to the internet, digital TV shopping services and using mobile phones. Almost all of this switching will be cannibalised from stores and not represent new customers. Most of the UK's top retailers have websites although not all allow transactions. Interestingly, Verdict report that as retailers currently with physical outlets move online, those who deal solely online at the moment may consider opening outlets.

Financial Times, 12/6/2000

Marketing at Work

Made-to-measure advertising

Imagine that companies only aimed advertisements at those consumers likely to buy their goods. What a wonderful world that would be, say marketers. No longer would advertisers waste money pitching their ads at indifferent viewers. Just as importantly, viewers would no longer have to sit and suffer through commercials about products in which their interest was slight to zero.

In fact, advertisers believe that cyberspace is moving them closer to their goal. The type of marketing known as customised advertising is being introduced to the Net. It works like this: cyberhosts – those who operate Net sites, primarily on the World Wide Web – 'know' who is entering a particular site, and screen the appropriate advertisement. Consumers anxious about their weight, for example, might see an ad for *Diet Coke*, rather than *Classic Coke*. Wintertime browsers in the northern US might see an advertisement for ski equipment while Florida's residents saw a sales pitch for scuba gear.

This is already happening. *Seven-Up*, for example, has a spot in the electronic version of *Wired* magazine, where an ad is displayed to students but not to business-people.

Action Programme 1

Using the PEST framework, determine some possible developments in the wider environment that might affect the communications of organisations operating in the following markets.

| | *Political* | *Economic* | *Social* | *Technological* |

Family saloon cars
Coffee
Kitchen furniture
Photocopier paper
Drinks vending machine

6 The ethical context   12/99

Marketing at Work

Ben and Jerry's go corporate but retain social values

The ice cream brand Ben and Jerry's, long hailed for its values based on social responsibility, is now part of the giant Unilever group. This has raised doubts in some quarters as to whether the brand's ethical values can be maintained under the giant's umbrella. Some consumers have suggested this move may lead to a loss of conscience. Unilever however intend to maintain the brand's credentials. Richard Goldstein, president of Unilever Foods North America states that 'it is our hope and expectation that Ben and Jerry's continues to engage in these critical, global economic and social missions.' There are also indications that the Ben and Jerry's social factor may influence their new owners' perspectives. Ben Cohen, one of B&J's founders, says Unilever have agreed to a social audit of its worldwide operations.

Marketing Business July/August 2000

6.1   The **ethical context is of increasing concern** to organisations. If it isn't of concern to your organisation, then it should be.

6.2   Ethics is about **what is right and wrong** and how we arrive at such judgements. It deals with questions of absolute values and their application in the real world.

Ethics in businesses

6.3   **Business ethics** is a relatively new area to exam syllabuses, however, many of the issues have always been of concern in practice. In the US, ideas of **corporate social responsibility** have been around for some time. The US context is important; the role of the state, for example in medical care, housing etc, has been far more constrained than it is in the UK, and it is only in recent years that commercial sponsorship of the arts, for example, has taken off in the UK. In the UK **social responsibility was the role of the state**: businesses and individuals paid taxes.

6.4 **All organisations have ethical standards**. They may not be enshrined in a formal written code, and they may be very low or even amoral standards but they are still there as part of the corporate culture. We shall say more about the link between culture and ethics later.

6.5 Reidenbach and Robin usefully distinguish between five different attitudes to corporate ethics.

(a) **Amoral organisations**, as you might expect, are prepared to condone any actions that contribute to the corporate aims (generally the owner's short-term greed). Getting away with it is the only criterion for success. Getting caught will be seen as bad luck. The most powerful myths in such an organisation will be the most outrageous examples of not getting caught after a narrow escape. In a nutshell, there is no set of values other than greed. Obviously, this company gets away without a written code.

(b) **Legalistic organisations** obey the letter of the law but not necessarily the spirit of it, if that conflicts with economic performance. Ethical matters will be ignored until they become a problem. Frequent problems would lead to a formal code of ethics that says, in effect, 'Don't do anything to harm the organisation'.

(c) **Responsive companies** are those that take the view - perhaps cynically, perhaps not - that there is something to be gained from ethical behaviour. It might be recognised, for example, that an enlightened attitude towards staff welfare enabled the company to attract and retain higher calibre staff, or that marketing communications designed to maintain a reputation for fair dealing helped the company to win business. If such a company has a formal code of ethics it will be one that reflects concern for all stakeholders in the business.

(d) **Emerging ethical** (or 'ethically engaged') **organisations** take an active (rather than a reactive) interest in ethical issues.

'Ethical values in such companies are part of the culture. Codes of ethics are action documents, and contain statements reflecting core values. A range of ethical support measures are normally in place, such as ethical review committees; hotlines; ethical audits; and ethics counsellors or ombudsmen.

Problem solving is approached with an awareness of the ethical consequence of an action as well as its potential profitability, and pains are taken to uphold corporate values.'

(e) **Ethical organisations** have a 'total ethical profile': a philosophy that informs everything that the company does and a commitment on the part of everyone to carefully selected core values.

Social responsibility and businesses

6.6 Arguably, institutions such as hospitals, schools and so forth exist because health care and education are seen to be desirable social objectives by government and the public at large, if they can be afforded.

6.7 However, where does this leave businesses? How far is it reasonable, or even appropriate, for businesses to exercise '**social responsibility**' by giving to charities, voluntarily imposing strict environmental objectives on themselves and so forth?

6.8 One school of thought would argue that the management of a business has only one social responsibility, which is to **maximise wealth for its shareholders**. There are two reasons to support this argument.

(a) If the business is owned by the shareholders the assets of the company are, ultimately, the **shareholders' property**. Management has no moral right to dispose of business assets (eg cash) on non-business objectives, as this has the effect of reducing the return available to shareholders. The shareholders might, for example, disagree with management's choice of beneficiary. Anyhow, it is for the shareholders to determine how their money should be spent.

(b) A second justification for this view is that management's job is to **maximise wealth**, as this is the best way that society can benefit from a business's activities.

(i) Maximising wealth has the effect of **increasing the tax revenues** available to the state to disburse on socially desirable objectives.

(ii) Maximising wealth for the few is sometimes held to have a '**trickle down**' effect on the disadvantaged members of society.

(iii) Many company shares are owned by **pension funds**, whose ultimate beneficiaries may not be wealthy anyway.

6.9 This argument rests on certain assumptions that are perhaps peculiar to the 'Anglo-Saxon' view of corporate activity.

(a) The first assumption is, in effect, the opposite of the stakeholder view. In other words, it is held that the **rights of legal ownership are paramount over all other interests in a business**: while other stakeholders have an interest, they have few legal or moral rights over the wealth created.

(b) The second assumption is that a **business's only relationship with the wider social environment is an economic one**. After all, that is what businesses exist for, and any other activities are the role of the state.

6.10 Henry Mintzberg (in *Power In and Around Organisations 1983*) suggests that simply viewing organisations as vehicles for shareholder investment is naive.

(a) In practice, he says, **organisations are rarely controlled by shareholders**. Most shareholders are passive investors.

(b) **Large corporations can manipulate markets**. Social responsibility, forced or voluntary, is a way of recognising this.

(c) Moreover, businesses do receive a lot of **government support**. The public pays for roads, infrastructure, education and health, all of which benefit businesses. Although businesses pay tax, the public ultimately pays, perhaps through higher prices.

(d) Strategic decisions by businesses always have **wider social consequences**. In other words, says Mintzberg, **the firm produces two outputs**:

(i) its goods and services;
(ii) the social consequences of its activities.

6.11 If it is accepted that businesses do not bear the total social cost of their activities, it could be suggested that 'social responsibility' is a way of recognising this. An example is given by the environment. Industrial pollution is injurious to health: if someone is made ill by industrial pollution, then arguably the polluter should pay the sick person, as damages or in compensation, in the same way as if the business's builders had accidentally bulldozed somebody's house. In fact, it could be argued that monetary compensation is incapable of rectifying the injury to the person's health.

Action Programme 2

Many of the privatised utilities (such as water and electricity companies) are still effectively monopolies (and therefore, in theory, in a strong position to manipulate their markets) and all have a wide social impact.

Study the promotional practices of organisations such as these to see how their marketing communications attempts to convey a positive attitude to social responsibilities. Compare them with the new approach to marketing gas, where competition is now widespread.

6.12 However, is there any justification for 'social responsibility' outside remedying the effects of a business's direct activities? For example, should businesses give to charity or sponsor the arts? There are several reasons why they should.

(a) If the stakeholder concept of a business is held, then **'the public' is the stakeholder** in the business. A business only succeeds because it is part of a wider society. Giving to charity is one way of encouraging a relationship.

(b) Charitable donations and artistic sponsorship are a useful medium of **public relations** and can reflect well on the business. It can be regarded, then, as another form of promotion, which like advertising, serves to **enhance consumer awareness** of the business while not encouraging the sale of a particular brand.

6.13 One of the arguments for the social responsibility approach is that in the long term it benefits the organisation. In other words it is argued that enlightened self interest leads to ethical decisions. This belief effectively evades any analysis of the **conflict between the objectives of the organisation (eg profit) and ethical obligations**. This cannot always be sustained: ecological improvements cost money.

6.14 Management is responsible not only to the organisation's owners (shareholders) but also, according to the stakeholder view, to a **wide range of publics**.

- Employees
- Customers
- Suppliers
- Competitors
- The local community
- The general public (and government)

Responsibilities towards the community

6.15 An organisation is a part of the community that it serves, and it should be responsible for:

(a) Upholding the **social and ethical values** of the community ♦

(b) Contributing towards the **well-being of the community**, eg by sponsoring local events and charities, or providing facilities for the community to use (eg sports fields)

(c) **Responding constructively to complaints** from local residents or politicians (eg about problems for local traffic caused by the organisation's delivery vehicles)

6.16 It is all very well to argue about social responsibilities, but there is a line to be drawn between:

(a) Socially **desirable** objectives

(b) The organisation's **moral duty** to promote them.

Those involved in the development of an organisation's marketing communications must be aware of the **ethical climate** and develop messages that are compatible with the **moral expectations of the organisation**, its stakeholders and the public.

Chapter Roundup

- Understanding the influences of the wider external environment can be managed through use of

- The law regulating marketing communications in the UK is not comprehensive. Many of the **statutory provisions**, because they are enshrined in a number of separate Acts of Parliament, are incomplete or contradictory. It is for this reason that **codes of practice** are of great importance to the regulation of this area of marketing activity.

- These codes of practice can be of two types - **statutory codes of practice** (such as the Code of Practice for Traders on Price Indications) or, more importantly in this area, **self regulatory codes of practice** endorsed by the various professional bodies in the industry.

- The aim of such codes is not to usurp the role of law but to **complement** it. Those marketing communications practitioners following both the letter and the spirit of the codes of practice should escape censure.

- Marketing communicators should adhere to the standards set down in the codes of practice of bodies such as the **Advertising Standards Authority**, the Institute of Purchasing and Supply and the Institute of Public Relations. In addition they may be bound by the **ethical codes of their organisations**.

- **Economic cycles** can affect purchasing activity, which suggests that promotional messages should reflect the changed needs of customers. **Social trends** should not be ignored and **technological advances** must be integrated within the array of communication methods and media used by an organisation.

- **IT** will continue to have a major impact upon all business activities.

- The **Internet** is a major new development in communications and most companies of any size now have a **website** and advertise its address in their marketing communications.

- **Digital TV** offers huge opportunities to marketing communicators in terms of **interactivity** and more **closely targeted** messages.

- **Ethics** is an important issue and increasingly organisations are recognising their **social responsibilities** towards a wide range of **publics**. Marketing communications has a key role to play in fostering and supporting values that are acceptable to those publics.

Now try Question 6 at the end of this Study Text

Quick Quiz

1   In what sense should marketing communications be 'honest and truthful? (see para 2.8)

2   What is the rationale for self regulation of marketing communications? (2.11)

3   Why is direct marketing affected by the EU? (2.13, 2.14)

4   Identify three social trends and determine how they might affect the marketing communications of a car manufacturer, a food retailer and a company providing financial services. (Section 4)

5   What are ethics? (6.2)

6   List five different attitudes to corporate ethics. (6.5)

7   Why is it naive for an organisation to think only in terms of pleasing its shareholders? (6.10)

8   Which groups feature in the 'publics' of an organisation? (6.14)

Action Programme Review

1   The PEST analysis is an ideal tool to enable you to brainstorm coherent influencing factors. To take the family saloon as an example:

- Political: The 'Rip off Britain' campaign
- Economic: Increasing tax burdens on car users
- Social: The environment damaging aspects of car use
- Technological: Alternative fuels and engine designs

When you have completed this exercise, consider what future changes might need to be considered and what are the implications for marketing communications strategies. Have another look at the issues discussed in Chapter 1 with regard to significant developments in marketing communications. Social and ethical issues may be of particular concern for many organisations in a range of different markets.

2   A number of companies involved in these markets have become involved in sponsorship of community based activities. As competition increases the probable response will be to add sales promotions to their activities in order to attract new customers.

Part C

Objectives and Strategies

Objectives and Positioning 7

Chapter Topic List	
1	Setting the scene
2	Promotional goals
3	Communication objectives
4	Positioning

Learning Outcome

☑ Determine promotional objectives, explain positioning and develop perceptual maps, and suggest ways in which offerings can be positioned in different markets

Syllabus Reference

☑ Determining promotional objectives and selecting positional opportunities

Key Concepts Introduced

- Adstock effect
- Positioning
- Market positioning
- Psychological positioning

1 Setting the scene

1.1 Having completed a **context analysis**, the goals for the Integrated Marketing Communications plan should have been uncovered. Some of the goals, such as the **marketing objectives**, will have been presented in the **marketing plan** derived from the **business context analysis**. Some will have been determined through the **organisational context analysis**, namely issues to do with corporate branding. Other tasks will have been revealed from the analysis of the **customer context**.

Links with other papers

1.2 The context for the goal setting process here is the overall goal setting activities discussed in *Strategic Marketing Management: Planning and Control*, and detailed at length in your BPP Study Text.

1.3 You will also see in your *Planning and Control* studies that **objectives are crucial** in both providing the foundation for a plan, and in **monitoring progress**.

2 Promotional goals

2.1 As we have seen corporate objectives are often financial but translate into objectives for each of the functions of the business, for example the production function and the marketing function. **Marketing objectives**, **such as increasing market share**, **translate into communications objectives**. In order to deliver an effective plan, it is important to establish marketing communications objectives. These will involve variables such as **perception**, **attitudes**, developing **knowledge and interest** or creating new levels of prompted and spontaneous **awareness**.

2.2 It should be clear that there are three different forms of objectives: corporate, marketing and marketing communications objectives. Collectively these are referred to as **promotional goals** or **objectives**.

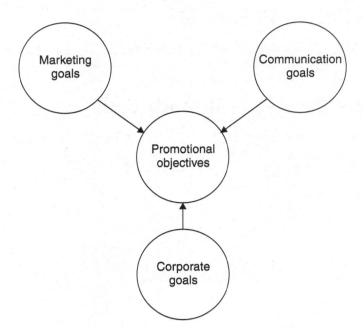

The role of objectives

2.3 Objectives play a clear role in the development of any management activity, including IMC. Objectives provide:

- A means of **communication and co-ordination** between internal and external groups

- A guide for **decision making** in that the goals constrain the number of strategies that can be realistically followed

- A **benchmark** in order that the programme can be **evaluated**

Types of objectives

2.4 Earlier it was identified that there were different types of objectives. These are **corporate objectives**, **marketing objectives** and **marketing communications objectives**. Each consists of one of two main components: they are either **sales** or **communication based**.

Action Programme 1

Select a television or print advertisement and think about the goals it attempted to achieve.

One of the first things that you might have thought of was that to increase sales was the main goal. What other elements might the advertisers be seeking to achieve?

Is it fair to expect marketing communications to achieve all the marketing plan's objectives?

Sales goals

2.5 Now, if you ask most people what the goal of marketing communications is, then most will respond 'to increase sales'. Ultimately this (and profit) is an important outcome, but ask yourself this: **Are sales generated by marketing communications alone**? What role does each of the other elements of the marketing mix play? How will sales vary if a competitor reduces its prices or you increase yours? What impact do marketing channel and product availability play in sales performance? **Marketing communications is important but it is not the sole contributor to marketing success or failure**.

2.6 One further difficulty associated with sales goals concerns the **impact of past promotional activities**.

Key Concept

This is referred to as the **Adstock effect**. Sales today might be the result of last year's (month's, week's) communications. It is just that the customer was not ready to buy then, but the significance of the communication enabled them to store salient messages and use them when they were ready. Setting sales-based goals fails to account for this important point.

2.7 **Sales goals** are important and performance can be easily measured. This might be via the following.

- Sales volumes Sales value or revenue
- Market share
- Profitability (such as return on investment (ROI))

Communication goals

2.8 In Part A we explored ideas about how marketing communications (advertising in particular) might work. The AIDA and other 'Hierarchy of Effects' models are no longer accepted as valid interpretations of the overall process. However, the essence of these **sequential models** is that in order to achieve a sale, each buyer must move, or be moved, through a series of steps. These steps are **essentially communication-based stages** whereby individuals learn more about a product and mentally become more disposed towards adjusting their behaviour in favour (or not) of purchasing the item.

2.9 Awareness is an important state to be achieved as without awareness of a product's existence it is unlikely that a sale is going to be achieved. To achieve **awareness** people need to see or **perceive** the product, they need to **understand** or **comprehend** what it might do for them (benefits) and they need to be **convinced** that such a purchase would be in their best interest and to do this there is a need to develop suitable **attitudes** and **intentions**.

2.10 There are problems associated with measuring each stage. The validity of assuming that individuals move hierarchically through the various stages is questionable and such a framework may be more applicable to high involvement decisions than to low involvement situations.

Corporate communication goals

2.11 **Analysis of the organisational context** will have determined the extent to which action is required to communicate with members and non-members. **Corporate communications**, particularly with employees, and **corporate branding** to develop the image held by key stakeholders, should be integral to such integrated marketing communication campaigns. These tasks form a discrete part of the communication programme.

2.12 In addition to this, it is the responsibility of the communication programme to **communicate the mission and purpose of the organisation in a consistent** and understandable form. In addition, the organisation needs to be able to listen and respond to communications from their **stakeholders** in order that they are able to adjust their position in the environment and continue to pursue their corporate goals.

Promotional goals

2.13 Sales, communication and corporate goals are important for the development of IMC. Sales goals can be taken from the marketing plan and corporate goals can be determined through the mission and business strategy. The communication goals need to be uncovered through the **context analysis**. For example, questions such as...'do we need to: Increase levels of prompted **awareness**? Change the way our **brand** is perceived? Change the **attitudes** held towards the brand or organisation? Provide new reasons to convince people that they **need** this brand (benefit orientation)?'…can only be determined by understanding the context within which the marketing communications will take place.

3   Communication objectives   12/99, 6/01

Setting SMART objectives

3.1   A useful acronym often applied to objectives, is SMART:

- **S**pecific
- **M**easurable
- **A**chievable
- **R**ealistic
- **T**imed + **T**argeted

Promotional objectives

3.2   Objectives need to be **specific** in that they must be capable of communicating to a target audience *(who)*, a distinct message *(what)*, over a specified time frame *(when)*. Promotional objectives must therefore include:

- Identification of the **target audience**
- A **clear message**
- **Expected outcomes** in terms of trial purchase, awareness and so on
- A measurement of **results**
- Mechanisms for **monitoring and control**

3.3   The objectives need to be **measurable and therefore quantifiable**. Statements such as 'increase consumer awareness' are vague, whereas 'increase awareness of the 55 - 65 year age group from 40% to 80%' is more precise and capable of measurement.

3.4   Objectives need to be **achievable**. Purely from an internal company perspective, if sales are targeted to increase by 25% over a designated time period then manufacturing capacity will have to be secured to meet this target. Likewise, attempting to gain additional shelf space within a retail outlet will require that additional resources are devoted to the sales force, to sales promotions and to advertising.

3.5   Objectives need to be set with a degree of **realism** rather than on the basis of wild imagination. Otherwise, a company would be better off having no targets at all. An unrealistic target would tend to ignore the **competitive and environmental forces** affecting the company, the available **resources** at the company's disposal and the **time frame** in which the objectives have to be achieved.

3.6   **Finally, objectives need to be timed over a relevant time period**. Although a plan of action may be drawn up for a year, it will be the case that the plan will be reviewed against target, for example monthly or quarterly, so as to enable corrective action to be taken.

3.7   The principle of SMART objectives applies not only to the overall communication strategy but also applies to the setting of objectives for each tool within the **promotional mix**. Once the overall communication strategy has been set then individual (yet integrated) plans need to be devised for each of the promotional tools. Using the SMART principle objectives can be set for advertising, sales promotion, public relations, direct marketing and personal selling.

4 Positioning

12/01, 6/02

4.1 You may recall that the final part of the target marketing process is **positioning**.

Key Concept

Positioning is how the product is perceived and evaluated by the target audience relative to competing products. This is why perception is an important and integral part of the context analysis.

It is crucial to review and analyse the way in which customers and other stakeholders perceive the product (or organisation). The way management think customers see a product is usually wide of the mark. Continuous (or at least periodic) research minimises the gap between reality (actual perception) and the way the product was **intended** to be seen.

Marketing at Work

The Samaritans have recently announced a new look, so that people have a better idea of what it does, as part of a broad repositioning strategy. The organisation asked itself:

- What do we stand for?
- How is it communicated?

The stakeholders in the organisation are diffuse – 'at risk' groups, volunteers (both fundraisers and counsellors) internal staff, the wider donating public, the government and social agencies, and other charities who may wish to share best practice in the field.

The need to communicate successfully with all these stakeholders has to be achieved within a limited outset and a climate of falling donations, whilst demands on its resources are increasing. The Samaritans has to identify its core message, but reconcile the needs of its different customer segments – and get its message heard through all the 'noise' in its particular marketplace.

4.2 Positioning has developed in importance because of **increasing competition** and the **increasing sophistication of consumers**. With the current speed of communication and advancing technology customers are able to perceive the similarities of physical form and function of competitive products. Therefore, it is important to position organisations as brands in the minds of customers.

Positioning statement

4.3 A **positioning strategy statement** can be as simple as a one-page document that will act as a guideline to measure the consistency of all marketing programmes.

Qualiburgers Positioning Strategy

Qualiburgers will sell premium-quality burgers and other ready-to-eat lunch-time products to upmarket business people in high-traffic urban locations.

Qualiburgers will be positioned versus other lunch-time street vendors as the 'best place to have a quick lunch.'

Qualiburgers is the best place because we have the cleanest carts, the most hygienic servers, the purest, freshest products and the best values.

Prices will be at a slight premium to reflect this superior vending service.

Qualiburgers will also be known for its fun and promotional personality, offering consumers something special every week for monetary savings and fun.

4.4 A carefully crafted business positioning strategy can be used as a guideline for judging the appropriateness of all marketing programmes, especially for promotion, advertising, and PR events. It will ensure that the business image is consistent with the target buyers/end users and help to build an enduring, memorable (and hopefully unique) message to sell the business's products.

Differentiation   12/99

4.5 The basic thesis of positioning is that companies **must differentiate their products or services** or they will be a provider of generic products or services to be sold at the lowest price.

4.6 Positioning entails the placement of a company - within the minds of prospects and customers in the target market - in terms of quality, service, capabilities, and price. **Positioning** aims to place a company's **products or services** in the **minds of people** to influence their behaviour.

Effective positioning

4.7 According to the basic principles of marketing, products and services are created to solve customer 'problems' (that is, to satisfy needs and wants) and provide benefits. Thus, to be effective, **positioning must promise the benefit the customer will receive**, create the expectation, and offer a solution to the customer's problem. If at all possible, the solution should be different from and better than the competition's solution, especially if the competitors are already offering their own solution.

4.8 Positioning should be a single-minded concept, an umbrella from which everything else in the organisation flows. Perhaps the most important aspect of positioning is that **a company should not try to be all things to all people**. A company that tries to be the high quality service provider to all niches while offering an array of special capabilities at a low price is likely to fail.

4.9 Properly targeted, single-minded positioning affects everything a product does or stands for, not only advertising, but also all its promotions. Positioning also affects policies and procedures, employee attitudes, customer relations, complaint handling, and the myriad of other details that combine to make up the customer's experience.

4.10 There must be a consistency among a company's various offerings and it is the positioning statement that guides this consistency.

4.11 **Tests of effective positioning**

- The position must be **believable** in the customer's mind.
- The **product must deliver that promise** on a consistent basis.

There is no point in implementing a particular positioning strategy just because a market analysis reveals that an **opportunity exists**. For instance, if an analysis reveals a potential opportunity for a high-quality premium-priced positioning strategy, the first thing to ask is **whether your company** is suited for such an approach.

4.12 It is imperative that everyone in the company 'buys into' the strategy. In other words, the positioning strategy should permeate the entire organisation, from the CEO to the sales force to the delivery driver. **The biggest positioning mistake a company can make is to create a false impression that it cannot live up to in the marketplace**.

Developing a successful positioning strategy

4.13 The positioning process consists of the various steps needed to develop an effective positioning strategy. This process must be continuous to keep up with changes in the environment, including the changing needs of the customer and the competitors' tactics.

Market positioning

4.14 Market positioning is the first step.

Key Concept

Market positioning is defined as the process of identifying and selecting markets or segments that represent business potential, to determine the criteria for competitive success.

This must be based on a thorough knowledge of the needs, wants, and perceptions of the target market, along with the benefits offered by the company's products or services.

(a) What is important to the target market?

(b) How does the target market perceive the product?

(c) How does the target market perceive the competition?

(d) What attributes should a product use to differentiate itself to make the best use of its limited resources?

4.15 The reality is that if the target market does not perceive the image, the image does not exist. If the target market does not believe that what the product has to offer is a benefit, it is not a benefit. If the target market doesn't believe that the benefit can be delivered, promises are meaningless. If the benefit isn't important to the target market, it isn't important. If the benefit is not perceived as being different from that of the competition, then differentiation has not succeeded. **In short, images, benefits, and differentiation are solely the perception of the customer, not the perceptions of production managers or marketers**.

Psychological positioning

4.16 This step utilises communications to convey a product's identity and image to the target market. It converts customer needs into images and positions a product in the customers' minds.

> ### Key Concept
>
> **Psychological positioning** is a strategy employed to create a unique product image with the objective of creating interest and attracting customers.

4.17 Since it exists solely in the mind of the customer, it can occur automatically without any effort on the part of the marketer and any kind of positioning may result. Two very dissimilar products may be perceived as the same; two similar products may be perceived as different. What the marketer hopes to do is to control the positioning, not just let it happen. Moreover, failure to select a position in the marketplace, to achieve, and to hold that position may lead to various consequences, all undesirable.

4.18 There are two kinds of psychological positioning: **objective positioning and subjective positioning**

(a) **Objective positioning**

  (i) **What is it?** Objective positioning is concerned, almost entirely, with the objective attributes of the physical product. It means creating an image about the product that reflects its physical characteristics and functional features.

  (ii) **How is it used?** If a product has some unique feature, that feature may be used to position the product objectively, to create an image, and to differentiate it from the competition.

  (iii) **Drawbacks**. Less successful objective positioning occurs when the feature is not unique. This is why many product promotions fail to create a distinct image or successfully differentiate the product. One of the first rules of effective positioning is uniqueness.

(b) **Subjective positioning**

  (i) What is it? Subjective positioning is concerned with subjective attributes of the product. Subjective positioning is the **image, not of the physical aspects of the product, but of other attributes perceived by the customer** (that is, attributes that do not necessarily belong to the product but to the customer's mental perception). These perceptions and the resulting images may not necessarily reflect the true state of the product's physical characteristics. They may simply exist in the customer's mind and not all customers' imagines will agree with a particular perception or image. What the marketer hopes is that the people in the **target market will agree on a favourable image** whether or not the image is true.

Marketing at Work

Positioning for growth in the drinks market

In the early to mid 90s, the alcoholic drinks market was based on three principal sectors; beer, wine and spirits. Consumer research suggested to Bacardi-Martini that they wanted great tasting, 'portable' alcoholic products. Premium packaged beers satisfied the portability factor but did not offer a wide range of differing tastes. Spirits offered a range of tastes but not the portability. The research further highlighted a blurring of the boundaries between drink categories. This provided the platform for Bacardi to develop and launch ready to drink products, most significantly the Breezer brand of fruit flavoured Bacardi spirit. Sales have doubled year on year in the UK since the launch in 1994 to current levels around £450 million. Others have readily joined in with brands such as Smirnoff Ice, Hoopers Hooch, Metz and WKD the dominant brands.

Not only were Bacardi competing against direct rivals such as Smirnoff but also against beer brands such as Budweiser. Early distribution battles were overcome as a result of demand created from advertising showing the product being consumed in bars and clubs. Their owners could not ignore this and fridge space had to be given over to the new brands alongside beer. The 'Latin spirit in everyone' theme has established Bacardi's brand values and distinguish it from other premium packaged spirits.

The positioning has very definitely reflected the value inherent in the principal Bacardi brand and as such represents brand extension just as Smirnoff has achieved with the Ice brand.

Bacardi - Martini are continuing to look for further opportunities by undertaking a marketing mapping exercise to test consumer needs for different products and purchase situations.

From *Marketing Business,* October 2000

Positioning strategies

4.19 Marketers may decide to select the most appropriate of the following strategies, depending on the information gathered during market and psychological positioning. (There is some overlap between the strategies: for instance superb after-sales service could be offered simply as a customer benefit or as something that a competitor does *not* offer).

- Attribute, feature or customer benefit
- Price and quality
- Use or application
- Product user
- Product class dissociation
- Competitor

Action Programme 2

For each of the positioning strategies mentioned below, identify a product and/or a service that fits into the category.

4.20 Positioning by **attribute or feature** involves positioning the product by clearly identifying it **with a distinct set of attributes which distinguish the product within the market**. BMW, the German car manufacturer, while positioned within the luxury end of the car market, make constant reference to the engine performance and design as part of their positioning statement. Likewise, Volvo the Swedish car manufacturer have for many years positioned themselves on safety features incorporated into the design of the car.

4.21 Another way to differentiate yourself from the competition is by providing **a unique range of services**. Depending on the characteristics of your local market, unique capabilities could include 24-hour operations, free pickup and delivery, or electronic commerce (online file transfer and on-demand output).

4.22 **Exceptional customer service** can be another differentiator. For obvious reasons, customers prefer vendors who follow their instructions and offer a simple ordering system, on-time delivery, easy problem-resolution, timely and accurate invoicing, and personalised service.

Marketing at Work

Positioning and differentiation strategies online

In an online context, retailers can position their products relative to competitor offerings according to four main variables: product quality, service quality, price and fulfilment time.

(These positioning options have much in common with Porter's competitive strategies of cost leadership, product differentiation and innovation).

The aim of positioning is to develop a perceived advantage over rivals' products. In an e-marketing context the advantage and positioning can be communicated by developing an **online value proposition (OVP).** For maximum effectiveness the OVP should clarify:

■ A clear differentiation of the online proposition compared to the conventional offline proposition.

■ A clear differentiation of the online proposition from competitors based on cost, product innovation or service quality.

■ Target market segment(s) that the proposition will appeal to.

■ How the proposition will be communicated to website visitors, and in all marketing communications.

■ How the proposition is delivered across different parts of the buying process

■ How the proposition will be delivered and supported by resources.

Price and quality

4.23 **Price and quality** are becoming increasingly important as companies attempt to offer more features, better value and improved quality at competitive prices.

4.24 **Price**. Some companies go for the bottom line: they attract customers by being the lowest cost service providers in the market. They do this by having highly efficient operations, so their cost-per-unit (eg per square foot, per page, etc) of output is the lowest. This does not necessarily mean those businesses spend less money than their competitors. For example, the price leader in a given market will probably do the most advertising, but because of the high volume of work the advertising helps bring in, the business will achieve the lowest cost per unit. However, a low-price positioning strategy always requires a high volume of business.

4.25 **Quality**. A company that provides exceptional quality to its customers can command a higher price for its services than its less quality-conscious competitors. However, quality is a variable that customers may take for granted after a while. When a competitor offers those customers a lower price, some of them might give the competitor a try, and may find out they 'get what they pay for'.

4.26 If a company intends to sell its quality program in order to charge higher prices for its services, then it must be willing to invest the time and money required to live up to the higher expectations of its customers. If it creates expectations of superior quality but fails to deliver, few customers will give the company a second chance.

Use or application

4.27 In the third case, the company attempts to position its product or service by deliberately associating it with a specific **use or application**. Kellogg's, the cereal manufacturer, in striving to defend their market position and increase sales, have positioned their main product Corn Flakes as an 'any time of day food', and not just to be eaten at breakfast.

Product user

4.28 Positioning by virtue of **product user** associates the product with a particular class of user. SmithKline Beecham have positioned 'Lucozade Sport' with the sporting fraternity, and have strengthened this through endorsement advertising using major sporting personalities.

Product class dissociation

4.29 It is possible to position a company brand against a product class or an associated product class, claiming that yours is different from the rest. Kraft foods, who produce 'Golden Crown', have positioned their product with respect to the associated product class, butter. Heinz, who produce a range of 'Weight Watcher' foods, are positioning these against traditional but more calorific foods.

Competitors

4.30 A **competitor's position** within a market may be used as a frame of reference in order to create a distinct positioning statement. Avis car rental use the slogan 'We're number 2, so we try harder'. Here the market leader is being used as a reference point to create a competitive statement. The key determinant for the marketer is whether claims made within a promotional campaign which use blatant comparisons can be substantiated through better quality, service, value, cost and so on.

4.31 This approach is used when it is necessary to meet the competition head-on; to bring out differences between products. For example, Visa credit cards compete with American Express by showing examples of places from around the world that do not accept American Express but do accept Visa.

Ice cream success is in the difference

The premium ice cream sector had been dominated by the sophistication of the Haagen-Dazs brand, and previous challenges had come to ground after challenging head on with similar approaches to branding and communications. Having established brand presence via limiting distribution and selective use of PR, Ben and Jerry's finally took on Haagen-Dazs but chose a very different approach. Rather than promote luxuriousness via sexual connotations which had been the Haagen-Dazs theme, B&J's built a position based on humour.

The communications aim to remain true to the original brand positioning of the niche, loveable underdog. The success of the brand has led to its acquisition by the giant food group Unilever who intend to maintain the difference in the approach and not seek to apply 'big brother' principles.

From an article in *Marketing Business,* July/August 2000.

Perceptual product mapping

4.32 Part of the positioning strategy involves **mapping the competing products** within a defined product class so that specific gaps may be identified into which the company may place a new product offering. These perceptual product maps identify the attributes that are strongly associated within a given product class. For example, below is shown a hypothetical product map that may be appropriate for the shampoo market.

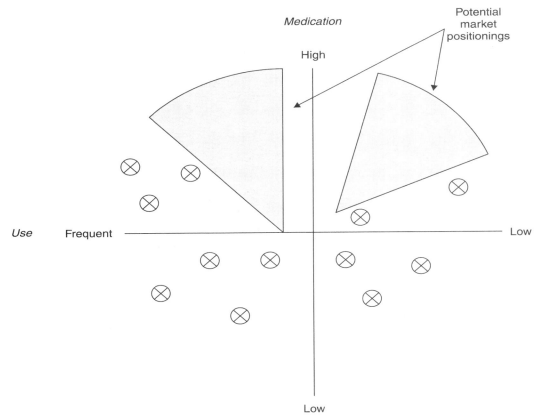

Hypothetical product positioning map 'Hair shampoo'

4.33 By plotting the competing products on this map, it would be possible to identify the **gaps that exist within the market**, and enable new products to be positioned accordingly in the mind of the consumer. Since the map illustrated is only two dimensional, it must be remembered that other factors will need to be taken into consideration, such as price, which will undoubtedly affect the optimal marketing mix employed for the new product.

4.34 The ultimate success of any promotional strategy will be dependent upon a number of inter-related factors, such as the creative stance adopted, choice of media, sales training and so on. However, these issues are dependent upon two main strategic choices: the **chosen segment** in which the company will compete, and the nature of the **positioning statemen**t, which will influence consumer choice. These two issues alone will determine to what extent the company is able to create for itself a definite competitive edge within its chosen market.

 Marketing at Work

Changing a product driven position

The Danish sound equipment and TV manufacturer, Bang and Olufsen, has long promoted itself on the design and technical excellence of its products. The reputation for quality has enabled them to build a loyal customer base and has provided the basis for advertising and marketing strategy. There are signs that the company is moving beyond this platform. The Chief Executive, Anders Knutsen, suggests that this image is insufficient in today's markets and envisages a shift toward promoting strong values and 'the promise of a better life.' He claims further that 'people demand to know the attitudes and beliefs of the companies they buy from'.

This thinking has led to advertising themes such as 'A life less ordinary' to promote distinctiveness as a value in itself. Brochures now describe the lives of customers and retail formats include 'concept shops'. The company products still offer customers premium quality and differentiation but also a reassurance that Bang and Olufsen understands who they are and what they look for, not just from a hi-fi system, but from life in general.

From an article in *Financial Times* 1/12/99

Chapter Roundup

- The **determination of promotional objectives** is an important part of integrated

- The goals to be achieved are derived from contextual analysis and take three main forms. These are **sales**, **communication** and **corporate communication** objectives.

- Promotional objectives need to be stated in such a way that it is easy to understand what is to be achieved and what was achieved. Using the **SMART approach** enables this clarity to be achieved.

- **Positioning** of a product is concerned with how it creates and establishes an image in the minds of consumers and how it is evaluated against competing products. Positioning may be according to attribute, price and quality, use or application, product user, product class or competition.

- The use of **perceptual maps** can assist the positioning decision.

Now try Question 7 at the end of the Study Text

Quick Quiz

1   Why is the use of objectives in promotional strategy recommended? (See para 2.3)

2   What is the Adstock Effect? (2.6)

3   What are SMART objectives? Define each. (3.1 - 3.6)

4   What is positioning concerned with? (4.1)

5   What are six positioning strategies? (4.19)

6   Draw a perceptual product map. (4.32)

Action Programme Review

1   Marketing communications can most effectively be expected to achieve objectives related to increasing awareness levels, changing attitudes and behaviour patterns. Increasing sales or market share is dependent on other marketing factors such as product acceptability, price and distribution.

2   Try and further identify similar kinds of products or services from competing companies. How does their approach to positioning vary? A skim through one of the Sunday newspaper supplements will show a range of different advertisements for motor cars that are all aimed at the same target audience but from a variety of positioning platforms.

Promotional Strategies: Pull, Push and Profile

8

Learning Outcomes

☑   Formulate marketing communications strategies with particular regard to consumers, business-to-business markets, members of the marketing channel and wider stakeholder audiences such as employees, financial markets, environmental groups, competitors and local communities

☑   Determine specific communication activities based upon knowledge of the key characteristics of the target audience. In particular, they will be able to suggest how knowledge of perception and attitude, levels of perceived risk and involvement can impact upon marketing and corporate communications

☑   Select, integrate and justify appropriate promotional mixes to meet the needs of the marketing communication strategies

☑   Advise on the impact corporate communications can have on both internal and external audiences and their role in the development of integrated marketing communications

Syllabus References

☑   Identify, select and formulate promotional strategies, ensuring reference is made to:

       (i)   push, pull and profile strategies

       (ii)   any existing or proposed branding strategies

       (iii)   the Internet and e-commerce activities relating to both consumer-to-business and business-to-business markets

☑   Select appropriate promotional mixes

Key Concepts Introduced

■   Pull strategy   ■   Key account

■   Successful brand   ■   Profile strategy

1   Setting the scene

1.1   Having established the objectives and positioning, the next step is to determine the **overall communication strategy**. The focus of this part of the management process is to consider the emphasis of the strategy, and the appropriate balance between the need to communicate with **consumers**, with **distributors** and with **all other stakeholders**.

Type of Audience		Message Focus
1.	Consumers and business-to-business customers	Products and Services
2.	Members of the marketing channel, such as dealers	Products and Services
3.	All stakeholders, in order to raise the visibility of the organisation	The Organisation

These approaches are referred to as the 3Ps of Marketing Communication Strategy:

1. **Pull communication strategies**
2. **Push communication strategies**
3. **Profile communication strategies**

Links with other papers

1.2   Communication strategy is a reflection of the objectives and positioning requirements set earlier in the marketing plan. 'Push', 'Pull' and 'Profile' strategies are not exclusive to each other and it is perfectly acceptable to choose an element of all three or just two approaches, depending upon what needs to be achieved. Do not forget that they can all be used in the international context.

Marketing at Work

Continental, the German tyre group with international sales of £6.3 billion in 2000, uses a combination of 'push' and 'pull'.

- **Push to:** the OE (original equipment) market, by supplying tyres to the big car manufacturers

- **Pull via:** replacement tyres, with consumers tending to opt for the same brand

The tyre-fitting trade plays a large role in the route to the customer. Continental carries out a lot of 'push' activity here, with incentive programmes, training and education to make sure that the fitters understand the brand segments (premium, quality, economy, budget, own-label). A greater challenge was to get consumers to think about tyres as more than those black things attached to their cars. TV and press advertising in Europe sought to change this perception.

Adapted from *Marketing Business*, January 2002

2 Pull based communication strategies   12/01, 12/02

Key Concept

A **pull strategy** is used to generate and sustain a dialogue with end user customers.

2.1 These might be consumers or they might be business-to-business customers where the customer is the end user and does not move the product on through the marketing channel. **Pull strategies encourage end-users to demand the product from the distributors**, pulling the product through the distribution network.

2.2 Where a pull strategy is specified, then the promotional mix and the message and media combination will need to be integrated. This will be explored later.

2.3 Typical strategies are to create higher levels of **product awareness** (spontaneous or prompted).

2.4 In order to ensure that the target market develops appropriate **attitudes** towards the brand so that it has the best chance of being selected, the marketer has a range of options.

Option	Comment
Modifying the brand	Redesigning the product so that it offers more of the attributes that the buyer desires.
Altering beliefs about the brand	Pursued if the consumer underestimates the qualities of the brand.
Altering beliefs about competitors' brands	Would be appropriate if the consumer mistakenly believes that a competitor's brand has more quality than it actually has.

Option	Comment
Altering the importance of attributes	Persuade consumers to attach more importance to the attribute in which the brand excels.
Calling attention to neglected attributes	Where the brand excels in these attributes. ('Have you forgotten how good they taste?').
Shifting the buyer's ideals	The marketer would try to persuade consumers to change their ideal levels for one or more attributes.

2.5 A particular pull strategy that has been developed and refined over many years is **branding**.

3 Branding and customer retention 6/01, 12/01

3.1 Branding originated as a means of differentiating products from commodities but it has come to be of major importance for reasons far wider in power and implication, especially since the introduction of mass media. In many markets it has taken over the role previously held by the direct selling operation.

What is a brand?

3.2 The following is a useful definition of a successful brand.

Key Concept

A **successful brand**:

- Is an identifiable product, service, person or place
- Augmented so that the buyer or user perceives
- Relevant, unique, added values, which
- Match the buyer's/user's needs closely

3.3 It is possible to depict this definition in diagram form. **The brand contributes the added value** and can be seen as adding clothes to a naked product.

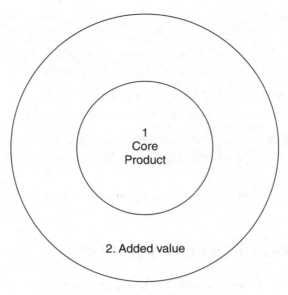

Added value concept

3.4   Levitt (in his 'Augmented Product Concept') takes this a stage further.

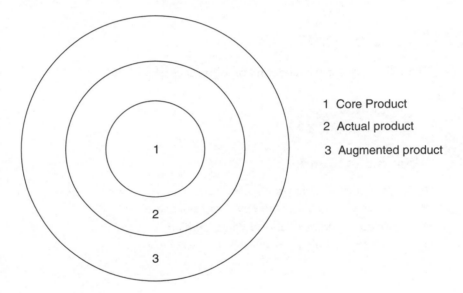

1   Core Product

2   Actual product

3   Augmented product

Augmented product concept

The core product satisfies the basic need of the customer. For a Jaguar car, for instance, this is transport from A to B. The actual product is a mechanical/electrical/electronic machine in certain colours built with certain features such as leather seats. The **augmented component adds the history and tradition** of the Jaguar name and heritage. The core has a unique shape and a distinguished history.

3.5   Another simple way of describing the difference between commodities and brands is the following diagram.

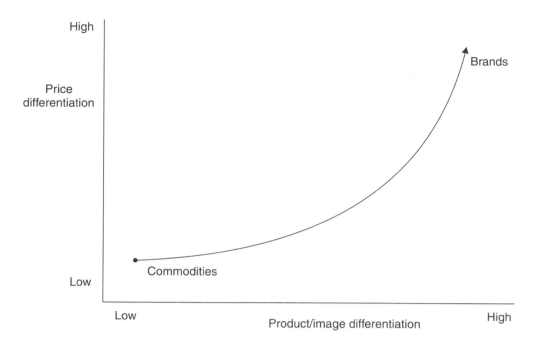

3.6 **Branding encourages the consumer to associate certain attributes with a product**. It differentiates very similar products into distinct segments of the market.

3.7 **The process of differentiation through branding allows the marketer to establish a unique position for a package**. Thus goods which in fact have very close substitutes, as in fmcg markets, can be positioned as though there was very limited competition.

3.8 **Brands are no longer simply a convenient device to differentiate, they are of importance in their own right**. It is often the brand that is bought, not the product.

3.9 The underlying justification for a brand is that it **builds profits**.

Types of brand

3.10

Type of brand	Comment
Individual brand name	This is the option chosen by Procter & Gamble, for example, who even have different brand names within the same product line, eg Bold, Tide.
Blanket family brand name for all products, eg Hoover, Heinz	This has the advantage of enabling the global organisation to introduce new products quickly and successfully. The cost of introducing the new product in terms of name research and awareness advertising will be reduced.
Separate family names for different product divisions	This is the option for the global organisation with 'inconsistent' product lines where a single brand name is not appropriate.
The company trade name	(For example, Kelloggs Corn Flakes, Rice Krispies). This option both legitimises (because of the company name) and individualises (the individual product name). It allows new 'names' to be introduced quickly and relatively cheaply.

Branding strategies

3.11 There are three main elements associated with successful branding: **differentiation, added value** and **integration.**

Differentiation

3.12 Through branding it is possible to differentiate a product from its competitors, make it distinguishable and **readily identifiable**.

Product	Comment
Generic	Core product, nothing added (functional aspects only)
Expected	Minimal value expected by buyer (features, design, packaging and price)
Augmented	Value that surpasses a buyer's basic expectations (service, guarantees, add-ons, delivery and availability)
Potential	Binding buyers to the branded item (brand name, quality and value

Added value

3.13 Branding needs to add value so that the consumers perceive a **meaning** in a brand that is **relevant** to them. This can be achieved through the way buyers perceive the performance of the brand, the psychosocial meanings attached to a brand and the level of **brand name awareness**.

	Comment
Perceived Performance	A function of the overall perceived quality and presence of important or significant attributes (eg Dyson).
Psychosocial meanings	A deduction of the social implications of brand ownership (eg Marlboro cigarettes and the differences between German/French cars).
Level of brand awareness	This can range from a state of unawareness through passive, active and Top-of-Mind awareness levels. This last stage is reached when the brand name becomes **synonymous** with the product category as with Walkman and Hoover.

Integration

3.14 For a brand to survive, the communications underpinning it must be consistent, uniform and reinforcing, so that it is very clear what it stands for.

Marketing at Work

Inmarsat is a satellite communication company which has expanded over the years beyond maritime communications into aeronautical, broadcasting, energy, emergency and aid relief sectors. Its nine satellites, positioned 36,000 km above the earth, give coverage everywhere apart from the North and South Poles.

Inmarsat wants to position itself by convincing companies that satellite communications are "neither too rarefied nor too expensive", and that it is able to deliver high speed global mobile data solutions. Its campaign, which ran in November 2001, aimed to show companies what they could do (positioning the brand in the market).

The advertisements, using the analogy of a 4x4 utility vehicle (which can be used both off road and in the city), looked like car advertising posters and ran in broadsheets and international business titles. The image was also used in public relations, direct marketing and channel marketing.

Because it operates through a range of distributors and service providers, Inmarsat helped to fund the marketing by these parties. The company also developed a range of initiatives to help employees understand the new branding (briefings, videos and competitions). Stephen Rogen, director of marketing communications, says that "The sense of positioning and brand values, how we talk, the tone of voice we use and how we communicate the message - this has changed quite substantially to show that we are far more 'real world' than many people expect."

Marketing Business, October 2001

Branding and marketing communications 6/00, 12/01

Exam Tip

In the June 2000 exam, branding was an important issue in a Section B question, on how marketing communications can contribute to a consumer or business-to-business brand. A key issue here is to read this question carefully. Branding in a business-to-business market is likely to be very different in nature from a mass consumer market.

3.15 The main idea behind branding is that a basic product can be converted with marketing communications into a brand. These communications can take one of two main approaches.

Approach	Comment
Functional	The aim is to provide **information** about the attributes and benefits associated with brand ownership. This is common where **persuasion** is important and where involvement and levels of perceived risk are also high.
Expressive	**Emotions and feelings** are central to the message and the prime goal is to develop audience **likeability** for the communication. Where involvement is low and perceived risk is minimal, it is common practise to try to engage the audience on an emotional level.

Brand strategies

3.16 Brand strategies may be summarised as follows.

Branding strategy	Description
Line extensions	Use of the same brand name to introduce new flavours, forms, colours and package sizes.
Brand extensions	Use of an existing brand name to ;launch new products in other categories (eg Mars into Mars Ice Cream, Honda into lawn mowers)
Multibrands	The introduction of additional brands into a particular market (eg Electrolux owns Frigidaire, Kelvinator, Westinghouse, Zanussi, White and Gibson)
New brands	The development of a new product into a market where none of the company's current brands would be applicable (eg Kellogg's entry into sportswear)
Co-brands	Occurs where two (or more) established brands combine together to generate increased impact. There are a number of variants:
Ingredient co-branding	Volvo advertises that it uses Michelin tyres, Intel and Nutrasweet are other brands which are promoted within a brand.
Same-company co-branding	When a company promotes two or more of its own brands in the same sector.
Joint Venture co-branding	Microsoft sponsorship of the NSPCC charity.

3.17 The relevance of branding does not apply equally to all products.

(a) The cost of intensive brand communications, principally advertising to project a brand image nationally, may be prohibitively high.

(b) Goods or services which are sold in large numbers, on the other hand, promote a brand name by their existence and circulation.

3.18 Where a brand image promotes an idea of quality, a customer will be disappointed if his or her experience of a product fails to live up to expectations. **Quality control** is therefore an important element in branding policy. It is especially **a problem for service industries** (eg hotels, airlines, retail stores) where there is less possibility than in a manufacturing industry of detecting and rejecting the work of an operator before it reaches the customer.

Business-to-business   6/01, 12/01

3.19 Business-to-business (B2B) communications is concerned with the promotion of exchanges that take place between businesses rather than consumers.

3.20 Differences between the consumer and business-to business based markets

(a) **The number of buyers**. There are relatively few buyers in the business-to-business market and normally a large number in the consumer markets. Individuals make purchase decisions in both areas, but the B2B buyers use an organisation's money and financial resources whereas consumers use their own.

(b) Whereas purchase decisions are made by individuals in the consumer market, such decisions are made by groups of people in the B2B setting, referred to as the **Decision Making Unit**.

3.21 These two types of customer require **different forms of marketing communications**. These are set out in the table below.

	Consumer orientated markets	Business-to-business markets
Message reception	Informal	Formal
Number of decision makers	Single or few	Many
Balance of the promotional mix	Advertising and sales, promotions dominate	Personal selling dominates
Specify and integration	Broad use of promotional mix with a move towards integrated mixes	Specific use of below-the-line tools but with a high level of integration
Message content	Greater use of emotions and imagery	Greater use of rational, logic and information based messages although there is evidence of a move towards the use of imagery
Length of decision time	Normally short	Longer and more involved
Negative communications	Limited to people close to the purchaser/user	Potentially an array of people in the organisation and beyond.

BPP
PROFESSIONAL EDUCATION

	Consumer orientated markets	Business-to-business markets
Target marketing and research	Great use of sophisticated targeting and communication approaches	Limited but increasing use of targeting and segmentation approaches
Budget allocation	Majority of budget allocated to brand management	Majority of budget allocated to sales management
Evaluation and measurement	Great variety of techniques and approaches used	Limited number of techniques and approaches

3.22 The development of IMC can be best observed in the communications serving the business-to-business markets. These have all necessitated the development of closely **co-ordinated marketing communication campaigns**. Factors to consider include the following.

(a) The use of exhibitions

(b) The balance between the types of advertising media that are available

(c) The role played by personal selling in demonstrating products (conveying technical information as well as creating awareness and generating sales leads).

3.23 The message strategy is often based on the **provision of product benefits**, and rational attribute claims. However, there is a trend towards the development of brands in this sector as a form of **differentiation**, and the **use of imagery and emotional claims is growing**.

Customer retention   12/02

3.24 Arguably, this is another 'pull-based strategy' predicated on the notion that 20% of customers provide 80% of profits.

3.25 **New customers cost more** because of advertising costs, sales administration costs, joining discounts etc, hence some firms enact customer retention programmes. Retention is not loyalty (which is 'emotional'), but it can be bought.

3.26 **Impact on marketing communications**

■ Customer retention requires **internal and external marketing**

■ Development of **reward packages** (eg Air Miles) and communication of these

■ More use of **direct marketing** (perhaps the Internet) with known customers as opposed to above the line advertising

■ The main communications burden may therefore be carried out by **service staff**

Exam Tip

We could cite Tesco as an example of where, in the long run, customer retention is a virtuous circle; if less money need be spent attracting new customers this represents a significant advantage over competitors and frees financial resources for other marketing activity (such as price cuts). The December 2002 exam featured a question on loyalty and customer retention in the context of a national lottery which has been losing customers.

4 Push based communication strategies 12/01, 12/02

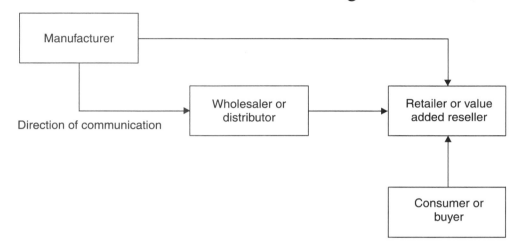

Push based communication strategies

4.1 Communication with members of the marketing channel, such as **dealers and retailers**, is absolutely vital if sufficient **exposure and visibility** are to be obtained for the product. Without suitable distribution it is unlikely that the marketing objectives will be met.

Exam Tip

The December 2002 exam contained a question about the provision of information to, and communicating with, the marketing channel.

4.2 It is therefore important to determine a promotional strategy to reach channel members in order to maximise the impact of an integrated marketing communications approach. This strategy is referred to as a **push communications strategy**.

Key Concept

A **push communications strategy** requires the identification of distributor needs and, through a combination of elements, an attempt to meet and satisfy these needs in order that both the supplier and the distributor are able to achieve their respective goals. The focus is on the intermediary.

4.3 **Members of a marketing channel** might be **independent** organisations and have their particular goals, but they choose to work together and are therefore **interdependent** and share a common goal: consumer/customer satisfaction.

4.4 Understanding the needs of the people who make up the decision making unit and then communicating effectively is an essential aspect of the push approach. **Partnership success** is achieved through co-ordination, trust, participation and the quality of information shared.

Marketing at Work

Everyone is happy with ARNIE – the new Automotive Repair national Information Exchange, recently rolled out by Suncorp Insurance to car repair shops around Australia.

The web-based system links all steps of the vehicle repair process, from quoting and assessment to parts ordering, completion and invoicing, reducing the cycle by two weeks on average.

The process is as follows:

1   Policy holder rings Suncorp call centre after accident

2   Call centre operator generates claim file

3   Appointed repairer photographs the damage, prepares quote and sends all via the Internet to ARNIE

4   ARNIE generates a new file and forwards it

5   Assessor receives notification of new file, and reviews and approves quote

6   Repairer received automated email 'go-ahead'

7   part numbers, prices and any variations are updated on ARNIE by repairer while repair is under way. When repair is completed, the repairer sends his invoice to Suncorp over the Internet.

8   Suncorp pays repairer electronically

When it comes to getting drivers back on the road after an accident, the quicker the repair, the happier the policy holder. And returning the car within seven days means that Suncorp doesn't have to pay for the hire cars it guarantees for long waits. Speed also has other advantages – a repair paid within a week of doing a job avoids cash flow problems. All these things should eventually have a positive effect on insurance premiums.

Adapted from: *"ARNIE'S insurance claim system is a smash hit"* Sydney Morning Herald, 23 April 2002

Key account management (KAM)

4.5 **Key account management** is an approach to determining which customer accounts are strategically important. These may be large revenue-driven accounts or they might be accounts that offer access to new markets or new technology, be competitively significant or represent a geographic advantage.

Key Concept

Key accounts are perceived to be strategically meaningful and the communications (primarily personal selling) are geared to sustaining and developing the relationship between the two parties.

4.6 Relationships with key accounts unfold and develop through a series of phases.

Stage	Activity
Pre KAM	Identification of potential key accounts
Early KAM	Tentative agreements and probing
Mid KAM	Account review and senior management involvement
Partnership KAM	Joint problem solving and sharing of sensitive information
Synergistic KAM	Synergy of shared values and a one entity perspective
Uncoupling KAM	A positive move recognising that there is no further value in the relationship

5 Profile based communication strategies   12/02

5.1 The context analysis may have uncovered issues concerning the way the organisation is perceived by a range of stakeholders, perhaps as a result of an **ethical issue or crisis that has struck the company** and the associated **media comment**. In these circumstances, one of the objectives of the marketing communications strategy will be to correct or adjust the perception held by influential stakeholder audiences.

5.2 The extent of the perception gap will have been uncovered during the analysis of the organisation context. This in turn should have been articulated as a corporate communication objective.

Key Concept

A **profile communication strategy** therefore addresses how the corporate entity is perceived by a range of stakeholder audiences.

5.3 For example, it is quite common for an organisation to develop a communications campaign that is targeted at the financial markets and the stock market in particular. This is referred to as investor communications.

Corporate identity

5.4 Corporate identity and corporate image are two different facets of the profile development strategy. Increasingly organisations are adopting the phrase **corporate branding** as a substitute for corporate identity.

5.5 **Corporate identity is about the way an organisation communicates with its audiences**. There are two main forms of communication, those that are **planned** and pre-determined by the organisation, and those that are **unplanned** and unexpected.

5.6 The individual communication methods that make up these planned and unplanned communications are referred to as cues.

   (a) Examples of **planned cues** are letterheads, logos, signage, product quality and the behaviour and level of knowledge of its employees.

   (b) Examples of **unplanned cues** are media comment, the cleanliness of the company's vehicles and any actions taken by competitors and consumer groups that may reflect or directly relate to the organisation.

Action Programme 1

Identify three corporate communication campaigns and the cues used by each to communicate with the different audiences.

5.7 The way in which these cues are perceived frames the way an individual sees and understands an organisation and helps form the image they have of an organisation.

Marketing at Work

Monsanto developed a strong corporate campaign in order to raise the social and scientific arguments related to genetically modified foods. This attempt at being perceived as fair minded and concerned about these issues was articulated using two-sided arguments and invited comment and discussion. This has backfired spectacularly in Europe with huge opposition to GM foods.

5.8 **Corporate identity therefore is about how an organisation presents itself**. Corporate image is what an audience believes an organisation to be as a result of their understanding of the cues. Sometimes the perception of these cues is correct and sometimes it is not correct. This may be because of the quality of either corporate communications or corporate performance. **Corporate reputation** is an extension of corporate image.

Marketing at Work

'No Logo' by Naomi Klein is anti-branding and 'anti-multinational'. She considers that by their very nature multinationals aim to destroy difference and impose a homogeneous culture on the world. Corporate ethics is therefore seen as a cynical, halfhearted exercise. For example, oil companies trading on their green and ethical intentions have been undermined by allegations of human rights abuses.

Corporate communication strategy

5.9 As well as communicating about its individual products and services, the company may wish to pursue a corporate communication strategy. This can take either of two forms.

(a) First, it can be a simple corporate communication campaign aimed at improving the company's identity and subsequently its image.

(b) Secondly, it may be a campaign whereby the company associates itself with a current and topical social issue.

Action Programme 2

Identify two major companies which have developed corporate campaigns related to social issues. What do you consider to be the benefits and potential problems associated with such a strategy?

Crisis communications

5.10 Closely allied to corporate identity is the field of **crisis management** (communications). Company image and reputation can be severely tarnished or even ruined if a response to a crisis is deemed inappropriate.

Marketing at Work

Mercedes

The initial response by Mercedes when its then prototype vehicle the A-Class turned over when driven by journalists was to deny that there was a problem. That denial, which lasted eight days, turned into a crisis as 3,000 orders were lost and the media refused to let go of the problem. The reputation of Mercedes was dented for the first time in a long time and only the acceptance of the problem, and a public statement about the actions the company was to take with regard to production and design, alleviated the pressure on the company.

5.11 Some crises can be anticipated, perhaps because of the **nature of the business environment** in which an organisation operates. For example, hospitals can plan for bed shortages caused by epidemics or local accidents. Airlines plan meticulously to cope with air accidents although their incidence is relatively rare. However, product sabotage and other seemingly unprovoked attacks on an organisation cannot be anticipated with such clarity.

5.12 The following table sets out the phases through which most crises pass. The duration of each phase will vary, depending upon the nature of the disaster and the quality of the management and planning processes.

Disaster phase	Actions
Scanning	Scanning of the environment to pick up signals that might herald a disaster. Many signals fail to materialise but those that do not surprise the organisation.
	Identify the nature of different crises that might hit the organisation. Where and when will it affect the organisation?
	Devise alternative crisis programmes for differing disasters. Establish appropriate communication channels, internally and externally. Chief Executive to formalise the programme and establish its significance throughout the organisation.
Pre-impact	Preparation of a specific crisis plan accompanied by the deployment of crisis teams in order to minimise the effects, and to inform stakeholders of the proximity of the crisis.
	Select key senior personnel and delegate responsibility. Instigate training programmes as necessary.
Impact	Implementation of the plan and continued communication with key stakeholder groups. The aim is to neutralise and localise the affect of the crisis but not to hide or diminish its significance. Maintain close contact with the media and provide stakeholders with access to specific personnel.
	Anticipate questions, do not speculate, use facts when answering questions and track media comment.
Readjustment	The speed of recovery is partly dependent upon the strength of the company's image/reputation before the crisis struck. However, internal and external (media, police) investigations characterise this phase. The organisation's attitude must remain consistent, positive and concerned.

Exam Tip

Corporate communications is a significant part of the Integrated Marketing Communications syllabus and questions about crisis management in some examination papers should be anticipated. Students are advised to prepare for this topic by learning examples and noting the manner and form of the way organisations cope with real crises.

The June 2000 exam featured a question on corporate identity and its use in reaching audiences. In December 1999, corporate identity was allied with ethics, as a differentiating factor.

Chapter Roundup

- It is possible to identify **three approaches to communication strategy**, based upon the

- These three, **pull**, **push** and **profile** strategies are not mutually exclusive. In practice, all three strategies are used, it is just that the balance between the three strategies will vary, according to the needs of each programme.

- **Pull based programmes are targeted at end user consumers** and business-to-business customers. Branding is often used as pull strategy as it is possible to convey a great deal of information in a concise way.

- **Push based programmes are directed at members of the marketing channel** where trust and commitment are essential ingredients for effective communications. Key account management techniques serve to help communications with strategically important accounts.

- **Profile strategies aim to influence the way the organisation**, as a whole, is **perceived** by either a small or large range of stakeholders. These strategies serve to develop the visibility and credibility of an organisation. **Crisis management** techniques are an aspect of this, as are corporate branding and associated image activities.

Try Question 8 at the end of this Study Text

Quick Quiz

1. Name three types of promotional strategy. (see para 1.1)

2. Identify six methods of changing consumer attitudes. What is one of the primary approaches used to communicate with consumers? (2.4, 2.5)

3. Define a brand. (3.2)

4. Name four types of branding. (3.10)

5. What differentiates strategies to reach consumers from business-to-business customers? (3.21)

6. Communication strategies to reach members of the marketing channel are characterised by . . . . ? (4.1 - 4.3)

7. What are the various phases through which KAM relationships are considered to proceed? (4.6)

8. Briefly explain corporate identity. (5.5)

9. What is the relationship between Corporate Reputation and Corporate Image? (5.8)

10. What are the phases of a crisis and how might communications vary across each phase? (5.12)

Action Programme Review

1   Look for campaigns from companies involved in similar fields and examine how they differ. Give some consideration to the possible differences in the objectives set.

2   Financial services companies such as the Cooperative Bank have developed campaigns based on their ethical investment strategy. Tesco, the food retailer, has been involved in promotional activity aimed at raising funds to provide computers in schools. Such strategies may find favour with different stakeholder groups and enhance corporate image. Drawbacks might include criticism if for example the Cooperative Bank is seen to be investing in an area or in a company where negative issues have been raised by pressure groups such as Greenpeace or Friends of the Earth.

Part D

The Promotional Mix

A Summary of the Tools of the Promotional Mix

9

Chapter Topic List	
1	Setting the scene
2	An overview of the promotional tools
3	Primary and support roles
4	How to integrate the tools
5	Advertising
6	Personal selling
7	Sales promotion
8	Public relations
9	Direct marketing
10	The Internet and e-commerce
11	Digital TV
12	Impact of interactive systems

Learning Outcomes

- ☑ Select, integrate and justify appropriate promotional mixes to meet the needs of the marketing communication strategies

- ☑ Be aware of the impact and contribution technology makes to marketing communications. Be appreciative and sensitive to issues associated with cross-border marketing communications

Syllabus References

☑ Identify, select and formulate promotional strategies, *ensuring reference is made to:

   (i)   push, pull and profile strategies

   (ii) any existing or proposed branding strategies

   (iii) the Internet and e-commerce activities relating to both consumer-to-business and business-to-business markets

☑ Selecting appropriate promotional mixes

☑ Determining message styles and key media goals

Key Concepts Introduced

■ Advertising   ■ Direct marketing

■ Personal selling   ■ E-commerce

■ Sales promotion   ■ Internet marketing

■ PR

1   Setting the scene

Links with other papers

1.1 There are a variety of tools that can be used to communicate with audiences. This chapter will remind you of the salient points about each tool. Those unfamiliar with this aspect of the programme should refer to one of the following titles.

■ BPP Study Text (2003) *Marketing Operations*

■ Fill C (2002) *Marketing Communications: Contexts, Contents and Strategies,* 3rd edition, Hemel Hempstead: Prentice Hall Europe

■ Smith P R (1998) *Marketing Communications*, Kogan Page

2   An overview of the promotional tools   12/01, 6/02

2.1 In this part of the Study Text the aim is to make you more familiar with the very broad range of promotional tools and to provide some guidelines for choosing the most appropriate promotional mix. With promotional tools this is not an easy job because usually it is not just one tool that is required but a combination. Indeed, several different combinations could probably achieve the same result.

2.2 Having chosen a suite of promotional tools and even allocated them as either primary or supporting, it is important to be able to integrate them into a comprehensive and cost effective whole.

The range of promotional tools

2.3 **The range of promotional tools continues to grow**. The variety of media that can be used for above-the-line campaigns has expanded, both in the printed advertising field and in the broadcast field. There are literally thousands of publications aimed at different target groups. In the personal computer field alone there are hundreds of magazines. In the broadcast field the number of television stations steadily increases through satellite, cable and digital television and the number of commercial radio stations has also grown considerably.

2.4 The diagram on the next page shows the range of tools that can be used to influence a customer or potential customer. These tools represent the deployment of **deliberate and intentional methods** calculated to bring about a favourable response in the customer's behaviour. The diagram represents the most obvious promotion methods, though other parts of the marketing mix, including the product itself, pricing, policy and distribution channels, will also have decisive effects.

Action Programme 1

(a) Actually read your junk mail, wander around the supermarket, read the paper, watch TV, and start collecting those leaflets that are constantly posted through your letterbox. How many examples of the tools shown above can you find? Be on the alert constantly for real-life examples and illustrations that you could use in your examination answers.

(b) Were you influenced by any of the examples that you found? Did you respond? You should be able to analyse your reasons in the light of Part B of this Study Text.

(c) Can you think of (or better, find examples of) any other promotional tools, not shown above?

3 Primary and support roles

3.1 What should already be clear is that influencing customers and potential customers is a complex business. Discussions of buyer behaviour have shown that there is not just one process that influences the customer but a whole series. It follows therefore that **each promotional tool will have a variety of roles**.

3.2 In terms of making management decisions and allocating budgets it is possible to consider promotional tools in two broad categories of **primary** and **support** roles. For example in a consumer campaign it may be that television is used as the main vehicle for launching the campaign, which is then sustained by a longer-lasting poster campaign.

Action Programme 2

One-to-One, the mobile phone company, ran a campaign of TV ads featuring a romance along the lines of the Nescafé Gold Blend couple. Then they ran a competition showing viewers extracts from the first series of ads and offering a prize to those who could put the extracts in the order in which they originally appeared. This (we were told) was a prelude to the second series of ads.

What are the primary and supporting promotional activities here? What do you think the prize was? Can you classify other campaigns that you have witnessed in a similar way?

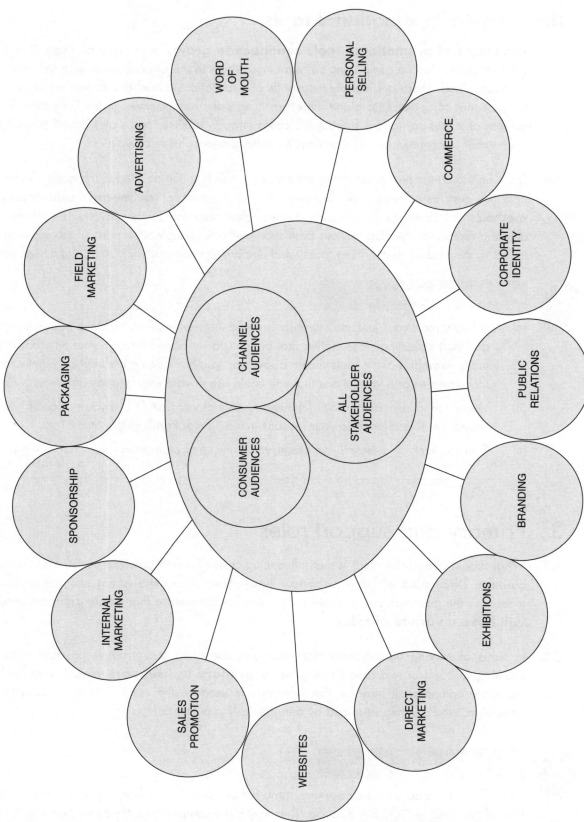

3.3 The choice of primary promotion tool can also be influenced by the stage of the product life cycle.

4   How to integrate the tools

4.1 Promotion work is exciting because the aim is to influence customers favourably towards your organisation's products or services. It is not an exact science. It retains many of the characteristics of an art or a game. It is necessary to integrate all the promotional elements to achieve the **maximum influence on the customer**.

4.2 Having recognised the need for integration and seen the role of the promotion mix within the broader marketing mix, it is now necessary to consider some more **practical steps to ensure that integration occurs**. The following diagram shows that integration can be a conscious choice during the promotion planning process, and it can also be a necessary part of the review and revision process.

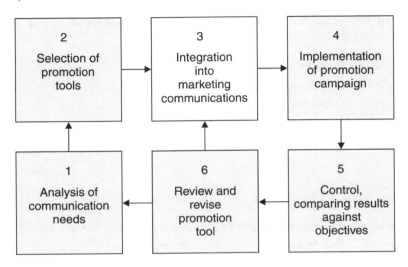

Integration of promotional tools into planning

4.3 **Practical steps can be taken to ensure the greater co-ordination of promotion tools**. The diagram below demonstrates the use of measures that can be taken to ensure integration. The first three involve asking questions about the effectiveness, economy and efficiency of the promotion tools. The efficiency can be forecast in the pre-campaign phase and then measured by means of tracking studies during the campaign. This will lead to a review, revision and further integration of the promotion tools.

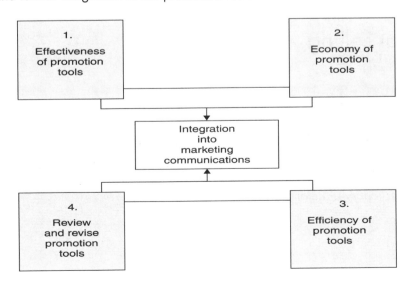

Criteria for integrating promotion tools

5 Advertising

Key Concept

Advertising may be defined as non-personal paid-for communications targeted through mass media with the purpose of achieving set objectives. Advertising is a means of reaching large audiences in a cost-effective manner. Personalised feedback from an advertising message is not usually obtained.

5.1 **The purpose of advertising is to achieve set objectives**. These objectives will vary depending on the following factors.

- The result of the **context analysis**
- The nature of the **product or service** to be advertised
- The stage it has reached in its **life cycle**
- The **marketplace** in which it operates
- The **role** advertising is to play

Action Programme 3

Choose some television or print advertisements and try to work out what each one might be trying the achieve. What type of goals might there be?

When you have attempted this refer back to Chapter 7, with regard to goals and objectives.

5.2 It is not the purpose of advertising to win awards for creativity (though winning any sort of award is good publicity). In this chapter we are concerned with the practicalities of arranging for advertising to be used as a promotional tool. More information about advertising, and in particular the **messages and media** used, follows this chapter.

6 Personal selling

Key Concept

Personal selling has been defined as 'the presentation of products and associated persuasive communication to potential clients, which is employed by the supplying organisation. It is the most direct and longest established means of promotion within the promotional mix' (Baron *et al*, *Macmillan Dictionary of Retailing* 1991).

6.1 All organisations have employees with responsibility for contacting and dealing directly with customers and potential customers. These employees, known as the **sales force**, provide a vital function to the organisation as they form a direct link to the buyers.

6.2 An organisation has a choice as to how it **organises itself for selling**.

(a) Employ a direct sales force, consisting of full or part-time paid employees who work exclusively for the company. This type of sales force may, in turn, consist of two groups: **inside sales personnel** who conduct their business from the company premises via the telephone, or **field sales personnel** who travel and visit customers.

(b) An organisation could employ a **contractual sales force**, which could comprise sales agents, dealers or brokers who are paid a commission on the sales they generate.

6.3 Irrespective of the type of sales force a company may use, the sales force needs the support of other groups within the organisation if it is to operate efficiently and effectively. Kotler (1999) identifies the following groups whose activities impact upon the effectiveness of the sales force.

(a) **Top management** who can be increasingly involved in the selling process, particularly with big orders or key accounts.

(b) **Technical sales personnel** who supply technical information and service to the customer before, during or after the sale of the product.

(c) **Customer service representatives** who provide installation, maintenance and other services to the customer.

(d) **Office staff** including sales analysts, administrators and secretarial staff.

Indeed, Kotler maintains that selling should increasingly be regarded as a **team effort** involving all these groups.

The tasks in the selling process

6.4 Personal selling is probably the area of the promotional mix that has the most stereotypes attached to it. The image of the 'travelling salesman' is an enduring one. However, this masks the reality that the term **sales representative** covers a broad range of positions, which vary tremendously in terms of tasks and responsibilities.

Role	Comment
Order collector	The salesperson's job is predominantly to deal with **routine orders** normally through **telemarketing**.
Order taker	The salesperson passively takes orders from the customer. This can be further divided into **inside order takers**, such as shop assistants, or **outside order takers**, such as those salespeople who call on regular customers to take an order periodically. The customer has already been persuaded to use the product, or has been using the product in the past.
Pre-order caller	The salesperson is not expected or permitted to take an order but is expected to **build goodwill or educate** the customer in the use of the product. Medical representatives from pharmaceutical companies may fall into this category.
Order supporter	The salesperson's main skill is the application of his **technical knowledge** relating to the product.
Order getter	The salesperson has to stimulate demand and **creatively sell** tangible or intangible products.

6.5   The 'degree of difficulty' of the salesperson's tasks increases the nearer the person gets to being an order getter. However, the art of 'selling' in its narrowest sense is only one of a number of tasks that the salesperson could perform. A salesperson could perform many different activities.

Activity	Comment
Prospecting	Gathering additional **prospective customers** in addition to sales leads generated by the company on his behalf.
Communicating	**Communicating information** to existing and potential customers about the company's products and services.
Selling	'**The art of salesmanship**', encompasses approaching the customer, presenting, answering objections and closing the sale.
Servicing	A salesperson may provide **various services** to the customer, such as consulting about their problems, rendering technical assistance, arranging finance and expediting delivery.
Information gathering	The salesperson can be a very useful source of **marketing intelligence** because of his or her links with the end customer. Many salespeople are responsible for supplying regular **reports on competitive activity** within their particular sales area.
Allocating	The salesperson may assist in evaluating **customer profitability** and creditworthiness, and may also have to control the allocation of products to customers in times of product shortages.
Shaping	An increasingly important role is to help build and sustain **relationships** with major customers.

6.6 While a salesperson may engage in all these tasks from time to time, **the mix of tasks will vary according to the purchase decision process, company marketing strategy and the overall economic conditions of the time**. For example, the skills needed for a straight rebuy situation (where the customer has bought the same product under the same conditions of sale in the past) will be totally different from those required to develop a new account.

6.7 **Sales force activity must also be undertaken within the context of the organisation's overall marketing strategy**.

(a) For example, if the organisation pursues a **'pull' strategy**, relying on massive consumer advertising to draw customers into the premises of marketing intermediaries to ask for the brands, then the **role of the sales force may primarily be a servicing one**, ensuring that retailers carry sufficient stock, allocate adequate shelf space for display and co-operate in sales promotion programmes.

(b) Conversely, with a **'push' strategy**, the organisation will rely primarily on the sales force to **sell the brands to the marketing intermediaries** who will then assume the main responsibility for selling on the brands to the end customer.

6.8 **The mix of a salesperson's tasks may vary with the prevailing economic conditions**. For example, in times of product shortage the art of selling may not be as important. However, such a view neglects the other roles of the salesperson that will be of greater importance in such circumstances, such as allocating, counselling customers, communicating company policy to customers and perhaps selling other products that are not in short supply.

7 Sales promotion

Key Concept

The Institute of Sales Promotion (ISP) defines **sales promotion** as 'a range of tactical marketing techniques, designed within a strategic marketing framework, to add value to a product or service, in order to achieve a specific sales and marketing objective.'

7.1 (a) Sales promotion encompasses a range of techniques appropriate for targeting **consumers**, for instance via price reductions, competitions or gifts with purchases. However, **trade and sales force incentives** are also implied under the general heading of sales promotion.

(b) Sales promotion is viewed by the ISP as a tactical promotional tool. The majority of companies will use sales promotion as a means of achieving a **short-term objective**, for instance to gain short-term sales volume or to encourage trial and brand switching by a rival manufacturer's consumers.

(c) Although it is used as a tactical tool, sales promotion works within a strategic marketing framework. **Sales promotion should start with due regard to the strategic objectives for the brand**.

(d)   Sales promotion always seeks to **add value** to a product or service. Thus consumers are offered something extra for their purchase, or the chance to obtain something extra.

7.2   Sales promotion includes the notion of both **sales pull** and **sales push** techniques. As we have seen, sales pull techniques incentivise the consumer to buy. Sales push techniques ensure that the distribution pipeline is well loaded, and sales are pushed along the distribution chain.

Exam Tip

Be aware of the potential for confusion between the terms promotion (used as a synonym for communication techniques in general) and sales promotion (which is a specialist term reserved for the specific techniques described in this chapter). In examinations some candidates read the question paper very quickly and mistake a question on sales promotion for one on promotional techniques in general. This unfortunate slip can result in a candidate scoring virtually no marks for a question.

Sales promotion objectives

7.3   **Examples of consumer sales promotion objectives**

(a)   Increase **awareness and interest** amongst target audiences

(b)   Achieve a **switch in buying behaviour** from competitor brands to your company's brand

(c)   Incentivise consumers to make a **forward purchase** of your brand, thus shutting out competitor purchase opportunities

(d)   Increase **display space** allocated to your brand in store

(e)   Smooth **seasonal dips** in demand for your product

(f)   Generate a **consumer database** from mail-in applications

7.4   Sales promotion objectives will link into overarching marketing and marketing communications objectives.

Marketing objective	To increase brand X market share by 2 percentage points in the period January to December 2003
Marketing communications objective	To contribute to brand share gain of 2% in 2003 by increasing awareness of X from 50% to 70% among target consumers.
Sales promotion objective	To encourage trial of brand X among target consumers by offering a guaranteed incentive to purchase.

Action Programme 4

Tesco and Sainsbury issue a type of loyalty card which shoppers present when they reach the check-out. Points are awarded for sums spent over a minimum amount and these are added up each quarter. Money-off vouchers to be used against future grocery bills are sent to the shopper's home. What do you think is the value of this? In 2000, Safeway decided to pull out of its loyalty scheme.

Why do you think these firms have used different strategies?

8 Public relations

Definitions

Key Concept

The Institute of Public Relations has defined **PR** as 'the planned and sustained effort to establish and maintain goodwill and mutual understanding between an organisation and its publics'.

8.1 The Public Relations Consultants Association (PRCA) says that:

Public relations is the name given to the managed process of communication between one group and another. In its purest form it has nothing to do with marketing, advertising or 'commercialism'. It will, however, often promote one group's endeavours to persuade another group to its point of view and it will use a number of different methods, other than (although often alongside) advertising to achieve this aim.

The scope of PR

8.2 The scope of public relations activity is very broad. The International Public Relations Association puts forward a number of spheres in which PR activity would be appropriate.

- Government - national, local, international
- Business and industry - small, medium, large
- Community and social affairs
- Educational institutions, universities, colleges
- Hospitals and health care
- Charities and good causes
- International affairs

8.3 Whilst the specific practice of the discipline of public relations will vary from sphere to sphere (and indeed, from organisation to organisation within each sphere, depending upon the specific circumstances of an individual organisation's situation) the IPRA lists fourteen separate types of activities that the PR practitioner may carry out at some time.

- **Counselling** based on an understanding of human behaviour
- Analysing **future trends** and predicting their consequences
- Research into **public opinion**, attitudes and expectations and advising on action
- Establishing and maintaining **two-way communication** based on truth and full information
- **Preventing conflict** and misunderstandings
- Promoting mutual **respect** and **social responsibility**
- Harmonising the **private and public** interest
- Promoting **goodwill** with staff, suppliers and customers
- Improving **industrial relations**
- Attracting **good personnel** and reducing labour turnover
- **Promoting products** and services
- Projecting a **corporate identity**
- Encouraging an interest in **international** affairs

8.4 From this list of activities it can be seen that the scope of **public relations activity**, if implemented effectively, should **embrace the whole organisation.** A number of criteria have been put forward in an attempt to define what constitutes 'excellent' public relations within an organisation, many of which relate to the role and position of the public relations department within the organisation.

(a) Programmes should be managed **strategically**.

(b) There should be a single **integrated** public relations department.

(c) Public relations managers should **report directly to senior management**.

(d) Public relations should be a **separate function from marketing**.

(e) The senior public relations person should be a member of the organisation's **dominant coalition**.

(f) Communication should adhere to the **two-way symmetrical model**.

Four models of PR

8.5 This last factor relates to the way in which public relations is practised. Given the diversity of the role of PR as emphasised above, it is logical to consider different ways in which PR could be practised. A framework for considering this has been propounded by Grunig and Hunt, *Managing Public Relations* (1984), who suggest that there are **four models of public relations practice**. Each model will be considered in turn.

Press agency/publicity

8.6 The role of PR is primarily one of **propaganda**, spreading the faith of the organisation, often through incomplete, half-true or distorted information. **Communication is one-way**, from the organisation to its publics: essentially telling the publics the information the organisation wants them to hear.

Public information

8.7 In this model the role of PR is the dissemination of **information**, not necessarily with a persuasive intent. As Grunig and Hunt state, 'the public relations person functions essentially as a journalist in residence, whose job it is to report objectively information about his organisation to the public'.

Two-way asymmetric

8.8 Grunig and Hunt describe the main function of the two-way asymmetric model as **scientific persuasion**, using social science theory and research about attitudes and behaviour to persuade publics to accept the organisation's point of view and to behave in a way that supports the organisation. The aim is to achieve the maximum change in attitudes and behaviour.

Two-way symmetric

8.9 In the two-way symmetric model the **PR practitioner serves as a mediator between the organisation and its publics** with the aim of facilitating **mutual understanding** between the two. If persuasion occurs it is as likely to persuade the organisation's management to change its attitude as it is to persuade the publics to change theirs.

8.10 Public relations is, therefore, the **management of an organisation's reputation with its publics** and this management involves a close consideration of the relationships involved. The organisation can be either reactive or proactive in its management of these relationships.

(a) **Reactive PR** is primarily concerned with the communication of what has happened and responding to factors affecting the organisation. It is primarily defensive, with little or no responsibility for influencing policies.

(b) In contrast, **proactive public relations practitioners** have a much wider role and thus have a far greater influence on overall organisational strategy.

8.11 Inevitably some techniques will be more appropriate in certain circumstances with certain types of publics than others. It is possible, therefore, to **classify the different types of techniques** or media according to the type of **project areas** in which they appear to be most effective. The most frequently used techniques are as follows.

(a) **Consumer marketing support area techniques**

- Consumer and trade press releases
- Product/service literature
- Promotional videos
- Special events (in-store competitions, celebrity store openings)
- Consumer exhibitions
- In-house magazines for sales staff, customers and/or trade
- Salesforce/distributor incentive schemes
- Sport, and to a lesser extent, arts sponsorships

(b) **Business-to-business communication area techniques**

- Corporate identity design
- Corporate literature
- Corporate advertising
- Trade and general press relations, possibly on a national or international basis
- Corporate and product videos
- Direct mailings
- Sports and arts sponsorships
- Trade exhibitions

(c) **Internal/employee communications area techniques**

- In-house magazines and employee newsletters
- Employee relations videos
- Formal employee communications networks and channels for feedback
- Recruitment exhibitions/conferences
- Speech writing for executives
- Company notice boards
- Briefing meetings

(d) **Corporate, external and public affairs area techniques**

- Corporate literature
- Corporate social responsibility programmes, community involvement
- Trade, local, national and possibly international media relations
- Issues tracking
- Management counselling
- Local or central government lobbying
- Industrial lobbying
- Facility visits
- Local/national sponsorships

(e) **Financial public relations area techniques**

- Financial media relations on both a national and international basis
- Design of annual and interim reports
- Facility visits for analysts, brokers, fund managers, etc
- Organising shareholder meetings
- Shareholder tracking research

8.12 While this is not a comprehensive list it does give an indication of the many types of PR techniques that can be used in various circumstances and how certain techniques will re-occur in various settings. Media relations, for example, is used in virtually all areas of activity.

9 Direct marketing   6/01

9.1 Theodore Levitt once stated that 'The sole purpose of a business is to create and keep a customer'. In brief, the **aims of direct marketing are to acquire and retain customers**. Here are two further definitions.

 Key Concept

The Institute of Direct Marketing in the UK defines **direct marketing** as 'The planned recording, analysis and tracking of customer behaviour to develop relational marketing strategies'.

The Direct Marketing Association in the US define direct marketing as 'An interactive system of marketing which uses one or more advertising media to effect a measurable response and/or transaction at any location'.

9.2   It is worth studying these definitions and noting some key words and phrases.

Definitions	Comment
Response	Direct marketing is about getting people to send in coupons, or make telephone calls in **response** to invitations and offers.
Interactive	It is a **two-way** process, involving the supplier and the customer.
Relationship	It is in many instances an **on-going process** of selling again and again to the same customer.
Recording and analysis	Response data are **collected and analysed** so that the most **cost-effective** procedures may be arrived at. Direct marketing has been called 'marketing with numbers'.
Strategy	Direct marketing should not be seen merely as a 'quick fix', a 'one-off mailing', or a promotional device. It should be seen as a part of a **comprehensive plan** stemming from clearly formulated **objectives**.

9.3   Direct marketing helps create and develop direct relationships between the company and each of its prospects, on an individual basis. It is a form of direct supply, embracing both a variety of alternative **media channels** (like direct mail), and a choice of **distribution channels** (like mail order). Because direct marketing **removes all channel intermediaries** apart from the **advertising** medium and the **delivery** medium, there are no resellers, therefore avoiding loss of control and loss of revenue.

Components of direct marketing

9.4   Direct marketing encompasses a wide range of **media and distribution opportunities**.

- Television
- Radio
- Direct mail
- Direct response advertising
- Telemarketing
- Statement stuffers
- Inserts

- Take-ones
- Electronic media
- Door to door
- Mail order
- Computerised home shopping
- Home shopping networks

9.5   In developing a comprehensive direct marketing strategy, organisations will often utilise a range of different yet complementary techniques.

9.6   **Direct mail tends to be the main medium of direct response advertising**. It has become the synonym for it. Newspaper ads can include coupons to fill out and return, and radio and TV can give a phone number to ring (DRTV is now very common). However, direct mail has a number of strengths as a direct response medium.

(a)   The advertiser can target down to **individual level**.

(b)   The communication can **be personalised**. Known data about the individual can be used, while modern printing techniques mean that parts of a letter can be altered to accommodate this.

BPP
PROFESSIONAL EDUCATION

(c)   The medium is good **for reinforcing interest stimulated by other media** such as TV. It can supply the response mechanism (a coupon) which is not yet available in that medium.

(d)   The opportunity to use **different creative formats** is almost unlimited.

(e)   **Testing potential is sophisticated**: a limited number of items can be sent out to a 'test' cell and the results can be evaluated. As success is achieved, so the mailing campaign can be rolled out.

9.7   The cornerstone upon which the direct mailing is based, however, is **the mailing list**. It is far and away the most important element in the list of variables, which also include the offer, timing and creative content.

9.8   A **database** is a collection of available information on past and current customers together with future prospects, structured to allow for the implementation of effective marketing strategies. **Database marketing** is a customer-oriented approach to marketing, and its special power lies in the techniques its uses to harness the capabilities of computer and telecommunications technology. Building accurate and up-to-date profiles of existing customers enables the company to

■   Extend help to a company's target audience

■   Stimulate further demand

■   Stay close to them. Recording and keeping an electronic database of customers and prospects, and of all communications and commercial contacts, helps to improve all future contacts.

Marketing at Work

Database applications

Computers now have the capacity to operate in three new ways which will enable businesses to operate in a totally different dimension.

'Customers can be tracked individually. Thousands of pieces of information about each of millions of customers can be stored and accessed economically.

Companies and customers can interact through, for example, phones, mail, E-mail and interactive kiosks. ... for the first time since the invention of mass marketing, 'companies will be hearing from individual customers in a cost-efficient manner'.

Computers allow companies to match their production processes to what they learn from their individual customers - a process known as 'mass customisation' which can be seen as 'the cost-efficient mass production of products and services in lot sizes of one'.

There are many examples of companies which are already employing or experimenting with these ideas. In the US Levi Strauss, the jeans company, is taking measurements and preferences from female customers to produce exact-fitting garments. The approach 'offers the company tremendous opportunities for building learning relationships'.

The Ritz-Carlton hotel chain has trained staff throughout the organisation to jot down customer details at every opportunity on a 'guest preference pad'.

The result could be the following: 'You stay at the Ritz-Carlton in Cancun, Mexico, call room service for dinner, and request an ice cube in your glass of white wine. Months later, when you stay at the Ritz-Carlton in Naples, Florida, and order a glass of white wine from room service, you will almost certainly be asked if you would like an ice cube in it.'

(Financial Times)

9.9 **Telemarketing** is the planned and controlled use of the telephone for sales and marketing opportunities. Unlike all other forms of direct marketing it allows for immediate two-way communication.

Telemarketing as an integrated marketing activity

9.10 Role of telemarketing

(a) **Building, maintaining, cleaning and updating databases**. The telephone allows for accurate data-gathering by compiling relevant information on customers and prospects, and selecting appropriate target groups for specific product offerings.

(b) **Market evaluation and test marketing**. Almost any feature of a market can be measured and tested by telephone. Feedback is immediate so response can be targeted quickly to exploit market knowledge.

(c) **Dealer support**. Leads can be passed on to the nearest dealer who is provided with full details.

(d) **Traffic generation**. The telephone, combined with postal invitations, is the most cost effective way of screening leads and encouraging attendance at promotional events.

(e) **Direct sales and account servicing**. The telephone can be used at all stages of the relationship with the prospects and customers. This includes lead generation, establishing buying potential for appropriate follow-up and defining the decision-making process.

(f) **Customer care and loyalty building**. Every telephone contact opportunity can demonstrate to customers that they are valued.

(g) **Crisis management**. If, for example, there is a consumer scare, immediate action is essential to minimise commercial damage. A dedicated hotline number can be advertised to provide information and advice.

10 The Internet and e-commerce
6/00, 6/01, 12/01, 6/02, 12/02

Exam Tip

In June 2000, an exam question came up covering the case for Internet-based marketing communications between businesses. The Internet and e-commerce is a certain topic for the examination, but the December 2002 exam turned it on its head by asking candidates why there is little online sales activity in luxury goods markets.

10.1 The Internet is the name given to the technology that allows any computer with a telecommunications link to **send and receive information** from any other suitably equipped computer. Terms such as 'the net', 'the information superhighway', 'cyberspace', and the 'World Wide Web (www)' are used fairly interchangeably, although technically the 'web' is what makes the 'net' user friendly (rather as Windows did for MS-DOS).

10.2 Access to the Internet will become easier and easier: most new PCs now come pre-loaded with the necessary software and developments in telecommunications networks will eventually render modems unnecessary. The decision to use the **Internet and related digital technologies** for either the whole or as a part of the business operations is a **strategically significant decision**.

10.3 The Internet can be used by organisations for business-to-consumer and/or business-to-business purposes. In the UK, some 80% of Internet activity is **business-to-business related** although as more members of the public get on-line and telephone and access costs reduce, so this divide should narrow.

Websites

10.4 As you are no doubt aware, most companies of any size now have a 'site' on the Net. A **website** is a collection of screens providing information in text and graphic form, any of which can be viewed simply by clicking the appropriate button, word or image on the screen. The user generally starts at the site's '**home page**', which sets out the contents of the site. For instance, Penguin Books have a home page which includes the following options.

| **Marketing at Work** |

The Penguin UK Home Page

About Penguin	Company history, jobs, press releases, how to order, how to get published
For children	Information on children's ranges
Free stuff	Competitions, quizzes and electronic greeting cards
Find a book	Search the whole Penguin site by author, title or keyword

There is also information on new releases, promotional offers, events and readers' groups, interviews and sample first chapters to read. The website also has links to related organisations such as the *Book Trust* and the *London Review of Books*, and writers' resources such as an online thesaurus.

Audience profile

10.5 The Internet is reckoned to be currently the fastest growing communications medium in Britain. It is thought that use is growing at between 10% and 15% per month. Estimates of the number of Internet users vary widely: one survey found that 4.6m adults in Britain (10%) of the population had Internet access. Many net users use it both at work and at home.

10.6 It appears that most users are male, aged over 30, and in a white collar occupation, although the number of women and younger people using it is steadily growing.

Internet Service Providers (ISPs)

10.7 Connection (if not available through a user's organisation) is made via an **Internet Service Provider** (ISP). The user is registered as an Internet subscriber and pays a small monthly fee together with local telephone call charges, even if contacting other users on the other side of the world.

10.8 ISPs such as CompuServe, America Online (AOL) and Microsoft Network (MSN) provide their own services, in addition to Internet access and e-mail capability. For instance, AOL also offers a main menu with options such as Life, Travel, Entertainment, Sport, Kids. It is rather like a quality Sunday newspaper, except that the sections are updated at least daily, and it provides much larger information resources (one option in the travel section, for instance, is to find out about train and plane timetables throughout the UK or worldwide).

Browsers and search engines

10.9 Most people use the Net through interface programs called **browsers** often provided by the ISP. Internet Explorer and Netscape Navigator are two examples. Surfing the Net is done using a **search engine** such as Yahoo!, Excite or Google. These guide users to destinations throughout the world: the user simply types in a word or phrase such as 'beer' to find a list of thousands of websites that contain something connected with beer.

Promotion: banner advertising

10.10 Companies such as Yahoo! make money by selling advertising space. For instance if you type in 'beer', an advertisement for Miller Genuine Draft may appear, as well as your list of beer-related sites. If you **click on the advertisement** you are taken to the advertiser's website, perhaps just to be told more about the product, perhaps to be favourably influenced by the **entertainment** provided by the site, or perhaps even to **buy** some of the product. The advertiser may get you to **register your interest** in the product so that you can be **directly targeted** in future. At the very least advertisers know **exactly how many people have viewed their message**, and how many were interested enough in it to click on it to find out more.

Marketing at Work

Banners to get bolder

Typically, advertising on the Internet has meant squeezing messages into thin rectangular strips that appear across the top of the screen. Compared to TV and print advertising, these formats have failed to generate sufficient revenues to meet costs. The sizing of the banner advertising has failed to attract customer interest as they have been more focused on website content than the peripheral advertising.

Publishers are hoping that moves to new bolder and bigger formats will both increase revenues and lead to greater consumer interest. The Internet Advertising Bureau, a trade group of web publishers have announced voluntary guidelines for seven new formats that will be closer to traditional print based formats. It is hoped these formats will be more attractive to the larger advertising agencies who have shunned banners previously as they fail to allow the creative execution required by their clientele.

The new formats are also intended to overcome the effects of ad-blocking software which has been developed to eradicate annoying banner style advertisements. If consumers can be persuaded that on screen advertising adds value and is interesting, they will be less inclined to use such software.

From an article in *Financial Times* 2/3/2001

E-mail as a promotional tool

10.11 E-mail is cheap, targeted and can be sent quickly to millions of people at relatively little cost, and therefore can be used in a number of different ways.

- To **advertise** a product/service, usually with a link to a website.
- To **update** a subscriber to a product/service with useful information
- To **confirm** an order
- To **invite** users to write in or to respond to a helpline

10.12 **Unsolicited e-mail** is probably more intrusive than traditional 'junk mail', though less so than the telephone. However, bad use of e-mail can have the habit of upsetting large numbers of people, to the extent that in Europe at least regulation is felt to be needed.

Curbing the cost of junk e-mail

10.13 The European Commission published a report entitled 'Unsolicited Commercial Communications and Data Protection', which highlights the significant issues of concern surrounding the **use of e-mail for consumer targeting**. The report estimates that in future the cost of downloading unsolicited e-mails could reach £6.4 billion a year. Regulations covering the use of direct mail are relatively clear in most countries with opt in/out clauses and mail preference services. The situation online is far from clear. Issues surrounding **costs to recipients** present a different aspect to this form of communication. Unwanted direct mail can be thrown away whereas e-mail incurs costs in viewing and downloading from the Internet. **'Spamming'** – the process of sending millions of unsolicited messages at one go - creates major problems for recipients imposing high costs.

10.14 In Europe, four separate directives cover unsolicited e-mail but are considered to be unclear and inconsistent. To date five countries (Austria, Denmark, Finland, Germany and Italy) have legislated for opt-in systems which allow for e-mail to be sent to consumers who have indicated they want to receive them. However the 'policing' of this issue is complex and will take some time to arrive at any kind of international agreements.

Internal communication: intranets

10.15 The idea behind an **'intranet'** is that companies set up their own **mini version of the Internet**, using a combination of the company's own networked computers and Internet technology. Each employee has a browser, and a server computer distributes **corporate information** on a wide variety of topics and also offers access to the global Net.

10.16 Potential applications include

- Daily company newspapers
- Induction material
- Online procedure and policy manuals
- Employee web pages where individuals post up details of their activities and progress
- Internal databases of the corporate information store.

Marketing and e-commerce

10.17 Before we look at some of the strategic issues associated with marketing communications and the Internet, it is important to establish what is meant by some key terms, namely, **e-commerce** and **Internet marketing**.

Key Concepts

- **E-commerce** is about transactions involving the **exchange of goods and services, for payment**, using the Internet and related digital facilities.

- **Internet marketing** is about the application of the Internet and related digital facilities to help determine and **satisfy marketing objectives**.

10.18 The problem that arises is that many organisations are trying to practise **relationship marketing**, and this concerns a one-to-one dialogue where transactions between parties are viewed over a long period of time. Although Internet marketing is not concerned with the mechanics associated with payments and security, the **boundaries between e-commerce and Internet marketing are becoming blurred**. As a result of this these phrases are often used interchangeably.

Strategic issues

10.19 The development of an interactive facility requires a major shift away from conventional commercial activities. It has been suggested that this is often achieved in three phases.

	Comment
Presentation	The use of a website to enable visitors/customers to **access information** provides an opportunity to stand out from competitors and **enhance corporate image**. It is an opportunity to illustrate the organisation's products and services. This facility is often referred to as **brochureware**.
Interaction	This phase is characterised by **two-way communication**. Questions and answers flow between the system and the user. Visitors to the site are able to enquire more deeply than at the presentation stage and **information about the visitor** is logged and stored on a **database** for future reference and for both on and offline communications.

	Comment
Representation	When this phase is reached the organisation will have replaced parts of its commercial activities with **full online transactions**. The organisation's traditional commercial trading methods and channels may still be in place and the new interactive facility provides a **complementary** and/or alternative method for **particular market segments**.

10.20 It should not be assumed that all organisations move through each of these phases. If they do, it is at different speeds. Those that do migrate do so according to a number of variables, including, the **nature of the markets in which they operate**, their strategy, technical resources, attitude to risk and competitive pressures.

10.21 Internet technology can also be used strategically to enable communication with particular audiences.

(a) The **Internet** itself enables public access to an organisation's website.

(b) An **Intranet** refers to a private internal network which is normally used to enable communication with employees.

(c) **Extranets** allow particular external audiences such as distributors, suppliers and certain customers access to an organisation's facilities.

Exam Tip

Extranets are important elements to consider when discussing communications with marketing channel partners, as featured in a question in the December 2002 exam.

10.22 The Internet offers two main marketing opportunities, namely **distribution and communication**. The ability to **reach customers directly** and so avoid many channel intermediaries reduces transaction costs and is a prime goal for most organisations.

10.23 The use of the Internet as a communications medium is equally attractive. It is more than a medium as it **facilitates interactivity and a two-way dialogue** that no other method of communication can support. Unlike other forms of communication, **dialogue is induced by the customer**, the speed and duration of the communication is **customer controlled** and the intensity of the relationship (with the on-line brand), is again customer managed. All the traditional tools of the promotional mix can be deployed over the Internet, with varying degrees of success, but it appears that **off-line marketing communications are required to support** the on-line communications and facilities. A combination of off and on-line communications need to be determined if the overall communications are to fulfil the **DRIP** roles (Differentiate, Remind/Reassure, Inform and Persuade).

10.24 The use of the Internet can perhaps be best observed when set alongside the **purchase decision process**. See the table below.

Use of the Internet to support stages in the buying process

Awareness

Not very effective at generating awareness and needs the support of offline communications to drive visitors to the site.

Positioning

As a means of presenting features and benefits the web is very good once a prospective customer has determined a need for a supplier search and is looking to compare offerings.

Lead generation

Once an active search commences leads can be obtained and used to reach prospects in the future.

Purchase decision support

By carrying vast amounts of information at low cost websites provide good opportunities to impress visitors and build credibility.

Facilitate purchase

Through the provision of basic transaction facilities (credit card payment) sales should not be lost once a decision to buy has been made.

Post purchase support and retention

Through the provision of free customer support and advice, levels of cognitive dissonance in customers can be reduced. Feedback from customers, email updates about product developments and the use of sales promotions to stimulate repeat site visits can improve reputation, enable cross selling and promote favourable word of mouth recommendations.

Adapted from Chaffey, Mayer, Johnston and Ellis-Chadwick, *What's New in Marketing* (2000)

E-commerce and website management

10.25 Management need to attend to three main decisions concerning their Internet and digital related facilities. These are their **development, maintenance and promotion**. All of these use resources and management need to be clear about the level of support that is appropriate. One of the key concerns is the web site itself. To be successful the web site should do the following.

(a) **Attract visitors** – with on-line and off-line methods

(b) **Enable participation** - interactive content, and suitable facilities to allow for transactions

(c) **Encourage return visits** - design targeted at needs of particular segments, free services and added value facilities

(d) **Allow for two-way information sharing** - personalisation reflecting visitor preferences, direct marketing and information retrieval provide visitors with the information they are seeking

Marketing at Work

Brand or business?

"It is all very well spending millions on marketing so every person in the country knows about your company. But if none of them are actually buying your products or services, it is money down the drain."

It has been suggested that the brief flourish of the "dotcom" revolution ended largely because those responsible for marketing concentrated too many resources on "brand blazing" rather than looking after customers. Few dotcom businesses bothered to analyse, profile or even contact their website visitors.

Adapted from *Marketing Business* October 2001

Business-to-business e-commerce   6/00

Exam Tip

This came up in June 2000. You had to develop briefing notes.

10.26 Many observers are taking the view that the future of Internet marketing lies in the **business-to-business** (B2B) sector. The belief is based on the premises that:

(a) Selling low value items to **consumers** requires significant **spending on advertising and promotion**, and costly **back up systems**

(b) Consumers expect **free content**

(c) Businesses which look for quotes can massively **increase their source of suppliers**, nationally and globally

(d) Suppliers have a **wider market** to appeal to

B2B is therefore expected to break down barriers and enhance supply chain management

Marketing at Work

Worldwidetender.com is an online B2B marketplace which allows businesses to buy and sell excess stock. Customers include retail chains, supermarket chains, convenience store groups, bulk catering companies and restaurant chains. Average sales are around £10,000 but can reach £250,000. With these higher value transactions, communications rely on the telephone and e-mail to encourage trading.

Many similar middle market companies are following the worldwide tender approach. The E-Business Report published recently by Birmingham Business School shows only some 25% of middle market firms are using the Internet for marketing and sales to consumers and almost 50% involved in B2B activity. Surveys by Forrester Research suggest the online market will account for approximately one third of all B2B sales by 2005.

Other significant issues that will determine the success of such activity include the integration of Internet services with traditional marketing communications tools including the telephone, creating the web-enabled call centre.

From an article in the *Sunday Times* 27/5/2001

Marketing at Work

Otis

Otis is the world's largest company in the manufacture, sales and service of people moving products such as elevators, escalators, shuttle systems and moving walkways. They have taken a dynamic and innovative approach to e-business.

Services include 24 hour access to maintenance records, an Internet-enabled flat-panel display elevator communication and entertainment system and the facility for customers to plan, price and track new equipment projects online. The global website can be accessed in more than 51 countries and in 26 languages. These initiatives have led to a re-evaluation of customer relationships and generation of new business. The process for ordering a new elevator had previously been based on the completion of 300 technical questions taking one to three months to complete. This now consists of 15 questions and an online ordering system that can be completed in 20 minutes. These changes now allow sales people to deliver excellent customer service.

From an article in *The Times* 11/4/2001

10.27 Benefits of using the Internet in e-commerce

Benefit	How generated
Loyalty	Faster response
Productivity	Better management of the supply chain
Reputation	Depends on competition and ability of web-based strategies to offer real customer benefit
Costs	Generally lower, easier for customers to obtain information

10.28 Organisational buying behaviour is generally more complex that consumer purchases. The Internet enables transparency. Moreover, **a website can be accessed by more people in the DMU**.

Exam Tip

Students are required to understand how Internet marketing can (and should) impact on Integrated Marketing Communications. Ideas about the Internet, intranets and extranets will be tested, normally through the mini-case questions. Individual specific knowledge about banner advertisements or the role of portals for example is not required. It is necessary to understand the strategic significance of Internet technologies, the impact they may have on current commercial systems and marketing activities and the role traditional marketing communications will continue to have in the strategic promotional activities of organisations.

11 Digital TV

11.1 In the past, television was 'analogue'. The development of digital technologies can be applied to television. **Digital TV takes a number of forms**.

- Digital terrestrial television delivered via the old 'analogue' arial

- Digital satellite televisions, in which digital signals are sent via an existing satellite dish (eg Sky digital)

- Digital cable television, in which digital TV is delivered via the cable network.

11.2 In outline, transmitting programmes by digital signal rather than by conventional means **dramatically increases the number of services which can be delivered to audiences**: as many as ten digital services will be able to occupy the frequency previously occupied by one conventional analogue service. In addition, digital broadcasting allows viewers greater choice over how and when they watch, eventually allowing them to interact with programmes and select their own programme content. More immediately, the new technology offers many viewers the prospect of improved reception.

11.3 The impact was described in depth in a BBC document, *Extending Choice in the Digital Age*, from which much of the following is derived.

11.4 **Digital technology removes the constraints** imposed by conflicting demands within the confines of a few television and radio networks. Viewers and listeners often miss programmes, and it is hard to schedule a range of programmes which suit everyone all the time. At present, programmes can only be scheduled in sequence, with the viewer having to make an appointment with the television to watch a specific programme at a set time. In the digital world, a spectrum can be used to allow networks to have many layers and branches: there is much more flexibility to **match services to the viewer's personal timetable**.

11.5 At the touch of a button, viewers are able to get **supplementary information** on the programmes they are watching. The BBC, for instance, envisaged that viewers could have instant access to the following.

- The musical scores for Young Musician of the Year
- A 'guess the value' game to accompany The Antiques Roadshow
- A summary of the story so far for viewers late to join a film or play
- Original language version of foreign films

Action Programme 5

If programmers can do this, then so too, of course can advertisers.

See how may applications you can think of for extra information at the touch of a button, alternative soundtracks and matter you can respond to if the viewer is watching advertisements.

12 Impact of interactive systems

12.1 The **ability to shop from home** and choose items directly with the use of scanners can be integrated with direct advertising. **Infomercials** (which combine information with a commercial) which the consumer has chosen from a databank will be relayed directly to the home down cable links. These may take the form of recipes, DIY hints, car repairs and so on. Consumers will also be able to purchase the necessary ingredients or parts simultaneously, simply by pointing a mouse on a computer screen at the desired goods and clicking its buttons.

12.2 It is, however, difficult to predict how successful and how big the market for home shopping will become in the UK.

(a) **Geography**. In the UK and other European countries, distances to retail shopping centres are small. (On the other hand, traffic congestion continues to be an issue.)

(b) However, people are often '**time poor**' and internet shopping with convenient delivery times is becoming popular for some consumer items, for example books, CDs and groceries.

(c) Success depends on consumers' **acceptance of technology** and the **reliability** of that technology. Technology that is hard to use or unreliable will discourage sales.

12.3 Advantages of interactive systems

- Saving time spent in shopping visits
- Saving use of cars and car parking
- Reduction in congestion and pollution
- Greater variety of products to choose from
- Ability to watch demonstrations from the comfort of one's home
- Ability to browse
- Ability to interrogate, get technical advice
- Getting bank balances immediately
- Transferring funds between accounts
- Paying bankers orders
- Access to directories of suppliers
- It may be possible to closely segment markets
- The specific needs of individual customers could be met
- The costs of stockholding could be reduced

12.4 Home shopping in America is a £1 billion business and is growing at the rate of 20% per annum. These shopping channels are increasingly being used by time poor professionals. The amount of broad band multimedia will accelerate the process, first, by increasing the **number of channels** available, and secondly, by increasing the **interactivity**. Instead of having to ring up to order, viewers will be able to punch in a code on their handset and pay by swiping their credit card through a slot in the set top box.

12.5 Limitations of interactive systems

There are limitations to such interactive systems, which may be related to the state of the technology or to ingrained social and cultural habits.

- There are inevitably high set up costs
- There is a lack of knowledge of the system
- Some people suffer from technophobia
- There is a lack of personal contact
- Expectations of quality may not be realised
- It is necessary to touch, feel, smell or taste some products
- Shopping for some people has social benefits
- Existing shopping centres may be destabilised

 Exam Tip

An understanding of the promotional tools and the ways in which they work is essential. However, knowledge of the individual tools is not part of this syllabus. What is important and part of the syllabus is an appreciation of the way in which the tools can be co-ordinated in order that consistent and meaningful messages be presented to target audiences.

This knowledge can be examined in a number of ways. One of the more obvious approaches is through the preparation of a marketing communications plan. Other ways include direct questions on integration or the effectiveness of the promotional tools discussed in Section 2.

Read *Campaign, Marketing Week, Marketing* and other trade journals on a regular basis and look out for case histories that track the use of a selection of promotional tools.

 Chapter Roundup

- There is an enormous range of promotional tools that the marketer can choose from. The skill is

- The choice should be made within the overall context of the **promotional objectives** and the strategies that have been determined.

- Promotional tools have a **primary or secondary role**. The product life cycle model might be helpful in choosing which tool plays the primary role.

- All the promotional elements must be **integrated** if the maximum effect is to be achieved.

Now try Question 9 at the end of the Study Text

Quick Quiz

1 What range of promotional tools is available? (see para 2.4)

2 How might you integrate the tools? (4.3)

3 What are the tasks of the selling process? (6.4)

4 List six different sales promotion objectives (7.3)

5 What are the four models of Public Relations? (8.6 – 8.9)

6 Define direct marketing. (9.1)

7 What features might you find on a website? (10.4)

8 What is a search engine? (10.9)

9 What is an extranet? (10.21)

10 List three advantages of digital TV for marketing communicators. (11.2, 11.4 – 11.5)

Action Programme Review

1 You will find it useful to maintain files of these examples. Try and find examples relating to differing market sectors including consumer products, services, public sector and not-for-profit. At your place of work collect examples based on business-to-business marketing communications. Collect examples for the same companies over a period of time. This will illustrate different use of communication tools and identify changes in strategy and tactics over time.

2 How does this approach differ from other companies in this sector. How was this integrated with other communications activities by One-to-One?

3 Consider the goals in relation to business, marketing and communications strategies.

4 On the launch of its 'Clubcard' Tesco said that it was a way of saying thank you to customers and that it wanted to 'recreate the kind of relationship that existed between consumers and local shops half a century ago'.

In practice, however, the schemes give supermarkets the chance to build up a massive database containing customers' names, addresses and detailed information on individual shopping habits. But did they really encourage loyalty? No. Safeway decided that the considerable expenditure in the loyalty card scheme could be better spent on sales promotions targeted at local level (eg leafleting of local households). Safeway reported substantial increases in sales – but this has to be set against the fact that Tesco, still using the Clubcard, is the UK's most successful retailer.

5 The following extract from an American article on Interactive TV (ITV) may give you some ideas.

'When it comes to peddling high-ticket items, Paula George Tompkins, CEO of The SoftAd Group, a Mill Valley (Calif.) creator of interactive marketing materials, says the most effective efforts aren't 'full-motion video and razzle-dazzle ads.' They're the information-laden programs that help buyers make complex decisions such as choosing a car or an industrial-products supplier.

Consider the flow chart for a typical car purchase: talk to friends, buy (and read) consumer reports, spend weekends checking out local dealerships and weekdays checking out other cars on the freeway, test drive a few cars, decide on a model, make arrangements with a lender, and - whew! - buy the car.

Now, eliminate a significant portion of that legwork. Using a mouse and TV screen, the consumer would be able to flip through manufacturers' catalogues - complete with backup data related to performance and pricing - 'trying on' the various models in terms of size and color. The shopper could then request a test drive via his or her TV. Later, the dealer brings a car over and, if the buyer is ready, goes online with a laptop to check inventory, leasing vs. financing options, and even fill out the paperwork. Voila!'

Messages and Media 10

Chapter Topic List	
1	Setting the scene
2	How marketing communications works
3	Messages
4	Media planning and strategy
5	Media planning concepts
6	Developing the media plan

Learning Outcomes

☑ Determine specific communication activities based upon knowledge of the key characteristics of the target audience. In particular, they will be able to suggest how knowledge of perception and attitude, levels of perceived risk and involvement can impact upon marketing and corporate communications

☑ Select, integrate and justify appropriate promotional mixes to meet the needs of the marketing communication strategies

Syllabus References

☑ Selecting appropriate promotional mixes

☑ Determining message styles and key media goals

Key Concepts Introduced

■ Source credibility

■ Frequency

1 Setting the scene

1.1 This chapter briefly considers some of the more contemporary ideas about and frameworks for how marketing communications might work. This is followed by an overview of **message structures** and some key aspects of **media planning**.

2 How marketing communications works

2.1 The purpose of marketing communications is to **inform**, **persuade** or **remind/reassure** audiences in order to **differentiate** a product, service or organisation. To accomplish these tasks it is necessary to deliver messages that enable audiences to understand and act upon information received.

2.2 Before considering the different types of messages it is necessary to consider briefly the ways in which marketing communications (and advertising in particular) is considered to work.

2.3 There is no set model or framework. For a long time the **AIDA model** (Awareness, Interest, Desire and Action) was considered to be an appropriate interpretation. Through this model, it was considered that prospective buyers moved through successive stages from learning about the existence of a product to actual purchase. However, AIDA and similar 'Hierarchy of Effects' models, are now considered to be too rigid, inflexible and an inappropriate explanation of the communication process.

2.4 The **Sales**, **Persuasion**, **Involvement** and **Saliency** frameworks are considered by some to be more acceptable.

Frameworks	Comment
Sales	Advertising works on the basis that it **affects sales directly**, and nothing else is worth considering.
Persuasion	Advertising works by **persuading people to act** (to buy products and services) in ways that they might not have acted had they not seen/heard the advertising message.
Involvement	Advertising works by **drawing people into an advertisement** and making associations between the advertisement and the product/brand.
Saliency	Advertising works by **standing out and being different** from other advertisements, especially those in the same category. For example, Pot Noodle or Tango.

Action Programme 1

Find two further examples for each of the persuasion, involvement and saliency interpretations of advertising.

2.5 Underpinning many of these views is the notion that advertising can persuade people to purchase products. This has been termed a **Strong Force**.

Marketing at Work

Although this may seem astonishing by European standards, only 35% of the under thirties in the US have a mobile phone. Richard Branson believes that he can change that. The brand-obsessed US could be a goldmine – insiders at Virgin believe Virgin Mobile will have a turnover of $3 billion within three years, dwarfing even Virgin Atlantic.

■ Guerrilla marketing, targeted at university campuses, will highlight the brand, reinforced by a commercial link with MTV.

■ The company is offering a simple pay-as-you-go price plan with no small print.

■ The venture will be supported by a network of 11,000 shops.

Plans are afoot to launch Virgin Mobile in South Africa and Canada.

Adapted from *The Observer*, 28 July 2002

2.6 Ehrenberg counters this view with an **ATRN** (Awareness, Trial, Reinforcement and Nudge) model, which interprets advertising as a '**Weak Force**'. This says that advertising **reinforces** previous purchase decisions and serves to **defend** them and **maintain market share**.

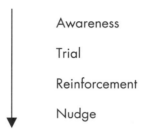

Awareness

Trial

Reinforcement

Nudge

The ATRN model of advertising (after Ehrenberg 1997)

2.7 Both models accept that **awareness is a necessary prerequisite** for purchase, although it may not always be through advertising.

(i) If a potential purchaser shows some interest in a product, perhaps because it is new or significant to them at that particular time, then they might try or **experiment** with the product.

(ii) If this is successful then a **repeat purchase** may be made.

(iii) With **reinforcement**, the purchaser might be encouraged to add the product to their **evoked set** (a small cluster of brands in each product category from which purchase decisions are made).

2.8 **Advertising can assist any of these stages** and can nudge people into buying one particular brand from their repertoire.

2.9 **There is no fixed model of advertising**. However, research suggests that advertising might be more effective when **combined with brands**, so that potential purchasers are enabled to develop links or associations between a brand and its advertising and related communications. IMC has a significant role to play in assisting the development of co-ordinated messages in order to help develop this brand/advertising association.

3 Messages

Source effects influencing consumer behaviour

3.1 The source of the communication directly influences the consumer's acceptance and interpretation of a message. **Credibility** and **attractiveness** are two major source factors influencing customers.

Key Concept

Source credibility is defined as the level of expertise and trustworthiness customers attribute to the source of the message.

Exam Tip

Part of the 40 mark case study question on the December 2002 paper asked why sports stars and celebrities are sometimes used to promote brands.

3.2 For example, some spokespersons may be regarded with high **credibility** in a particular field, but the **trustworthiness** of their product endorsements may be questioned because they are being paid by the advertiser. Indeed, product messages sponsored by the advertiser are seen as less trustworthy than product messages from sources that are perceived as impartial, such as the Consumers' Association. Research appears to show that the **greater the perceived credibility of the source, the greater is the likelihood that the receiver will accept the message**.

3.3 **Source attractiveness** is determined by its **likeability** and its similarity to the consumer. Research has shown that when consumers perceive salespeople as similar to themselves, they are more likely to accept and be influenced by the sales messages.

Balance of the message

3.4 Our understanding of the **level of involvement** that may exist in the target audience can be used to determine the **overall balance of the message**. If there is **high involvement** then interested members of the target audience will **actively seek information**. Messages therefore tend to be **rational**, proclaiming **product benefits** and the **key attributes**.

3.5 Where there is **low involvement** the audience are not really interested and **need to be drawn to the communication message**. In these cases, **image-based** appeals tend to be more successful and the use of **emotion** rather than logic predominates.

3.6 The strategic implication is that if integration and consistency is to be achieved then **adherence to an emotional or rational approach has to be maintained** throughout all the promotional tools.

3.7 There are a number of ways in which the rational and image based messages can be presented to audiences. These are referred to as **message appeals** and some of the more common approaches are **rational based appeals** and **image based appeals**.

3.8 **Rational based appeals**

Issue	Comment
Factual	The benefits are presented using reasoned, factual arguments (eg nicotine patches).
Slice of life	Allow the target customer to identify with the characters and a common problem. Brand X is then perceived as a suitable solution (eg washing powders).
Demonstration	Show the audience how the product solves a problem (eg floor cleaners, before and after use).
Comparative	Through comparison it is possible to achieved enhanced status and superiority (eg credit and charge cards).

3.9 **Image based appeals**

Issue	Comment
Fear	The suggestion of physical danger or social rejection might be alleviated through use of the brand (eg life assurance, drink driving, anti-dandruff shampoo).
Humour	Attention and mood can be maintained by relaxing the target audience (eg Batchelors).
Animation	For low interest products/services animation can attract attention and convey complex products/issues in a novel manner (eg Clover, Self Assessment, Tetley Tea Bags).
Sex	Used primarily to attract attention and to be salient (eg Diet Coke, Wonderbra, Citroen Xsara).
Music	Provides campaign continuity and a degree of differentiation through recognition (eg Ford Cougar, Peugeot 406).
Fantasy	Used to engage an audience and to encourage the question 'what is going on here?' (eg Bristol & West Building Society, Gieves and Hawkes, Silk Cut, Ericsson).

Action Programme 2

Using a variety of media, identify two examples of all the message appeals listed above. Can you identify anything that is common to your selections?

The December 2002 exam contained a question in Section B asking candidates to evaluate the heavy use of advertising in the luxury goods market, and to provide examples.

4 Media planning and strategy 12/99, 6/00

The media planning function

4.1 Media planning as a function is becoming increasingly complex.

(a) The **media environment changes** all the time, with new media technology, new formats and new owners.

(b) More **media fragmentation** means fewer truly mass market channels.

(c) **Consumers are becoming increasingly sophisticated** and adept at avoiding or discounting advertising messages.

(d) **Media research methods are evolving** to keep pace with media and audience developments.

(e) **Clients are more media aware**

4.2 Media is the vehicle which delivers the advertising message. However good the creative execution, an **advert will fail if the media planning and buying function has been carried out wrongly**.

4.3 The **planning and buying** role may be carried out by the media department of a **full service** advertising agency. Alternatively, a client may choose to use a **media independent**, who as the name implies, provides only media services and is independent of the traditional agency structure.

4.4 Media departments or independents may choose to split the media role down into further **specialist functions**. The media planning role, which is rather abstract and analytical in nature, calls for a slightly different set of skills from those required in competitive media buying negotiations. Alternatively, media staff may be organised in **client groups**, performing both planning and buying tasks across a full spectrum of media.

Action Programme 3

Make a list of the types of media that are available to clients to convey their messages.

Media strategy

4.5 The objective of a media strategy is to achieve the **best fit between media vehicles and the target audience at the lowest price**. It is, therefore, tied in with the overall marketing strategy.

5 Media planning concepts 6/00

5.1 There are a number of concepts associated with media planning and an understanding of these (and the jargon) will help you to appreciate some of the strategic issues associated with this important aspect of the communication process.

Reach

5.2 When a new product is launched or a new variant introduced to the market, the communications objective is very often to generate high levels of **awareness**. The complementary media strategy is called a **reach (or coverage) strategy**. This means ensuring that as many people as possible in the target audience have an **opportunity** to see/hear the message during the relevant time period/campaign.

Frequency

5.3 The ability of people to retain (and of course forget) information varies widely. In view of this, **advertising messages need to be repeated**.

> ### Key Concept
>
> **Frequency** is used to refer to the number of times a person is exposed to the message, within a particular campaign or period of time.

5.4 Calculations in media planning are based upon an individual's **opportunity to see** (OTS) the advertisement. This means **seeing the media vehicle** (Marie Claire, FHM) which, of course, is not the same as actually seeing or reading a particular advertisement.

5.5 The relationship between **reach** and **frequency** is important. All campaigns need to generate a certain number of OTS and these are determined and measured by what are referred to as **ratings** (or Gross Rating Points). **Ratings are the multiple of reach and frequency**.

Reach × Frequency = Ratings (in television these are known as TVRs)

5.6 One of the important tasks of the media planner is to determine the number of times the target audience should be exposed to the message. This is referred to as the **level of effective frequency**. There is no set answer and a debate about whether it should be 1, 2 3 or 10 times in any one purchase interval, continues.

You need to be aware of the issue and be able to justify your media schedule when preparing a marketing communication plan.

6 Developing the media plan

6.1 Many of the initial considerations in media planning will be identical to those which apply when starting communications planning.

Market background

6.2 **Market size, shares and trends must all be taken into account**. If a client is trying to break into a highly competitive marketplace, such as washing powder, perfumes or confectionery, then heavyweight multi-media advertising may be the only way of making a presence felt. On the other hand, if a small advertiser is trying to establish himself in the market for a highly specialised service (for example genealogical research services for the family historian), a tightly targeted campaign through a specialist medium will probably suffice.

Marketing at Work

For the large advertiser trying to track competitive media expenditure, Register MEAL provides a useful reference point. Advertising expenditure levels across a wide variety of product and service groupings are monitored and published quarterly. Figures are calculated using ratecard prices published by the different media, or by using industry benchmark estimates. As most advertisers do not usually pay ratecard prices, accuracy for specific campaigns can be questionable. However, it is a helpful guide to relative levels of expenditure within an industry or product grouping.

6.3 Although some advertisers are forced into specific media choices in order to mirror and offset the actions of their **competitors**, other advertisers may choose a little-used medium in order to capitalise on 'stand out value'.

6.4 **Media must be able to deliver the target market required**. Some audiences are more difficult to deliver than others, owing to their media viewing habits. Young adults tend to be light television viewers and may be best targeted with cinema advertising. Mass media will rarely deliver niche audiences, special interest magazines being a more appropriate media vehicle.

Action Programme 4

Suppose you work for a cinema chain. What information might it be useful to collect to help potential advertisers decide when and whether to use some or all of your cinemas as an advertising medium?

Product/service background

6.5   The role which advertising is to play for the product or service will to some extent dictate media strategy.

   (a)   If the campaign's objective is to ensure that the audience is **constantly reminded** about the product being advertised, then media may be used continuously in a low key manner.

   (b)   If the objective is to **inform about a new product or service**, then a mass media launch will be more suitable. When the Government launched the telephone, gas, electricity and water share offers, there was heavy use of all media in order to communicate the privatisation message to the public.

6.6   There may be product or service characteristics which lend themselves to **specific media environments**. As we have said, television is demonstrative, as is cinema. A press advert would be able to go into lengthy body copy detail about the attributes of, say, a mountain bike. However, a television advert could visibly demonstrate its features.

6.7   An advertiser may wish to play to geographical strengths or alternatively bolster weak sales areas. Retailers with nationwide branches are able to examine weekly sales figures and adjust regional advertising accordingly.

Budget

6.8   Clients should always specify the amount of money that they intend to spend on media, as opposed to the production budget for a campaign.

   (a)   A budget of £100,000 would tend to dictate a campaign that runs on a local basis only, or a national campaign which utilises only one medium (for example, a national press campaign with a limited number of titles).

   (b)   A budget of £2m would allow for a national campaign across a mix of media. You should try to get a feel for this by reading the marketing press.

Media characteristics

6.9   Media choice is also governed by a number of factors arising from the different properties of the various media options.

6.10   **The nature of the medium in its own right is an important consideration**. People purchase magazines for their entertainment value, or because they serve as an information source. In terms of information value, editorial stance, style, language and personality, the magazine environment will tend to rub off onto the advertising, and particular magazines will be chosen for their compatibility with the products and services being promoted.

6.11   Similarly, the **positioning of adverts within television**, **radio or cinema contexts** can make a difference to how they are perceived. An advert scheduled in the middle of a TV game show will deliver an audience with a different mind set from one scheduled in the centre break of a documentary. Take notes next time you watch either on commercial TV.

6.12 Another consideration is **how people use media**. Whether the medium is used as sole activity or in conjunction with other activities will affect the ability of that medium to deliver the advertising it contains.

(a) Many popular radio stations are used as a background to other activities (driving a car, talking to friends, carrying out activities at work or in the home). People are generally unlikely to be giving their main attention to listening to the radio.

(b) By contrast, reading a newspaper is a main activity in its own right.

Other characteristics

6.13 **The amount of time spent with the medium** can be a factor. Daily newspapers are a relatively quick read in the busy environment of the working week. Saturday and Sunday papers are a more leisurely read.

6.14 Television and cinema allow advertisers to use the power of sound and vision together to create an impression. **Special effects** originally created for film or pop video production can be used to give adverts an 'up to the minute' feel.

6.15 Other characteristics that must be considered when judging a medium on its **creative scope** are as follows:

- Potential for **colour** advertising
- Potential for **movement and sound**
- **Space and time** limitations
- **Reprographic** standards

6.16 **Booking and production lead times** may rule out the use of certain media. Magazine space is generally booked months in advance. Television and cinema commercials with high production values will take months to prepare, film and edit.

6.17 As well as taking into account the inherent features of each medium, **media channels must be evaluated quantitatively** for their ability to deliver against criteria such as coverage, frequency and cost.

(a) **Coverage** (also called reach or penetration) is a measure of the percentage of a particular target audience reached by a medium or a whole campaign.

(b) **Frequency** is the number of times the target audience has an opportunity to see (or hear) an advertising message.

(c) **Cost** will not only be measured as an absolute, but also in terms of the cost per thousand contacts of the target audience.

6.18 Media planners will use recognised **media research sources** such as the National Readership Survey, Target Group Index and BARB to calculate media efficiency.

Client preferences

6.19 Clients may have their own specific reasons for dictating or declining the use of specific media options. One company booked a poster site directly opposite one of their main competitor's offices on an 'until cancelled' basis. Every morning and evening, employees were greeted with the sight of their rival's latest advertising campaign.

6.20 Other advertisers may rule out the use of a specific medium because of bad experiences in the past, or they may dictate that a particular trade magazine be included on the media schedule because of its popularity with important trade distributors.

Media scheduling

6.21 As the media planner works through the available choices, a **media schedule** begins to evolve. This is the **formal listing of which adverts are to appear where**. Media schedules can be constructed for short-term campaign bursts or for a whole year's advertising cycle.

6.22 Budget will be a major determinant in the seasonality of advertising. A very **small budget** may dictate that advertising is limited to certain **key times of the year** (eg pre Christmas; peak sales periods). A **large budget** that allows for year round advertising is usually allocated in one of two ways.

(a) A **burst campaign** concentrates expenditure into promotional bursts of three or four weeks in length.

(b) A **drip campaign** allows for a continuous but more spread out presence.

6.23 Other scheduling questions that need to be addressed include the following.

(a) When is **media value** at its greatest?

(b) How fast is **advertising decay**?

(c) Will **over-exposure** to advertising be counter productive?

(d) Does advertising timing need to link into **other communications events** such as PR, sales promotion or salesforce cycles?

Exam Tip

When a marketing communications plan is requested as an answer to the mini-case in Section A it is expected that a timetable of proposed marketing communications activities will be presented.

An example is shown below, and there are plenty of others in the BPP *Practice & Revision Kit*.

Example media schedule

	September				October
Observer	•	•	•		
Independent				•	• •
S Times		•	•	•	
Telegraph		•	•	•	
You	•	•	•		
Womens' mags					
Vogue			•		
Tatler			•		
Elle		*September issue*	•		
Marie Claire			•		
Cosmopolitan			•		
Television					
Granada	←----------------→				
Central	←----------------→				
Yorkshire	←----------------→				

Action Programme 5

Choose a product or service with which you are familiar. List the media planning considerations which apply within that product/ service market. Use the following checklist to structure your thoughts.

(a)   Market background
(b)   Target audience

Chapter Roundup

- Understanding some of the ideas about how marketing communications might work is important. In particular, the **strong and weak forces** approach helps guide thought about what

- The message to be delivered to target audiences must be perceived as **credible** if it is to be **effective**. The use of **rational** and/or **image based** appeals can assist the communication process.

- The **dynamic nature** of the media environment means that **media buying** is a complex specialist function within advertising.

- The **media planning** role is sometimes separated from the buying function because of the different skill and task requirements.

- Market, product and target audience characteristics; budget and client preferences need to be taken into account when **planning media campaigns**, as do the attributes of each individual media option.

- A **multi-media campaign** is likely to achieve a greater level of synergy than one which concentrates on options within one medium.

Now try Question 10 at the end of the Study Text

Quick Quiz

1 List four frameworks used to explain how advertising works. (see para 2.4)

2 What is the Strong theory of advertising? (2.5)

3 Explain the ATRN model of advertising. (2.6)

4 Using examples, describe three types of rational messages and four types of image based appeals. (3.8, 3.9)

5 List four reasons why media planning as a function is becoming increasingly complex. (4.1)

6 What market and product/service characteristics affect the initial planning of a media campaign? (6.2 - 6.7)

7 How might the way in which people use media play a part in media choice? (6.12)

8 What quantitative measures can be used to evaluate media choice? (6.17)

Action Programme Review

1   Quite often the advertising is supplemented with sales promotional activity in order to further incentivise purchase and/or encourage brand switching.

2   Include these examples in the files you are keeping of differing communications activities.

3   This should include 'above-the-line' advertising media such as TV, newspapers, magazines, radio, posters, cinema. Direct mail, inserts, telemarketing, sponsorship are all examples of 'below the line' media. These are no longer considered to be discrete definitions with many communications activities being considered as 'through-the-line'.

4   Possibilities include attendance numbers on different days, age-range, likely audience characteristics for different types of film, differences between audiences in different locations. You may have had further ideas.

5   Having listed these considerations what would be your recommendations for actual media selection?

Part E

Managing Resources

The Financial Imperative

11

Chapter Topic List	
1	Setting the scene
2	Who decides budgets?
3	When to decide budgets
4	How to decide budgets
5	Strategic considerations
6	Controlling the budget
7	Practical advice

Learning Outcome

☑ Determine appropriate levels of marketing communications expenditure/appropriation.

Syllabus Reference

☑ Deciding upon the level and allocation of the promotional spend

Key Concepts Introduced

- Budget process
- A/S ratio
- Share of voice

1 Setting the scene

1.1 Like all other areas of business activity, marketing communications needs careful housekeeping. The amount of money available is the **key constraint** on marketing communications, and we have mentioned a number of times that there is growing pressure on total communications expenditure. This is because of fluctuating world economies, increasing media costs and also because methods of **measuring the effectiveness** of spending have been improved and wastefulness is more transparent.

1.2 In this chapter we consider **who** sets the budget and **how**, and **what** can be done to control expenditure and get the **best value for money**.

2 Who decides budgets?

2.1 Who decides the level of budgets often **depends on the size of the organisation**. In the smaller organisation it is the owner/manager but even in quite large companies the decision on the level of marketing communications expenditure is taken at quite **senior levels**. This is in part because of the experience needed to **integrate the decision into the company plan** and also because the results of the decision have a high profile to everyone inside and outside the company.

2.2 However, in helping to shape the ultimate decision, four parties are involved.

- **Senior management**, approving budgets
- **Marketing managers**, putting forward budgets
- The organisation's **advertising agency**, providing advice
- The **media**, providing the basic cost structures

2.3 **Implementation of the budget**, once decided, is sometimes delegated to more specific and more junior members of the client's staff. These will work with the agency's account executive in detailed programmes, often with weekly or monthly project management meetings.

3 When to decide budgets

3.1 Marketing communication expenditure, like other substantial expenditures, is usually budgeted for on **an annual basis** as part of the overall budgeting process.

Key Concept

Budget process. The marketing team will put forward plans for approval some months before the start of the financial year. These are debated, modified and agreed and form guidelines for the year's operations.

3.2 As the year progresses, **individual decisions on particular items of expenditure** are made by the marketing team, usually with the help of the advertising agency. These individual decisions are taken within the framework of the agreed annual budget. The individual decisions are then usually reviewed on a month by month basis, comparing the **actual versus the budgeted** expenditure.

3.3 In some markets there will be a burst of marketing communications at particular seasons, for example at Christmas for toys, at Easter for garden products, or in January for holiday booking.

3.4 Some companies also make **specific provisions for opportunistic decisions** at future as yet unknown dates. These are to take advantage of market changes such as a competitor's difficulties or the availability of a special media offer.

3.5 Finally, with the help of sales results and tracking studies, **management can monitor the effectiveness of the marketing communications activities** and may decide to modify the budget to suit the current circumstances.

Action Programme 1

For several organisations with which you are in contact, carry out a review of how they decide their marketing communications budgets. Determine if there are any similarities and decide what the reasons are for any variety in methods. Comparing data with friends and colleagues at college will be valuable, but don't give out confidential information.

4 How to decide budgets

4.1 There is no one uniform method of deciding what to spend on marketing communications. This is not so surprising. The following are some of the **considerations that can affect the amount of expenditure**.

- What variety of marketing communications is to be used?
- What tasks are to be undertaken?
- How competitive is the market place?
- How well known is the organisation?
- Are there any special requirements?

4.2 Costs to be budgeted

- Air time and broadcast media
- Space and printed media
- Production costs
- Staff salaries
- Overheads and expenses

Theoretical approaches to budgeting

4.3 Theoretical approaches to setting budgets have not found favour in industry because the effects of **any marginal increase on expenditure are likely to be swamped**, or at least hidden, by many other marketing variables. The effects of any expenditure will have both long-term and short-term effects. It is worthwhile emphasising the view here that **marketing communications should be treated as an essential long-term investment**.

Marketing at Work

Marketing Metrics

The total amount spent on marketing in the UK last year was £20bn - probably. But it could have been £25bn or even £30bn, no one really knows.

This uncertainty is evidence of a curious paradox. On the one hand, marketing is vital to business and accounts for truly staggering sums of money; on the other, much of it is ill-defined and unaccountable.

There is little understanding, outside the discipline, of how marketing budgets are arrived at, even though they are sometimes the largest single company expenditure.

There is no standard vocabulary and no agreement on how to measure the effectiveness of these vast budgets. There isn't even an agreed definition of what constitutes 'spending on marketing'.

It probably includes advertising, direct marketing, promotions and public relations. But what about price maintenance and a host of other activities?

Now the professional bodies concerned with marketing in the UK have decided enough is enough and have quietly formed a coalition to finance a research programme that could finally nail those issues.

'Marketing Metrics' is a 30-month project funded by the Marketing Council, the Marketing Society, the Institute for Practitioners in Advertising and the London Business School.

It aims to set common standards for terminology and develop models of best practice, particularly in the important area of measuring effectiveness.

If successful the project will shed much needed light on the arcane processes by which huge marketing appropriations are arrived at. For although no company will admit that the setting of marketing budgets amounts to little more than guess work, there is consensus among commentators that the process leaves much to be desired.

Financial Times

4.4 **Methods of deciding budgets** have, however, been developed over a period of time and, in the absence of clearer guidance, are useful in approaching a budget decision for the first time. After several years' operations it is possible to use experience to make decisions. One, or a combination of more than one, of the following methods can be used to approach the problem.

- Completely arbitrarily
- All you can afford
- Historical basis
- Matching the competition
- Percentage of sales
- Experiment and testing
- Modelling and simulation
- Objective and task method

Recent research has indicated a growing trend towards database methods and especially favours the **objective and task method**.

Completely arbitrarily

4.5 There are many examples of budgets being set in an apparently **arbitrary way by senior management**. There may be a link between the **personality** of the **decision maker and**

the level of expenditure. This link may not be obvious to people elsewhere in the organisation. Subsequent arbitrary cuts in expenditure if trading becomes difficult and the profit margins begin to suffer are more worrying.

All you can afford

4.6 This often applies to a new company starting up or to an existing company advertising for the first time. The conscious decision has to be taken to forgo immediate profits or to forgo an investment in another area in favour of an investment in marketing communications. This often means **investing at a minimum level**. This will necessarily limit the **scope** of the work, however, and limit the **results** to be achieved.

Historical basis

4.7 We have already indicated that with **experience**, managers are able to form their own judgement of the effectiveness or otherwise of particular expenditure levels and different promotional methods. Year-on-year figures provide the basis for **following trends** and making decisions accordingly.

(a) The **danger of inertia**: a temptation just to keep it the same, in which case all the elements of the environment and the costs associated with the task facing the organisation are ignored.

(b) A slight improvement is to use a **media multiplier**, which at least recognises that media rate card costs may have increased.

Matching the competition

4.8 In many cases an organisation is trying to reach exactly the **same customers** through exactly the **same channels**. In order to obtain a certain market share it is then necessary to **match the competition** and particularly the market leader.

Percentage of sales method

4.9 The **percentage of sales** is a commonly used method of determining a marketing communications budget because:

- It is easy to calculate
- It is precise
- It can be quickly monitored
- It can be varied in progressive steps
- It appears logical
- It is financially safe

However, the percentage chosen should be conditioned by all the usual variables (not least by whether the market is a consumer or industrial one) and it should be dependent upon how competitive the market is. The following figures are suggested based on experience of different accounts.

Percentage of sales on total communications budget

State of competition	Consumer markets	Industrial markets
No competition	1%	0.5%
Little competition	2%	1%
Average competition	5%	2%
Heavy competition	10%	3%

Action Programme 2

Use the above table to determine the approximate marketing communications budget for a number of market situations with which you are familiar. Include consumer and industrial markets.

Action Programme 3

What do you think is the logical flaw associated with the percentage of sales method as an effective technique for budget allocation?

4.10 If all companies in an industry use a similar calculation then **expenditure** will approximate to **market share positions**. However, it must be clear that the real position is very complex and sales are the result of marketing communications and not the other way round. The method is in reality over-simplistic but does form a good basis of calculation.

4.11 Once a sales forecast has been made then the approximate budget level can be obtained. It can then be moderated for special circumstances such as the **degree of competition** experienced in the previous year or expected in the next year.

Experiment and testing method

4.12 This method involves selecting **a set of matched markets**. Different final promotional budgets can be set for each of these markets and the results carefully monitored. The resulting levels of **awareness and sales delivered** can be compared. For example, this method can be used to **evaluate alternative media schedules**. Problems associated with this method include:

- The **cost** of conducting the experiment
- The **time** it takes to get results
- The premature **informing of competitors**
- The fact that markets can never be completely **matched**

Modelling and simulation method

4.13 With advancing use of computer databases and more precise promotional media it is possible to build **models** to forecast the likely performance of different media schedules. There are likely to be an increasing number of PC based modelling programs available which will allow a number of business variables to be examined including:

- Sales levels
- Purchase frequency
- Awareness levels
- Profits achievable

The objective and task method

4.14 The **objective and task method** is probably the one which is most **logical and appropriate** to the complex situation found in planning marketing communications programmes. Basically the logic of the method is as follows.

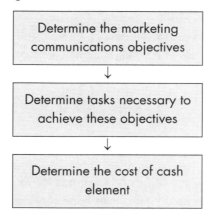

Determine the marketing communications objectives

↓

Determine tasks necessary to achieve these objectives

↓

Determine the cost of cash element

4.15 This approach is simple to understand and uses carefully considered and linked objectives and tasks. It is necessary to be **realistic about the objectives** and **accurate in the costing** of the tasks. This is an extremely difficult process in reality because of the large number of unknowns.

Action Programme 4

To demonstrate the logic and difficulty of this method choose a marketing communications problem with which you are familiar.

(a)   Define the precise marketing communication objectives.

(b)   Determine the tasks necessary to achieve these objectives.

(c)   Cost out the problem both in terms of the individual tasks and in total.

4.16 A systematic approach to applying the objective and task method will pay dividends because of its rigorous nature. Although it will not necessarily produce perfect results it will lead to disciplined thinking and provide an excellent communication and decision device.

Ten steps in applying the objective and task method

Step 1.   Define marketing and promotion objectives

Step 2.   Determine the tasks to be undertaken

Step 3.   Build up expenditure by costing the tasks

Step 4.   Compare the results against industry averages

Step 5.   Compare the results as a percentage of sales

Step 6.   Reconcile differences between steps 3, 4 and 5

Step 7.   Modify estimates to meet company policies

Step 8.   Specify when expenditures are to be made

Step 9.   Maintain an element of flexibility

Step 10. Monitor actual results against these forecasts

 Action Programme 5

Compare the advantages and disadvantages of the various methods that can be used to determine the appropriate levels of marketing communication budgets.

5   Strategic considerations

5.1   You may notice, say, that you see British Telecom ads far more frequently than ads for most of its competitors such as the cable companies' telephone services. BT is, of course, the largest player in the market. But then, French car ads are more often to be seen than ads for Japanese cars, yet the Japanese have a larger share of the market. How can we **analyse** these strategies?

Advertising to sales ratios (A/S Ratios)

5.2   One of the important factors that always needs to be considered is the **amount spent on communications by competitors**. It can be difficult determining the amount spent by competitors on below-the-line activities, although reasonable guesstimates can often be made by those actively involved in the market.

5.3   **Above-the-line** activities can be measured (data bought from various marketing research agencies) and can be used to gain an insight into possible strategies.

5.4   The **A/S ratio** for an industry provides a **benchmark** against which it is possible to determine **how much should be spent** or stimulate consideration of **why certain amounts have been spent**.

Key Concept

The **A/S ratio** is different for each market sector. It is calculated by working out the total amount spent on advertising (usually at rate card cost) as a proportion of the sales in the market. Therefore, if sales in a market are valued at £150 million per year and the amount spent on advertising is £14 million then the A/S ratio is said to be 9.33%.

5.5 Part of the strategic decision is to decide whether an individual company's A/S ratio should be higher, lower or the same as the industry average.

(a) **Reasons to spend more** might be that a **new product or variant** is being introduced to the market so greater effort is require to **develop awareness** (reach) and then perhaps knowledge and or establish brand values.

(b) **Reasons to underspend** the industry average might include trying to maintain an established market position or **directing spend to other products** in the portfolio or deciding to **put more work below-the-line**.

Share of voice

Key Concept

Share of voice. Within any market the total of all advertising expenditure (adspend), that is, all the advertising by all the players, can be analysed in the context of the proportions each player has made to the total.

5.6 If one advertiser spends more than any other then more of their messages will be received and therefore stand a better chance of being heard and acted upon. If a brand's **share of market (SOM)** is equal to its **share of voice (SOV)** an equilibrium can be said to have been reached.

5.7 It is possible that organisations can use their advertising spending either to maintain **equilibrium (SOV = SOM)** or to create disequilibrium.

5.8 The following matrix (Shroer, 1990) shows how **different spending strategies are appropriate** depending on your competitors' **share of voice** and your own **share of market**.

BPP
PROFESSIONAL EDUCATION

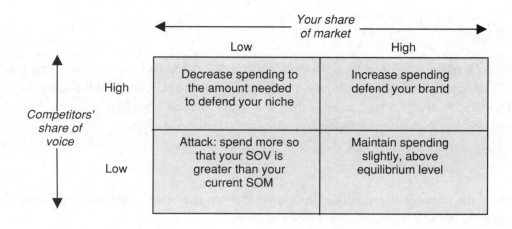

5.9 Note that **careful monitoring of the fortunes of competitors is needed**: if you know that a competitor is spending large sums on restructuring, say, they may not be in a position to retaliate to a sudden advertising burst by your company.

6 Controlling the budget

6.1 Marketing communication budgets may be very substantial and have a major effect on profitability. Controlling the effectiveness of the budget may be difficult if not impossible. What is possible is to use normal budgetary control techniques and to **review its effectiveness regularly** even if this is only by means of informed judgement. A simple way of representing this twin track is shown below.

Controlling the budgets and effectiveness

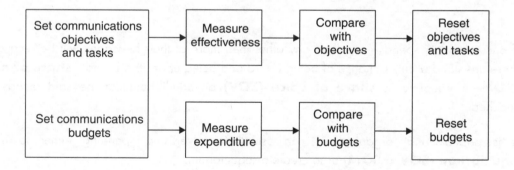

7 Practical advice

7.1 In this section we are going to give a few statistics and examples. The intention is to give you some ballpark numbers and stimulate you to keep an eye out for up-to-date information.

Overall spending on advertising

7.2 The Advertising Association publishes *The Advertising Statistics Yearbook* (NTC Publications). This is expensive but your college or a library may be able to obtain a copy.

7.3 Chris Fill offers the following approximate ratios of advertising spending to sales income for various sectors. (For example, if you spend £10 on advertising and sales are £100 the advertising to sales (A/S) ratio is 10%.)

	A/S ratio
Female Fragrances	8.7%
College	3%
Cereal	8%
Office equipment	1 - 2%
Steel and heavy machinery	0.2%

7.4 Here are some extracts from news pages in marketing magazines, to give you an idea of the likely cost of high-profile campaigns.

> 'Barclays Bank has hired former Labatt marketing directing David Radford to control its £18m advertising budget.'

> 'the introduction of a new velcro device to ... Huggies ... will be backed by an advertising campaign through Ogilvy and Mather in London which will run in the UK, France, the Netherlands and Belgium. The three month burst will cost Kimberly £25m.'

> 'Publisher Reader's Digest is reviewing its estimated £6m advertising and direct marketing business ... '

> 'Coca-Cola is scrapping the role of international media director, with the result that there will be no single person in charge of the company's £1.3bn worldwide media budget.'

Exam Tip

Mini-case questions in the exam will typically ask you to give some indication of the budget. An example may give you an idea of what is required. Remember, though, that different scenarios will present different challenges: this is definitely not a pro-forma to be learned.

Consider the promotion of a luxury car brand on an international basis over the next five years.

Planned worldwide sales by the year 2008	100,000 vehicles
Current price range (per vehicle)	£50,000 - £80,000
Product development investment to 2008	£700m
UK advertising	£3m
UK below-the-line activity	£750,000

You are told the company wants better use of its 36,000 customer database and that significant new products are planned for launch in 2006.

Here is a suggested five-year-budget.

	2003 £m	2004 £m	2005 £m	2006 £m	2007 £m
Advertising					
■ UK core market	3.0	3.5	4.0	4.5	5.0
■ USA/Japan/Germany	6.0	7.0	8.0	9.0	10.0
■ New market entry	1.0	2.0	3.0	4.0	5.0
Total advertising	10.0	12.5	15.0	17.5	20.0
Direct marketing					
■ UK	0.3	0.4	0.5	0.5	0.5
■ International	0.3	0.6	0.9	1.2	1.5
Motor shows	3.0	4.0	5.0	6.0	7.0
Public relations	1.0	2.0	3.0	4.0	5.0
Sponsorships	1.0	2.0	3.0	4.0	5.0
New product launches	1.0	2.0	3.0	5.0	5.0
Total	16.6	23.5	30.4	38.2	44.0
Contingency fund	1.4	2.5	2.6	2.8	4.0
Total promotion	18.0	26.0	33.0	41.0	48.0

Consider another example, concerning the proposed launch of a combined PC and TV into the European consumer market.

The budget is £10 million per year for 2004 and 2005. How should it be divided? Here is a suggested solution.

Budget for PC/TV communications in 2004 and 2005

	Activity	Expenditure £'000	Percentage of total sales
1	Trade Campaign	800	4%
2	Public Relations	400	2%
3	Television	4,000	20%
4	National Press	8,000	40%
5	Specialist Magazines	1,600	8%
6	Literature	400	2%
7	Sales Promotion	2,400	12%
8	Research	800	4%
9	Contingency	1,600	8%
	Total budget	20,000	100%

Chapter Roundup

- **Four parties** are involved in deciding the level of budgets: senior management (approving), marketing managers (**proposing**), the advertising agency (**advisory**) and the media (**setting

- **Budgeting** is usually done on an **annual** basis, with **monthly reviews**. Seasonal factors must be taken into account and some organisations have contingency funds for one-off opportunities.

- **Methods of budgeting**.

  - Spending an arbitrary amount
  - Spending all you can afford
  - Determining the spend on a historical basis
  - Matching competitors' expenditure
  - The percentage of sales method
  - By experiment and testing
  - By modelling and simulation
  - The objective and task method

- The **objective and task method** is the most rigorous. As its name suggests this entails determining the **marketing communications objectives**, determining the **tasks** necessary to achieve those objectives and determining the **cost** of each element.

- **Budgetary control is essential** because of the large sums involved. In essence this involves establishing satisfactory measures of the effectiveness of the marketing communications process.

Now try Question 11 at the end of the Study Text

Quick Quiz

1   Who implements a promotional budget? (see para 2.3)

2   What factors influence the timing of budgets? (3.1 - 3.4)

3   What factors influence the size of promotional budgets? (4.1)

4   List the eight methods of determining budgets. (4.4)

5   Why are budgets sometimes decided arbitrarily? (4.5)

6   Why is percentage of sales an attractive method? (4.9)

7   What are the disadvantages of the experiment and testing method? (4.12)

8   List the steps in implementing the objective and task method. (4.16)

9   What is share of voice? (5.6)

Action Programme Review

1   Having identified the different approaches to budgeting, what are the significant differences in the way in which the budget is spent? It will be interesting to compare the different kinds of businesses and the way in which different kinds of communication tools are used.

2   You will be able to identify sales turnover figures from company Annual Reports. Also look at market sector reports from Mintel or Keynote.

3   The main deficiency of the percentage of sales method is that it turns the traditional cause and effect relationship on its head.

Promotion causes sales. Hence, the amount of sales is a function of the amount spent on promotion. The strict implementation of the percentage of sales method means that the promotional spend becomes a function of the level of sales. Therefore, if sales decrease, then the amount spent on promotion is also decreased, whereas it might be wiser to keep the promotional spend constant in the face of declining sales.

The problem in forecasting future sales is the uncertainty of knowing what resources will be available to achieve the sales targets. Hence, this method should only be used to determine how much needs to be spent if conditions remain static. Beyond that, the budget needs adjusting in view of the new objectives.

4   This could involve looking at your own organisation or use a past examination paper mini case study.

5   This can be achieved by checking back to the points made in this Chapter.

Marketing Communications Agencies

12

Chapter Topic List	
1	Setting the scene
2	Research agencies
3	Briefing the research agency
4	Creative agencies
5	Agency selection
6	Managing the relationship

Learning Outcomes

☑ Determine the context in which marketing (and corporate) communications are to be implemented in order to improve effectiveness and efficiency, understand the key strategic communication issues arising from the contextual analysis and prepare (integrated) marketing communications plans

☑ Formulate marketing communications strategies with particular regard to consumers, business-to-business markets, members of the marketing channel and wider stakeholder audiences such as employees, financial markets, environmental groups, competitors and local communities

Syllabus References

☑ Managing internal and external resources necessary for successful promotional activities

☑ Agency structure and support

BPP
PROFESSIONAL EDUCATION

Key Concepts Introduced

- Qualitative measurement
- Tracking studies
- Advertising content research

1 Setting the scene

1.1 External agencies exist to provide services that a client cannot, or decides not to, set up in house. Broadly speaking there are only two types of agency that a marketing communicator will deal with: **creative agencies** and **research agencies**.

1.2 This chapter will concentrate mainly upon creative agencies, a term which includes among others full service advertising agencies, hot shops, à la carte agencies, sales promotion experts, media specialists, and public relations specialists. Research agencies should be familiar from your earlier studies, but a few comments may help to jog your memory.

2 Research agencies

2.1 It is essential that a marketing communicator has a thorough understanding of the role, scope, and reliability of both **quantitative and qualitative research**. Thus equipped he can develop a healthy distrust of data that is presented in the form of research.

The cost of research

2.2 **Cost** is a major problem in securing accurate **primary research**. Budget constraints sometimes reduce a sample size to a very low level and however impressively they may be presented, the results can be misleading. **Secondary sources**, such as syndicated surveys, tend to carry a high price, and **value** must therefore be the criteria of purchase.

Action Programme 1

Wait for the next publication of ABC audit figures and examine how each major newspaper presents the results. What conclusions can you draw from what you observe?

Research decision sequence

2.3 Prior to commissioning research the decision sequence should be this.

Step 1. Do we **need** research?
Step 2. If so, **what for**?
Step 3. By **when** is it needed?
Step 4. How much can we **afford**?
Step 5. Can we locate a **quality researcher** who is free at the time needed?

Step 6. Is our **budget** (cost and time) sufficient?

Step 7. Do we go ahead and **commission** the research?

2.4 When deciding on sources of research it is essential to consider **what is really needed** in terms of sample reliability, rather then availability or cheapness. It is essential to check the credentials of any research organisation: can it deliver what you want at the time that you want it?

2.5 **All advertising agencies have links with the other specialists that are needed**. Clients should therefore remember that the benefit of engaging specialists who are used to working together could be outweighed by the specialists' desire to continue working together, whether or not it is appropriate to the client's needs to do so.

Qualitative measurement

Key Concept

Qualitative measurement is used to ascertain:

- Whether a target group is aware of a package
- What is their attitude towards it
- What response is achieved

2.6 **Qualitative measurement includes measuring awareness, attitudes and responses**

What is measured?	How it is measured?
Awareness	Measured through **recognition and recall tests**, and also from responses to omnibus **surveys** (see below) or specific surveys. ■ **Recognition tests** aim to determine whether the package, or its advertising is recognised without help from the researcher. ■ **Recall tests** check whether, given a non-directional reminder, the target can recall the subject of the survey, even if it was not recognised immediately.
Attitude	Complex to measure. **Attitudinal studies** on a Likert based like/dislike scaling are commonly used. **Depth interviewing** is of value, but tends to be used more in pre-launch evaluation and testing.
Response	Advertisers can attempt what is known as a **split run test**, where different advertisements for the same product are placed in different print runs of the same magazine or newspaper.

Quantitative measurement

2.7 Obtaining **quantitative information** on audience size is less difficult. The degree of **accuracy**, however, is a question that is very much open to debate. We have discussed this already to some extent in Chapter 4 on segmentation and targeting and in the previous chapter in the context of media measurement.

Measuring the sales result

2.8 Sometimes ex-factory sales are accurate: industrial and most business-to-business selling organisations have the advantage of tight control over their own goods up to the point of sale. For those who have to sell through a distribution chain, however, the situation is much more complex.

Retail audits (eg A C Nielsen)

2.9 (a) These measure **stocks moving through retail outlets**. However, Nielsen have been denied access to certain major stores such as Marks and Spencer so their data has to be adjusted.

(b) **Such research can be self-fulfilling**. However. When Nielsen declare the market shares for each segment, shops tend to adjust their shelf-space allocation so that the market share percentage is given to each brand stocked.

2.10 Consumer panels comprise shoppers who complete diaries showing purchases in detail. Alternatively, researchers are sent into the home to carry out 'pantry checks' in similar fashion to retail audit.

2.11 Omnibus surveys are vehicles provided by a research organisation that carries out a regular survey on a syndicated basis.

(a) Client companies are invited to **buy questions at a fixed price**. Discounts are usually available for several questions and/or for repeating the questions in a series of surveys.

(b) The research is carried out at a **far lower cost** than could be achieved by individual commission. They are particularly suitable for those who want to ask a limited number of questions of a large, representative sample of the population. The largest is the ICD Survey.

(c) There are many general omnibus surveys available and each claims to offer unique benefits. Potential clients should consider not only the **sample size**, but also its quality in terms of **structure** and method of **data collection**.

(d) There are a wide variety of specialist omnibus surveys working to **niche markets** such as motorists or mothers with children under two.

Marketing at Work

Audience Selection, who specialise in research by telephone, offer their key directors omnibus survey.

Sample   -   400 directors from the top 10% of British business: 200 managing directors and 200 financial directors.

               -   Questions may be placed to one or both groups.

Timing   -   January, April, July, October.

               -   Closing dates for questions are the second weeks of the above months.

               -   Results are available in the first week of the following month.

Data   -   Can be analysed by any combination of a wide range of business demographics, or by cross-analysis of the client's own questions.

Costs   -   On a fee per question basis.

               -   No joining fee.

The Target Group Index

2.12 The **TGI** is a national **product and media survey** which collects information from 24,000 adults each year. The TGI is a 'single source' measurement and all elements of the survey can be cross-referenced, for example media usage to product usage; brand usage to demographics. The TGI measures the following.

(a)   Heavy to light usage for over 3,000 brands in more than 200 FMCG product fields; additionally, usage of over 450 other brands in banking, building societies, airlines, holidays, cars, grocery and other retail outlets.

(b)   The 1,400 or so brands with more than a million claimed users, broken down demographically and by media.

(c)   The readership of more than 200 newspapers and magazines.

(d)   The weight of viewing of ITV and Channel 4, and half-hourly viewing behaviour.

(e)   The weight of listening to commercial radio.

(f)   The level of exposure to outdoor media and the cinema.

(g)   The full range of standard demographics together with special breakdowns such as terminal education age and working status.

2.13 There is also a **lifestyle section** which consists of nearly 200 separate attitude statements. The degree of agreement or disagreement to each is sought from each respondent. Standard cross-analysis can be used, but cluster analysis has been found to be especially revealing. Once attitudinal similarities have been determined the groups can then be analysed against demographics, media, and brands to provide an overall perspective.

2.14 **Geo-demographics**: the data can be accessed on-line and so breakdown by geo-demographic classification is simple. ACORN, PINPOINT and MOSAIC all offer TGI data cross-referenced into their own system of geo-demographics. The combination provides a selection of very powerful tools.

Key Concept

Tracking studies follow the behaviour of a target audience over time.

2.15 '**Before, during and after**' studies are necessary if achievement is to be known. For the major brands tracking is continuous, and for all packages some form of tracking is mandatory if they are to respond to market change and to market need.

2.16 **Pre-launch research** is concerned with every stage of development; evaluation of product concept, product sampling, package design, pricing and promotion. Before moving into the test market stage there may well be **placement tests** of very limited quantities. All will be done under considerable security, and where possible an independent research company will be engaged. The usual method will be the **depth interview**, usually in small groups.

2.17 The biggest danger at this stage is in distinguishing between **expressed intention** to buy and **actual purchase**. Members of the panels may like the package very much, they may give cast-iron guarantees that they will buy it and yet not do so when it hits the market.

2.18 One cannot know that an advertisement will work, but one should identify and eliminate the ones that definitely will not. Design and layout must be tested in detail: the copy platform should be thoroughly tested before representative audiences from the designated test market. Alternative appeals should be tested and details of layout should be checked thoroughly. Similarly all other aspects of promotion should be researched, modified and researched again. When all is ready, the final stage of pre-launch research is the **test market**.

Key Concept

Advertising content research focuses on the ability of the advertisement to achieve impact and to project the desired message.

Action Programme 2

Here are two small ads from a recent edition of *Marketing Week*. (The names have been omitted.) What sort of companies/products might use these services?

Market Research Limited **Trade Research Specialists**	**CHILDREN AND YOUTH** **BRITAIN AND CONTINENT**
• Retail audits • Product availability surveys • Mystery shopping • Shop testing • Trade interviews • Tailor made studies • Overnight pricing checks • Customer interviews • Consumer research	**GB** *Core Sample:* 1200 7 - 19 year olds with bi-monthly extensions to include ages 3 to 6 and 20-24. Any age range within these limits. *Field dates:* every 2 - 4 weeks. *Rates:* from £290 per question according to age range covered. **Continent:** Five country child and youth surveys

3 Briefing the research agency

3.1 The marketing communicator's prime task is to **brief the researcher** on the questions that require answers. The researcher's prime role is to propose the research that will achieve the objectives set.

3.2 The researcher should come back with queries on the brief and offer suggestions for improvement. The client may well help to improve the research methodology. The fact remains, however, that it is for the **researcher to propose the methodology**.

The approach to briefing

3.3 (a) Ensure good communication: take time to give a thorough briefing on the background to the problem.

(b) Do not allow pre-conceived ideas to preclude objective discussion with researchers.

(c) Specify the type of data and the degree of confidence that will be adequate.

(d) Ask for a formal research proposal that specifies the following.

■ The research to be undertaken
■ The methods of enquiry
■ The sample design
■ The data to be collected
■ The time to be taken
■ The likely cost
■ The internal security controls (ie checks on the effectiveness of the interviewers)

(e) Only after the proposal has been checked against the brief should authority be given to proceed.

3.4 The contents of a research brief are shown in the table below

Issue	Comment
Security	Any security implications must be made very clear.
Objectives	These should state the exact purpose of the research, that is, the **management** questions that need to be answered so that a decision can be taken. (The detailed questions that will be asked by the interviewers will be devised by the researchers.)
Background	The **marketing problem** should be defined in sufficient detail for the **objectives** to be seen in context.
Budget	Only a guideline need be given at this stage, although a maximum figure may well be quoted; this may also be stated in the contract.
Deadlines	Deadlines should be set for the receipt of and agreement to the proposal. The researcher should be asked to detail the time to be taken and the **latest date** for receipt of any reports.

Need to know

3.5 Gathering research on a **need-to-know basis** is directive, purposeful and cost effective. Going off at a tangent to gather data that would be 'nice to know' wastes resources, takes time and clutters up the report with data that are of no immediate use.

Exam Tip

International advertising agencies have featured in exam questions but agencies in general had not until December 1997 when a surprise question picked up on a number of articles that had appeared in the marketing press, as follows.

'Over the last decade, marketing communications agencies have lost out to Management Consultants when clients seek advice on strategic aspects of their business. Write a short report on why this occurs and state what agencies can do to combat this loss of strategic level business.'

4 Creative agencies

4.1 Types of agency

In-house	If a potential advertiser has sufficient expertise, he may decide to handle advertising in-house.
Full Service	Alternatively, an advertiser may decide to use a full service agency. This is an agency which provides a **complete advertising service** encompassing creative work, production, media planning and buying. The full service agency may also provide or sub-contract research services for a client. Some large advertising agencies will provide other communications services, for example direct marketing, public relations or sales promotion.
Hotshops	Smaller operators which have been set up by **creative staff** from larger agencies.
Media independents	Media independents provide **media services only**.
A la carte	A client may decide to share out his communication tasks, choosing to **cherry pick** services *à la carte* from the different providers available. Responsibility for controlling and co-ordinating the activities of these service providers rests with the client, usually in the form of the brand or marketing manager.

5 Agency selection

5.1 The pages of the trade magazine *Campaign* regularly carry news of client accounts on the move from one agency to another. There are a number of reasons why clients may **change agencies**. The client may feel the agency is lacking in new ideas, or is overcharging. Alternatively, a new client won by the agency may result in a conflict of interests between new and old clients. Often, a change in personnel on either the client or the agency side can result in an account moving on.

Search

5.2 **Sources of information** include the following.

(a) Publications such as *Campaign Portfolio* provide a listing of agencies and the types of business they handle, alongside addresses and contact numbers.

(b) The Advertising Agency Register (AAR) is a specialist intermediary type service which clients can use to help them with their search. For a fee, AAR will provide a list of candidate agencies and a selection of their work.

(c) Many agencies engage in self promotion via advertising, direct mail or even cold calling.

(d) Personal recommendation may bring some agency names to light.

(e) Some agencies now produce CD-ROMs containing case studies, examples of work and background information about them and their offices.

Shortlist

5.3 From the initial search, a shortlist of perhaps six to eight agencies will be drawn up, usually on the basis of their current work and past track record. The prospective client will then visit those agencies for a series of what are known as **credentials presentations**. A preliminary evaluation of the agencies may be carried out using the criteria below.

(a) **Previous work** handled

(b) **Experience** in relevant fields of business (for example, do they handle other clients with similar target audiences to mine? Have they carried out work in the FMCG/industrial/business-to-business market before?)

(c) Agency **costs**/terms of business

(d) **Resources** in house as opposed to bought in

(e) Staff **expertise**

(f) **Personalities**

Agency pitch

5.4 Following these initial visits, it is likely that a smaller number of agencies will be formally invited to **pitch** for the client's business. There is some controversy regarding whether an agency should be reimbursed for a pitch. Some agencies will only carry out pitches if they can claim some of the expense back from the potential client. Other agencies will only carry out an ideas pitch as opposed to presenting creative work.

5.5 Normally, three or four agencies will be invited to compete for the client's business. All will receive a standard **brief** and will be given a set period in which to reply to the brief.

Detailed selection process

5.6 It is essential that each agency is judged by the same criteria. The criteria should be established by the client in advance, and they must be understood and agreed by all who will be part of the selection team.

5.7 **Criteria for assessing an agency**

Item	Comment
Present work	■ Is it exciting/interesting? ■ Is it effective? What proof is there? ■ It is allied to our marketplace?
Present clients	■ Are there any clashes that will worry us or the agency or the other client(s)? ■ Do previous clients come back for more or are agency/client relationships short-lived?

Item	Comment
Chemistry	■ Is the chemistry between us good? ■ Will we feel able to trust the agency all the way? ■ Will the trust be reciprocated?
Staffing	■ Will the people who worked on the pitch work on the account? ■ How stable will our account team be? ■ What depth of experience can the account team offer?
Evidence	■ Have we seen evidence of creativity, of production, of media planning, of management, of the particular skills we need?
The pitch	■ Is it a package or tailored specially? ■ Does it arouse us to buy?
The agency	■ Is its size, age and structure suitable? ■ Does it have to have international capacity? ■ Is it a full service agency or a specialist? ■ What is its workload? Does it have time for us? ■ Does it possess the necessary business skills? For example, has it negotiated a fee for specialised work necessary to meet the requirements of our invitation to pitch for the account?
Specialised knowledge	■ Has it demonstrated realistic and satisfactory understanding of our organisation and market?
Price	■ Does the asking fee represent value for money when the above points are taken into account? ■ Does the agency know its value to us?
Judgement	■ Is this the agency for us?

Final selection

5.8 The final selection will involve a judgement about how well the client believes the agency has responded to the brief in terms of the **strategic thinking** involved, the creative work (if presented) and the agency's all round **understanding of the client's industry**.

6 Managing the relationship

6.1 The specialist agencies providing support services (advertising, public relations, sales promotion, research) usually all work to much the same principles. There will be an **account manager** directly responsible for the client's account and working directly to the **brand manager**. All contact between client and agency is via these individuals.

6.2 **The account manager is vitally important because a full service agency will provide the services of many departments**, and these need to be co-ordinated around a client focus. The departments commonly found in a full service agency are as follows.

- ■ Creative
- ■ Typography
- ■ Presentation
- ■ TV and radio production
- ■ Press production
- ■ Press buying
- ■ Marketing
- ■ Media planning
- ■ Market intelligence

- Studio
- Account management
- Economic forecasting
- Research

- Print buying
- Art buying
- TV and radio buying
- Sales promotion

- Personnel
- Finance
- Administration
- Management

6.3 **Establishing a relationship with a creative agency takes time**. The end result has to be an on-going relationship based upon mutual understanding and respect. Therefore both the selection process and for the day-to-day relationships have to receive very careful attention.

6.4 **A creative agency should be a full member of the client's marketing team**. As such, members of the agency have to be trusted with market information and, to some extent, with profit information as well. If an agency understands the costing of a package it is less likely to spend time devising a promotion that the client will not be able to afford.

6.5 An agency and its personnel must be **trusted**. If they are not then information will be withheld and the relationship will suffer. The creative work will suffer too, and sales and profitability will fall.

6.6 The only reason an agency is engaged is because it can do a job or provide a service better than the client can do it for himself. It follows that the client should not meddle with their work. If the client does not like it, of course, he must say so, but **the test must be 'will it work with the target audience?'**

6.7 **Key principles for managing the relationship**

1	Management is by the client.
2	The agency team must work closely within the client's marketing department.
3	Briefings must be specific and unambiguous.
4	All research data and management control information available to the brand manager must be provided to the agency.
5	The agency should sit in on the client's strategic planning meetings as an equal member, and of right.
6	Time and cost requirements must be reasonable and must be accepted by the agency.
7	The client should not meddle in the creative process and the agency should not interfere with the production of the package, although both may make an input, as appropriate, as part of the strategic planning process.
8	Full credit must be given when the agency is successful, and shared responsibility must be accepted as appropriate.
9	Fees and commissions should be agreed in advance and accounts should be paid promptly.
10	Copy should never be changed once it has been approved. It should be fully checked before it is signed off. Changes after that stage are not only expensive but, more importantly, they are damaging to the brand manager's personal credibility with the agency.

6.8 Given that the agency is accepted as part of the marketing communications team it should take full responsibility for the production of **cost-effective work** that meets the **brief** and hits **time targets**.

Payment of creative agencies

6.9 Historically, agencies have earned their money through **commission on media space** purchased for their clients. The practice arises from the time when the advertising agent was a media broker who also provided other services. This method of payment also highlights the agency's legal standing. The agency is liable for bills to the media if the client defaults on payment.

Agency commission

6.10 Some large clients have argued that they should pay the agency a discounted rate of commission, because of the volume of media throughput that the agency handles. Other clients, themselves under pressure to make advertising money work harder, have argued for commission rates of 10% or 13%, compared to the previous standard of 15%.

Fee payment

6.11 Some advertisers and their agencies prefer to work on a **project by project fee system**. This ensures the agency earns money, whether or not the work is media based.

Marketing at Work

David Ogilvy is on record as saying 'I pioneered the fee system but I no longer care how I get paid, providing I make a reasonable profit. With a fee system the advertiser pays only for the services he wants, no more and no less. Every fee account pays its own way. Large profitable accounts do not subsidise small, unprofitable ones. Cuts in client's budgets do not oblige you to cut staff. When you advise a client to increase his advertising he does not suspect your motive.'

6.12 It is essential for the agency to have an efficient system to capture accurately and promptly all data relating to the allocation of staff time, and the utilisation of other resources. It is reasonable for a client to expect to be shown the control method in use, but not to have access to the agency's detailed profitability. A typical **fee calculation** is shown below.

Advertising agency: typical fee calculation

	Actual hours	Amount £
Direct time cost*		
Account management	1,000	40,000
Creative	1,500	60,000
Media	300	12,000
Production	400	16,000
Research and planning	750	30,000
		158,000
Overheads at 110% (including secretarial, managerial, accounting and administration payroll; also establishment and general costs)	-	174,000
Direct expenses (including directly attributable travel and presentation costs)	-	14,000
Total hours/cost	3,950	346,000
Gross profit at 25%	-	86,500
Total (£109.50 per hour)	3,950	432,500

* Includes direct and indirect payroll costs of all staff who allocate their time.

6.13 The sums charged per hour will obviously vary from agency to agency and over time. It will be seen that a new product development can occupy many hours. Even more hours will be used within the client, but they are unlikely to be controlled as rigorously. There is therefore considerable unquantified investment in any new creative development. The only party able to account for its involvement accurately is the agency.

Payment by results

6.14 **Payment by results** schemes have been used mainly in the USA, although they are becoming more common in the UK. With performance-related payment, the agency is judged on **the effect its advertising has on client company sales**. Different rates of commission then come into force, depending on performance to target, over-achievement or under-achievement. The major drawback to this method of remuneration is that it pre-supposes a direct correlation between advertising effort and sales.

 Marketing at Work

Every year *Campaign* conducts a survey on choosing an agency. The results shed some further light on the best approach to managing the relationship - or not managing it, as the case may be.

Marketing directors were asked a series of questions and given suggested answers. The questions and the percentages agreeing with the answers are as follows.

(a)   *Why do you change agency?*

(i)	It is not devoting enough time/resources to your account	87
(ii)	It has lost its enthusiasm for working on your product/service	85
(iii)	It is working on a conflicting account	61
(iv)	There is a personality clash	44
(v)	It lacks *integrated* communication skills	32
(vi)	It lacks the technology to service your account	15
(vii)	You change agency regularly as a matter of course	2

(b)   *How do you go about drawing up a shortlist?*

(i)	You take into consideration advertising you admire	86
(ii)	You ask acquaintances for recommendations	77
(iii)	You read the marketing press	59
(iv)	You read *Campaign*	45
(v)	You take into consideration creative/effectiveness ad awards	44
(vi)	You use the Advertising Agency Register	38
(vii)	You use *Campaign Portfolio*	36
(viii)	You appoint a selection consultant	5

(c)   *What do you look for at the pitch?*

(i)	Evidence the agency understands and can enhance your brand	95
(ii)	Quality of thinking	94
(iii)	Good chemistry between both parties	90
(iv)	Presence of senior agency staff who will stay on your account	81
(v)	Evidence of sound business/management skills	75
(vi)	Strategy that offers value for money	73
(vii)	A powerful creative idea	68
(viii)	An agency culture which fits your own	64

(d)   *What do you look for in a new agency?*

(i)	It is fundamentally committed to creative excellence	74
(ii)	It has previous experience working in your market sector	46
(iii)	It offers a remuneration system based on fees not commissions	41
(iv)	It has embraced new technology and uses it	38
(v)	It offers a fully *integrated* service, including below-the-line	35
(vi)	It is able to advise you on the information superhighway	22
(vii)	It offers international resources	16

(e)   *How could your agency improve its service to you?*

(i)	Unprompted original ideas	78
(ii)	Cut costs	66
(iii)	Not be afraid to challenge your viewpoint	56
(iv)	Devote more time/resources to your account	49
(v)	Embrace new technology and use it to your advantage	44
(vi)	Offer a more through-the-line approach	41
(vii)	Spend less time wining and dining and more time working	21

(f)   *In which of the following areas could your agency improve its skills?*

(i)	Creativity	55
(ii)	Strategy	50
(iii)	Research	42
(iv)	Planning	36
(v)	Below the line	27
(vi)	Media	23

Perhaps not surprisingly *quality* seemed to be main issue in each case. Notable trends were the interest of a sizeable minority in *integrated* communications and in the possibilities of information technology.

Agency structures

6.15 Within the agency, a variety of personnel will be involved in handling the client's business. The account executive or account manager is the lynchpin between the numerous agency personnel and their client. His role is to liaise with client staff and to brief, supervise and co-ordinate the appropriate agency staff at appropriate times.

6.16 The internal structure of an agency can best be explained by considering how the agency handles a piece of client work.

(a)   **The client problem**

A client and agency who have been together for some time will have built up a good working relationship. The agency will understand the client's business, and the motivations and decision-making processes of end consumers. A new product or service, new situation or changing market conditions may provide the starting point for a new role to be performed by advertising. The client needs to brief the account executive on the task in hand.

(b)   **The internal briefing**

The account executive will brief the members of the account team who work on the client's business. These members are:

(i)   An **account planner**, responsible for using market research to develop advertising strategy for the clients.

(ii) A **creative team** or duo of art director and copywriter, responsible for conceiving a creative idea which meets the advertising brief and working that idea up into visual form and written copy.

(iii) A **media planner/buyer**, responsible for recommending an appropriate media strategy and ensuring media is bought cost effectively.

(c) **The client presentation**

The account executive will present back to the client. He will show examples of how the final advertising execution will look, using rough visuals or storyboards and will explain the rationale for the ideas presented. Depending on the client's reaction to the team's interpretation of the brief, the team will either be asked to go ahead in developing the work, or will be asked to rework their ideas.

The go-ahead stage may include a decision to test the advertising in research prior to full production of the advert.

(d) **Production of advert(s)**

Some simple advertising executions will be carried out almost entirely in-house by the advertising agency. For more complex executions, the agency will buy in specialist functions on behalf of the client.

Whilst production is ongoing, the media department will be involved in the actual commitment of the media budget. Dates, times and positions will be agreed with media owners.

During this stage, there will be continuous liaison between the account executive and the client. The client is likely to attend some of the key production stages such as filming or photography of the commercial.

If time allows, further research may take place to identify the need for any additional changes.

(e) **The campaign appears**

The time span between the briefing of the account executive by the client and the campaign appearing can be as little as six or eight weeks for a simple photographic newspaper execution, to 20 weeks plus for an animated TV commercial. Once the campaign has appeared, it is important that it is properly evaluated against the objectives initially set.

6.17 Members of the account team, who work directly on the client's business in creating a campaign, are those the client is most likely to come into contact with, although the main point of contact will of course be the **account executive**. There are other behind the scenes staff with whom the account executive must liaise but who will not have direct client contact.

(i)   **Accounts department**, responsible for billing the client and paying agency invoices

(ii) **Vouchers department** checks that press adverts appear

(iii) **Traffic department** ensures that jobs are taken through their different stages on time.

(iv) A large agency may additionally have an **information** or **library** service, and **legal** department.

6.18 Agencies have been searching for a structure that best meets the integrated marketing communications needs of their clients. No one single framework has been determined although various models have been tried and tested by agencies.

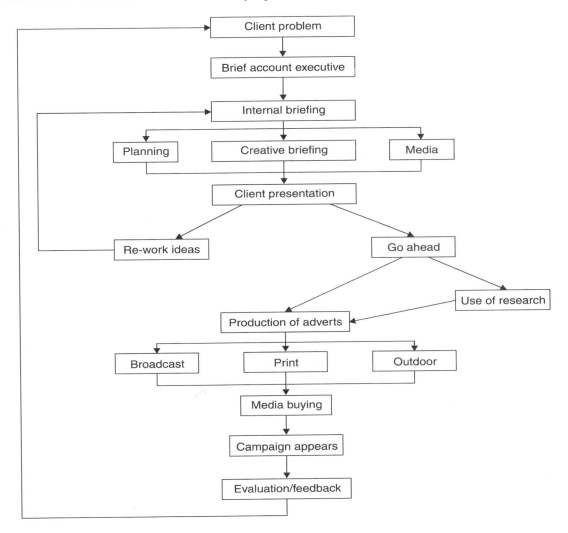

Handling a piece of client work

Marketing at Work

Here is an extract from *Campaign* in June *1996*.

'Howell Henry Chaldecott Lury, the agency that turned its back on traditional agency structures, has created a new role within its project teams to cope with the extra demands of integrated communications.

HHCL has split the role of account director for each of its six core multi-disciplinary project teams – HHCL's alternative to traditional account teams – into strategy and implementation roles.

The new project managers will take on the implementation functions, while the account directors will focus exclusively on strategy.

HHCL's managing partner, Robin Azis, said the move was sparked by the increasing workload that has been generated by the agency's growing number of integrated communications accounts.

'Until recently we would produce a couple of ad campaigns a year for a client like Tango. When we moved into integrated communications we found we needed extra resources as we were doing five campaigns, posters, on-pack promotions, and PR type events for Tango,' Azis said.

6.19 Integrated agency structures tend to form along a continuum. At one extreme the agency is structured along **client needs**, where there is a high level of centralisation and hence integration but where staff tend to be generalists. At the other end of the continuum the structure is orientated to **functional specialists** but in order to make this work agencies align themselves as part of a **network** where integration opportunities are much lower.

Chapter Roundup

- Marketing communicators need to be fully aware of the range of **qualitative and** research.

- **Briefing researchers** entails explaining what questions need to be answered. The researcher should devise the method. 'Need to know' may be an important principle, since external researchers may also be engaged by a company's competitors.

- Clients can choose to handle their advertising function in a number of ways. Very large advertisers may keep the function **internal** to the company. Alternatively, a client can buy in expertise from a **full service advertising agency**, or combine services from a **creative shop** and a **media independent**.

- A variety of **agency staff** will handle the workflow on a client's account.

- It is the responsibility of the client to provide a full **campaign briefing** for any new piece of advertising work. An oral brief is usually backed up by a written document. The account executive in turn will provide a creative briefing for the specific use of the creative team.

- The process of **selecting a new agency** involves initial search; credentials presentation and shortlist; competitive pitch and final selection. The client will gauge competing agencies against set criteria such as expertise in the client's field of business, previous work handled, resources provided and costs. The final selection decision will involve a judgement about how well the agency has answered the client brief. Personal chemistry between the individuals involved will also play a part.

- **Managing the relationship** requires trust, a free flow of information, proper allocation of responsibilities and careful control.

Now try Question 12 at the end of the Study Text

Quick Quiz

1   Describe three qualitative measures. (see para 2.6)

2   List some types of quantitative research. (2.8 - 2.16)

3   What approach should be taken to briefing a research agency? (3.3)

4   What sources of information are there? (5.2)

5   What items might be included in an agency selection checklist? (5.7)

6   What principles underpin the management of a client/agency relationship? (6.7)

7   What are the advantages of the fee system? (6.11 – 6.12)

Action Programme Review

1   Each newspaper will have presented the aspects of the data which showed itself in the best light. The *Sunday Times* may have increased overall circulation, and increased the percentage of AB readers. The *Sunday Telegraph* may have lost circulation (you will know from the *Sunday Times*), but have increased its colour magazine readership. The *Guardian* may show a large *percentage* gain in readership, and an increasing number of ABC1 readers. Only by researching back to the original ABC report will you be able to ascertain the truth, but you can come close by cross-referencing the data provided by each, and filling in the gaps from the rivals and by inference. Beware the switch from real numbers to percentages!

2   Market Research Limited will provide retailers of different kinds of products with useful information as well as the product manufacturers, most likely consumer goods given this description. Children and Youth - companies producing goods and services aimed at the youth markets who want to conduct research but may not have the resources to undertake surveys independently.

Part F

Evaluation

Evaluating Different Communications Campaigns

13

Chapter Topic List	
1	Setting the scene
2	Understanding communications effectiveness
3	Consumer communication case studies
4	Business-to-business communications strategies
5	Marketing communications for service organisations
6	Marketing communications for non profit organisations
7	Marketing communications for small businesses
8	Communications in the 21st century

Learning Outcome

☑ Evaluate a variety of promotional campaigns drawn from different sectors.

Syllabus References

☑ Evaluating the outcomes of promotional activities

☑ Knowledge and understanding of different campaigns from different context (including FMCG, business-to-business, services and public sectors, and not for profit organisations)

☑ Consideration of the competitive conditions, available resources, stage in the product life cycle and any political, economic, social or technological factors that might be identified as influencing the development of a campaign

Key Concepts Introduced

- Pre-testing
- Post-testing

1 Setting the scene

Exam Tip

In every *Integrated Marketing Communications Strategy* examination paper, Part A will be based on a mini case study based around a real life scenario. Often, Section B questions will also involve shorter case histories. You will frequently be asked to provide examples of and evaluate campaigns of different kinds with which you are familiar. The module requires an understanding of marketing communications relating to different marketing sectors and types of business. Many of the cases used will relate to consumer situations as these are the ones most candidates will be most familiar with.

1.1 This chapter will provide a range of case histories from differing market sectors – consumer, business-to-business, services, not-for-profit and small businesses. Much of the text to date has focused on consumer marketing communications and the cases presented here are not supported by further discussion of the principles involved. With regard to the other marketing sectors, you will find additional discussion outlining significant issues which influence the communications used in such situations.

1.2 The cases and examples used are further designed to illustrate the application of appropriate promotional mixes discussed in Chapter 9. They also in most cases illustrate implementation, control and overall planning perspectives.

2 Understanding communications effectiveness   12/02

A summary of marketing communication effectiveness

2.1 Ultimately communications are designed to meet three objectives.

Awareness	Increase brand **awareness** and establish brand **recognition**
Trial	Stimulate **trial purchase**
Reinforcement	Stimulate and **reinforce** brand **loyalty**

2.2 To succeed in achieving these goals, communications must:

- Gain attention
- Communicate a message
- Improve attitude to the brand
- Reinforce the already positive attitude to the brand

■   Obtain the readers'/listeners'/viewers' liking for the message and its execution

2.3   How to assess the effectiveness of communications campaigns

Principle	What it means
Value linkage	Communication must represent the value of the brand.
Sense making	Communications must be meaningful and relevant.
Simplification	Strict simplification is necessary in view of the avalanche of information.
Acceleration	The message must be transmitted in a few seconds.
Visualisation	We must communicate visually first and foremost.
Humanisation	Communication must relate to the lives and dreams of real people.
Emotionalisation	Communications should activate the receiver's feelings more.
Conditioning	Effective use requires strong, unambiguous, vivid stimuli.
Refreshment	Receivers can become bored or tired of campaigns.
Branding	The brand has to be an integrated part of communications.
Entertainment	Entertainment can be extremely effective in some cases.
Consistency	Consistency has been the mainstay of major brands.

2.4   The difficult part is measuring the effectiveness of the marketing communications process. The following are some possible techniques.

Marketing communications method	Examples of measurement
Personal selling	Sales targets
Public relations	Editorial coverage
Direct marketing	Enquiries generated
Advertising	Brand awareness
Sales promotion	Coupons redeemed
Exhibitions	Contacts made

Exam Tip

The December 2002 exam contained a question on measuring the effectiveness of advertising and public relations campaigns for a children's clothes manufacturer.

2.5   Engel, Warshaw and Kinnear's book on *Promotional Strategy* contains a substantial chapter on the 'Measurement of Promotional Effectiveness' from which the following table is taken. This shows possible advertising effectiveness and control methods. **Testing** is an important part of the communications development process.

BPP
PROFESSIONAL EDUCATION

Classification of advertising effectiveness measures

Types of measure	Advertising related	Product related
Laboratory measures	Pre-testing ■ Consumer panels ■ Portfolio tests ■ Readability tests ■ Physiological measures eg eye movements	Pre-testing ■ Theatre tests ■ Hall tests ■ Laboratory scores
Real word measures (Respondent unaware of testing)	*Pre-testing* ■ Dummy advertising ■ Inquiry tests ■ On air tests *Post-testing* ■ Recognition (clues given) ■ Recall tests (no clues)	*Pre- and post- procedures* ■ Sales measures ■ Test markets

Key Concepts

Pre-testing is the assessment in advance of whether what is proposed is likely to work.

Post-testing evaluates afterwards whether it has done so, and provides feedback for future activities.

Exam Tip

The examiner has said that candidates should use suitable examples to demonstrate the points they are making. The age of an example is not important, nor is the culture or country from where the examples are drawn. What you must do is give more than a description. You should show your understanding through a **structured interpretation** and evaluation of a campaign.

Action Programme 1

For a campaign of your choice answer the following questions. (You might have to do this in an exam.)

(i)   Describe the organisation concerned and its competitors.
(ii)   What factors and issues have shaped the campaign?
(iii)   What are the marketing communications objectives?
(iv)   What are the main elements of the communication strategy?
(v)   How can you measure the effectiveness of the campaign?

3 Consumer communication case studies

You have already been encouraged to keep up-to-date by reading the business press and, in particular, trade magazines such as *Marketing, Marketing Week* and *Campaign*. These contain regular reviews of marketing communications activities including varying campaigns from different types of organisations. You are also encouraged to obtain and study cases histories in more detail than you would normally find in such sources.

3.1 Some of the cases illustrated here are taken from the Institute of Practitioners in Advertising (IPA) Advertising Effectiveness Awards. These are awarded each year. Although these focus largely on advertising, they do provide coverage of other communication tools and their effectiveness in a wider marketing communications context.

3.2 The IPA cases used here are presented in a format which would provide a **framework for marketing communications planning**:

- Situation analysis
- Communications objectives
- Marketing communications strategy
- Communications tactics – promotional mix
- Action – implementation
- Control – measurement and evaluation

Marketing at Work

BRITISH TELECOM: 'IT'S GOOD TO TALK' (IGTT)

Situation

After privatisation, OFTEL required BT to reduce its call charges significantly. In order to increase call revenues, BT's residential division sought to encourage its existing customers to use the phone more.

BT believed that certain underlying negative attitudes towards telephone communication were restricting usage, and that these would need to be addressed if a real step-change in phone usage was to occur. BT needed advertising that could break down these barriers to calling.

Objectives

(a) To persuade people to make more and longer calls.
(b) To ease the tension between 'gatekeeper' and 'key caller', thus releasing pent-up demand.
(c) To change price perceptions.

Strategy

There are two major barriers to a better appreciation of phone communication.

(a) Men tend to use the phone in a very functional way, whereas women tend to be more 'chatty'. Because many men cannot understand women's usage, they try to restrict it, and act as 'gatekeepers' to the phone.

(b) High-price perceptions inhibit usage. Although BT call charges have fallen, perceptions remain high because total phone bills keep rising.

'IGTT' therefore aimed to ease the tension in 'gatekeeper' households by promoting the value of female-style communication, and by reducing price perceptions.

Tactics

'IGTT' achieved its advertising aims in two ways:

(a) Through the use of an objective 'guide to better communication', Bob Hoskins pointed out to us the benefits of better phone usage.

(b) By comparing individual call charges to other everyday low-cost items. In this way, the abstract price of a call was related to real life.

Action

BT invested £44 million in 'IGTT'. The campaign maintained a constant presence, apart from three-months when it made way for National Code Change advertising.

Control

Analysis covered the period of all campaigns since privatisation. Assessing advertising effectiveness was a difficult task, because the telecommunications market has seen much change. It was necessary to establish and quantify, where necessary, the impact of these changes on call growth. Econometric analysis determined the contribution of advertising, price, the economy and other variables to call growth. The analysis demonstrated that 'IGTT' had generated by far the highest return of all campaigns since privatisation. It showed that every 100 TVRs of 'IGTT' in any given month produced an eventual return of 1.75% of monthly sales.

The sales uplift from 'IGIT' produced an advertising-generated income of £297m. With hardly any variable costs, this was pure profit and represented a return on investment of 6 to 1.

'IGTT' worked in the way intended.

(a) People claimed to use the phone more, and for longer, as a result of seeing the advertising. This was especially true of the group whose calling levels were expected to be most depressed - women.

(b) There was a substantial increase in the degree of relaxed attitudes towards using the phone, particularly among men, suggesting a softening in 'gatekeeper' attitudes.

(c) Correspondingly, women now feel less guilty about using the phone.

(d) BT price perceptions fell steeply during the campaign.

Action Programme 2

Compare the current BT communications mix with those of mobile phone companies such as Vodafone, Orange and One2One.

Marketing at Work

MURPHY'S IRISH STOUT: 'LIKE THE MURPHY'S, I'M NOT BITTER'

Situation

Murphy's Irish Stout, licensed in the UK by Whitbread since 1987, had not been performing as Whitbread had anticipated. The sales force was becoming demoralised and the brand was facing delisting in the trade. Murphy's survival as a brand depended on finding a new way forward to accelerate growth. A daunting task, however, in the shadow of Guinness.

Objectives

(a)   To break Guinness's consumer monopoly and open the market to a competitive stout brand.

(b)   To develop Murphy's as the stout brand that people would prefer to drink instead of Guinness.

Strategy

For years, Guinness has made a great virtue of its acquired taste. Despite consumer belief that this is an enormous benefit of the brand, in reality 'an acquired taste' is simply another way of saying that it's 'difficult to drink'. Knowing that Murphy's was smoother and easier to drink than Guinness presented a very considerable opportunity for Murphy's to become the accessible entry-point into the stout market, thus segmenting the market on taste. Stout, by virtue of the slow manner in which it is commonly consumed, is associated with sociable, laid-back values. These values had been neglected by Guinness in its attempt to appeal to new, younger drinkers.

The vision for the future of the Murphy's brand was first to become the accessible, easy-drinking, easy-going stout brand, and in doing so open the market (and the minds of consumers) to embrace an alternative player. The groups most likely to need help with accessing stout were targeted. Regular Guinness drinkers were already of the Guinness 'club', and unlikely to be tempted away, but it was found that many occasional drinkers were inhibited by the Guinness taste. There was also a group of non-drinkers who aspired to drinking stout, but the taste of Guinness put them off. So these groups were prime targets for Murphy's: Men, not lads, who drink Guinness now and then or who'd like to drink it but don't like the taste (stout wannabees).

Tactics

The advertising idea itself highlighted the easy-drinking nature of Murphy's. The endline: 'Like the Murphy's, I'm not bitter' worked by also associating the brand with an aspirational state of mind. The campaign ran on television and was supported by press advertising, incorporating full-colour double-page spreads.

Action

TV buying revolved around programming that the target audience specifically chose to watch and included programmes particularly relevant to the positioning.

Control

The strategy led to Murphy's significantly increasing its share of the on and off trade stout market, to the detriment of Guinness. Advertising impact was confirmed by the fact that over 60% of those people claiming to have seen any Murphy's advertising could repeat the endline word-for-word. Importantly, when put head to head against Guinness, the Murphy's brand held an over-whelming lead over Guinness as 'less bitter tasting' and 'easier to drink', and most spectacular, given Guinness's heritage, 37% of beer drinkers saw no difference between the two brands as 'authentically Irish'.

Action Programme 3

Choose another drinks market sector and look at the positioning of different competitors and the different communications tactics they employ.

Marketing at Work

WALKER'S CRISPS: GARY LINEKER

Situation

In 1989 Walkers and Smiths Crisps moved under the umbrella of PepsiCo Foods International. In 1993, the two brands were merged. With a turnover in the region of £300 million, Walkers Crisps had become the biggest single food brand in the UK.

By August 1994, Walkers had experienced two years of double-digit growth, and the brand's share had reached 22%, over three times that of its nearest branded rival. However, there were several clouds looming on the horizon:

- Plateauing distribution
- Success of promotions
- Advertising uncertainties.

Marketing communications objectives

To maintain volume and share growth on a par with that achieved in the previous two years, primarily through ROS (rate of sales) growth. In particular it needed to do this in two ways:

(a)   Theme advertising that would work harder than before and would generate ROS increases in its own right.

(b)   Through promotional advertising that would be part of the same campaign and hence more strongly branded than before, and that would generate even more pronounced short-term ROS uplifts than the previous promotional advertising.

Marketing communications strategy

In March 1993 Walkers had embarked on a successful series of 'Instant Win' promotions, producing unprecedented uplifts in volume and ROS. 'Instant Win' promotions were seen as another engine for dynamic growth. But it was unclear how important the novelty factor was to their success, and whether repetition would see declining effectiveness over time, and it seemed inevitable that competition would try to copy them.

There was little doubt that the promotional advertising had been successful in boosting sales. However, to protect the salience of Walkers' own promotions in the face of copying by competitors, stronger branding of the 'Instant Win' promotions was felt desirable, best achieved by a single brand umbrella bringing promotional and theme advertising together.

When Walkers put the advertising account out to pitch in mid 1994, it was to develop an integrated brand campaign incorporating new theme and promotional advertising.

It was decided to create advertising that would appeal to a mass audience of adults as well as children. From qualitative research conducted amongst crisp-lovers of all ages, 'irresistibility' was identified as the quality that embodied everything they most enjoyed about snacking. It was shorthand for the perfect crisp. A creative vehicle that would generate PR and media coverage was desired. Given the importance of fame and the need for a mass audience, TV was chosen as the main medium.

The idea for the campaign can be summarised as 'Walkers are so irresistible they make even nice guys turn nasty when it comes to crisps'.

What set the idea apart was the thought of casting ex-England and Leicester footballer Gary Lineker as the nice guy turned nasty.

As the ambassador and genuine 'nice guy' of the game, Gary was as attractive to mums as to kids. His well-publicised return from playing in Japan offered unique PR opportunities. Most important of all, his down-to-earth personality and roots in Walkers' Leicester heartland provided a seamless fit with the desired brand personality and the unpretentious values to be established.

Tactics

Prior to the 1996 IPA Awards five TV executions had been produced in the series including two for further 'Instant Win' promotions:

Execution	Airdate	TVRs	Objective
'Welcome home'	Jan 95	472	Launch improved cheese & onion
'Nun'	Mar 95	520	Support 'Instant cheque' promotion
'Garymania'	May 95	451	Launch Crinkles range
'Dial-a-Prize'	Sept 95	361	Support 'Dial-a-Prize' promotion
'Salt & Lineker'	Jan 96	553	Launch improved S&V flavour

Action

From the outset, the Lineker campaign generated an amount of TV and press coverage much in excess of anything previously seen in the market. TV coverage ranged from News at Ten to Fantasy Football League, The Big Breakfast and How Do They Do that? Press coverage appeared in all national press, from *The Times*, *The Independent* and *Daily Telegraph*, to the *Daily Mail*, *Daily Mirror* and the front page of *The Sun* ... twice.

Control

Analysis of growth in different advertised varieties of Walkers crisps, showed that the advertising clearly influenced consumer behaviour. Two econometric models showed directly that the advertising was responsible for a large proportion of the brand's growth. The part played by other variables showed no other activity could have been responsible for the effect claimed for advertising.

The marketing objectives of sustaining volume and increasing market share growth were successfully exceeded.

Volume grew by 22.5% in the year following Gary Lineker's appointment.

Walkers continue to use Gary Lineker in their ads.

Action Programme 4

This is an integrated campaign. Identify as many features of integration as you can, both from the above or from your own experience of the Walker's brand.

Marketing at Work

Dulux reveals true colours

Situation

Historically, Dulux the paint manufacturer had used advertising to associate the brand with white and 'Natural Hints' ranges. If they were to achieve ambitious targets for 1999, focus on the coloured paint sector was also required. Paint sales were expected to grow at the expense of wallpaper and the coloured sector was important as it was the most profitable sector and likely to see a significant proportion of the forecast growth. Brighter colours were more fashionable as a result of programmes such as Changing Rooms, which particularly appealed to a younger target audience. The image of Dulux was safe and respected but irrelevant to the younger market.

Target Audience

Focus was placed on the under 35 for a number of reasons. Unless younger customers could be attracted this would lead to longer term loss of share as these were the customers of the future. First time house purchase was on the increase fuelled by lower interest rates creating younger home owners. It was also the sector where Dulux had the lowest share and therefore most opportunity for growth. Further segmentation targeted females who were seen to be the decision makers and to seek consumers with a more adventurous mindset in order to move away from the 'safe' image.

Promotional mix

A TV campaign spearheaded the repositioning efforts, demonstrating the range of colours available and the consumer need this range met. The theme was bright, bold and controversial, very different to the gentle and romantic execution of earlier advertising.

A website allowed consumers to test different paint mixes and advise on suitability for different surfaces and calculate the quantity required. PR included a challenge to personalities to dye their hair for a day in aid of charity. Further media coverage arose from a body-painted naked lady visiting key media offices with the famous Dulux dog to deliver specially created paint mixes.

Measuring Effectiveness

Tracking studies four months into the campaign showed a 12% increase in the numbers agreeing that Dulux 'had the widest range of colours' and a 15% rise in those agreeing that Dulux 'always has the right colour for you'. As a result of the campaign, over 80% of those recalling the ads remembered the key message that Dulux can 'match the colour you want.'

In February 2000, Dulux volume share topped own label (Homebase /B&Q)sales for the first time.

Dulux was one of the winners of the CIM/Marketing Week Marketing Effectiveness Awards 2000.

From an article in *Marketing Business* February 2001

 Marketing at Work

Last laugh for Skoda

Situation

For years the butt of jokes based on the car's unreliability, the success of the brand over the last two years, provides a remarkable example of how to turn a brand around. Even after motoring journalists began praising the improvements made in product design and engineering, sales hardly moved. The advertising was doing little to overcome brand prejudice and although drivers might have recognised that the product had improved, they would still not want to be seen driving a Skoda. It was further recognised that the pan-European approach that had been taken did not reflect the fact that the brand meant something different in each market.

Budget constraints

A reduced promotional budget compared to earlier launches made the task even more of a challenge when launching the new Fabia model. £4.5 million was half of the £9 million Toyota spent on launching the Yaris and little more than a third of the £17 million spent by Renault on relaunching the Clio.

A risky approach

There was little doubt that it would take something different to change consumer attitudes toward the brand not made easier by the low budget available. The Fallon advertising agency created a campaign with the strapline ' It's a Skoda. Honest'. This centred on reducing the gap between consumer expectations and reality using self-deprecating humour in seeking revaluation of the brand. Research of the concept proved positive.

Promotional mix

£2.85 million was spent on a TV campaign, supported by £600,000 spent on posters and £274,000 in colour press. PR was used to extend and amplify the message and further activity included retail staff training and high profile location product placement.

Measuring effectiveness

In addition to improving sales of most models and creating a waiting list for the new Fabia, significant changes in attitude toward the brand were achieved.

Before the campaign 54% of people agreed that Skodas were better than they were commonly perceived. This increased to 79% after the campaign. Only 20% said they could imagine themselves driving a Skoda before the campaign with this increasing to 33% after.

The success of the communications has prompted Skoda to seek further improvements by building their database and nurturing customers (who may currently be warming to the brand), closer to point of purchase.

This campaign won the Grand Prix in the CIM/Marketing Week Marketing Effectiveness Awards 2000.

From an article in *Marketing Business*, December/January 2001

---

4 Business-to-business communications strategies

4.1 Although the principles of marketing communications are the same for both consumer and industrial markets there are significant differences in the details of how promotion is carried out. In order to understand these differences it is valuable to look again at the major differences between industrial (or business) marketing and consumer marketing.

Major differences between industrial and consumer marketing

	Area	Industrial marketing	Consumer marketing
1	Purchase motivation	Multiple buying influences Support company operations	Individual or family need
2	Nature of demand	Derived or joint demand	Primary demand
3	Emphasis of seller	Economic needs	Immediate satisfaction
4	Customer needs	Each customer has different needs	Groups with similar needs
5	Nature of buyer	Group decisions	Purchase by individual or family unit
6	Time effects	Long term relationships	Short term relationships
7	Product details	Technically sophisticated	Lower technical content
8	Promotion decisions	Emphasis on personal selling	Emphasis on mass media advertising
9	Price decisions	Price determined before Terms are important	Price substantially fixed Discounts are important
10	Place decisions	Limited number of large buyers, short channels	Large number of small buyers Complex channels
11	Customer service	Critical to success	Less important
12	Legal factors	Contractual arrangements	Contracts only on major purchases
13	Environmental factors	Affect sales both directly and indirectly	Affect demand directly

Business decision-making process

4.2 Perhaps the most significant differences are the nature of the **buying motivation** and the linked nature of the **buying decision process**. In industrial buying there are many motivations. These stem partly from the technical use of the product but also from financial, security of supply and, to a lesser degree, emotional reasons. The decision-making unit can be equally multi-faceted.

Decision makers and buying motivation

	Decision makers	Buying motivation
1	Operations Manager	Uses the product in the organisation's processes - wants efficiency and effectiveness.
2	Technical Manager	Often has to test and approve the product – wants reliability.
3	The Managing Director	May approve major expenditure or change of supplier.
4	The Purchasing Manager	Approves conditions of purchase. Monitors supplier performance.
5	Legal Manager	Draws up or approves legal contracts with supplier.
6	Finance Manager	Approves expenditure and controls debt payment.
7	Health and Safety Manager	May have a role to play with hazardous supplies.

Implications for marketing communications strategy

4.3 It will be obvious that marketing communications strategy for industrial marketing must reflect this considerably more complex decision-making process.

Strategic importance

4.4 Business or industrial marketing can be regarded as involving more **strategic decisions** in its implementation. Consumer products, by definition, are mass market products often purchased in a routine and habitual manner. This is unlikely to be the case in industrial marketing. Business customers have differing needs and in some cases these needs may be conflicting within the organisation.

Impact of time

4.5 The **length of time** involved for the purchase evaluation and for the life of the product is much greater in industrial markets. Consumers often make buying decisions on the spur of the moment. Industrial buying decisions may take over a year. This then alters both the **type of marketing communications** and the **relationships** between the buying and selling organisations.

The buying organisation

4.6 Business buyers have several different methods of **organising purchasing**, and this can affect communication strategy. Some firms purchase on a highly centralised basis. This allows for maximum price advantage and negotiation strength because of economies of scale. Other organisations allow decentralised purchases, which leads to local needs being better met. In these cases, two different forms of selling organisation are needed and the communication strategy needed to reach the right person will be different in each case.

Variety of products and services

4.7 The variety of products in business markets is extremely large. Business products vary from product inputs to items for resale. They can be broken down into three main types.

- **Capital equipment** (major purchases of fixed assets)
- **Production inputs** (becoming part of the buyer's process)
- **Business supplies**/services (ongoing use by the buyer)

Again, each type of purchase will need a different communications strategy.

The business-to-business communications mix

4.8 The chart below shows the relative importance of differing elements of the promotional mix between consumer and industrial markets. These differences are reflected in developing marketing communication strategies for industrial markets.

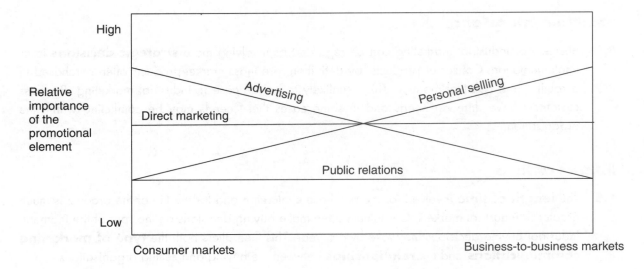

Relative importance of promotional elements

4.9 The clearest difference is the **importance of personal selling in industrial markets** because of the complexity of the decision-making process, the differing industrial needs and the higher value of individual purchases. Advertising, though still important in industrial marketing, is less so than for consumer marketing.

4.10 The diagram also shows that both **public relations** and **direct marketing** have important continuing roles in both consumer and industrial marketing. It is clear from the above list that the methods to communicate with industrial markets will be of a much greater variety than for consumer markets. This in turn means that industrial marketing decisions can be really challenging and the need for effective integrated marketing communications is important.

4.11 The range of promotional methods is described below.

Method	Comment
Personal selling	This is a major component of industrial marketing because of the need to deal with technical and other issues on a face-to-face basis.
Internal selling	Increasingly it is recognised that a salesperson has an internal role to play in representing his customers' needs to the company.
Advertising	A wide variety of publications exist which can be used to target individual market sectors including: (i)　　trade journals (ii)　　business press (iii)　　directories Advertising is used to create awareness, provide information, generate leads, assist channel members and sometimes to sell off the page.
Telemarketing	Telemarketing has been proved to be a very cost effective method of order processing, customer service, sales support and account management.

Method	Comment
Direct mailing	Direct mail, another form of direct marketing, has been used by industrial marketers for a long time but its use has substantially increased. It can be used to provide information and generate enquiries. It can be tailored to individual customer needs.
Public relations	Sometimes in industrial markets this is referred to as publicity. It often focuses on getting editorial coverage in appropriate magazines but it has a wider role of building customer relations.
Sales promotion	Sales promotion is an important area of communication in industrial markets. There are a wide range of methods that are of well established use in industrial campaigns. ■ Literature ■ Exhibitions ■ Videos ■ Discounting ■ Events ■ Business gifts ■ Trade shows Technical literature is clearly important in specifying the product. Complicated equipment can be captured on video and applications shown. Trade shows and exhibitions continue to grow in importance. Discounting and special price promotions are used extensively in industrial markets. Business gifts continue to have their value if not used excessively.

Integrated marketing communications

4.12 Finally, it should be stressed that the concept of Integrated Marketing Communications is equally, if not more, important in industrial marketing. This is because there is likely to be a more complex promotional mix and definitely a more complex audience. Consistent delivery of images on a limited budget is therefore important.

Summary of strategic implications

4.13 The **principles of industrial marketing communications are the same as for consumer marketing** but the strategies differ. The table below summarises some of the strategic implications.

Principle	Strategic implications
Purpose of industrial promotion	Builds up the company's image in the mind of the purchaser.
Communication objectives	Must be geared to specific business objectives.
Communication methods	Different balance than for consumer markets. Personal selling more important.
Choice of media	Important to determine the best media to reach the participants in a complex decision-making process.
Measuring effectiveness	Essential to measure the contribution of communications in achieving business objectives.

5 Marketing communications for service organisations

5.1 The promotion of goods and services have many similarities. We do not need to discriminate between the two when considering:

- The **role of promotion** in meeting marketing objectives
- The need to **design** effective promotions
- The **managerial challenge** of efficient implementation
- The broad **choice** of methods and media
- The **agencies** available to support promotion

5.2 **Promotional objectives** for services are related to those for products, as the following examples show.

- Build awareness and interest in the service and the service organisation
- Communicate and portray the benefits of the services available
- Build and maintain the overall image and reputation of the service organisation
- Advise customers of new channels
- Advise customers of special offers or modifications to the service
- Persuade customers to use or buy the service

5.3 In spite of these similarities there are significant differences caused by the special nature of services. Gronroos, a Swedish writer on service marketing, draws attention to some of the complexity in the diagram below demonstrating service relationships.

5.4 In service markets there are four **elements of the service** that need to be taken into account in planning.

- The **core service concept** and any auxiliary service.
- The **accessibility** of the service.
- The **interactive communications** that take place in delivering the service.
- The **influence of the consumer** and other consumers receiving the service.

5.5 Four promotional methods are then used to influence the customer.

- Traditional selling
- Advertising and direct marketing
- Public relations and sales promotions
- The communication aspects of pricing policy

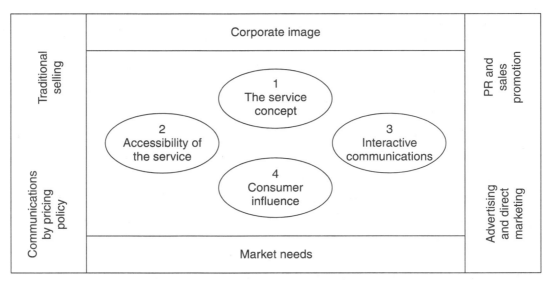

Model of service communications

5.6 There are differences in promotion necessitated by the characteristics of service industries and services companies.

Characteristics	Consequence
Lack of market orientation	Managers are untrained, unskilled and unaware of the role of promotion.
Professional and ethical constraints	Places limitations on certain promotion methods. Sometimes legal restrictions.
Small scale of many service organisations	Limits size of promotion budgets.
Nature of capacity available	Capacity for delivering the service may be limited. Promotion may produce too much demand.
Attitude to promotion methods	Limited knowledge of and attitude to wide range of promotion methods.
Nature of the service	Services may be very specific, which excludes mass advertising.
Consumer attitudes	Consumers may rely on subjective judgements made at the point of service delivery.
Buying process	The need to develop a professional relationship with the service provider makes customer care important.

Source: D Cowell, *The Marketing of Services*, 1989

5.7 These differences lead to a number of guidelines that must be considered when designing communication campaigns for service markets.

(a) Use **clear unambiguous messages** to communicate the range, depth, quality and level of services.

(b) **Emphasise the benefits of the services** rather than their technical details.

(c) **Only promise what can be delivered**, to avoid disappointment.

(d) **Advertise to employees**, as they are particularly important in many people-intensive services.

(e) Obtain **maximum customer co-operation** in the service production process as the service is often an interactive system.

(f) Build on **word of mouth communication** from one satisfied customer to another.

(g) Provide **tangible evidence to strengthen promotional messages**. Use well known personalities to support the messages.

(h) Develop **continuity in promotion** by the use of consistent and continuous symbols, themes, formats or images.

(i) **Remove post purchase anxiety** by reassuring the buyer of the soundness of choice, especially where there is no tangible product.

(j) **Personal selling** becomes more important in the promotion of services as the following table shows.

5.8 **Differences between selling goods and services** are shown below.

Issue	Comment
Customer's purchase perception of services	Customers view service as having less consistent quality ■ Service purchasers have higher risks ■ Service purchasing is less pleasant ■ When services are bought greater consideration is given to the particular salesperson ■ Perception of the service company is an important factor when deciding to buy a service
Customer's purchase behaviour with services	■ Customers may do fewer price comparisons with services ■ Customers give greater consideration to the particular seller of services ■ Customers are less likely to be influenced by advertising and more by personal recommendations
Personal selling of services	■ Customer involvement is greater ■ Customer satisfaction is influenced by the salesperson's personality and attitude ■ Salespeople may have to spend more time reducing customer uncertainty

6 Marketing communications for non profit organisations
6/02

6.1 The major principles of marketing communications for non profit organisations are the same as for consumer and industrial marketing. There are, however, **considerable differences of emphasis**. The **sum of money** available for organised communication may be less. **Public scrutiny** of policies may be higher.

Marketing at Work

In the face of a severe shortfall in revenue (due to wildly optimistic forecast visitor numbers) the amount of grant funding to the New Millennium Experience Company rocketed to £628 million. Sir John Bourne of the National Audit Office said in a report:

> "Building and opening the Millennium Dome on the very short timescale required was a tremendous achievement. But the New Millennium Experience Company has experienced severe financial difficulties this year and has required considerable additional lottery funding.
>
> The main cause of these difficulties is the failure to achieve the visitor numbers and income required. The targets were highly ambitious and inherently risky leading to a significant degree of financial exposure on the project. In addition, the task of managing the project has been complicated by the complex organisational arrangements put in place from the outset, and by the failure to establish sufficiently robust financial management."

What went wrong? The whole issue illustrated the need for proper marketing communications planning. Strong negative word-of-mouth also had an impact. The following general points should have been considered.

■ Promotional strategies to attract visitors (pull strategy), communicate with those issuing tickets (push strategy), and promote the image of the 'Dome' and that of the Millennium Experience Company (Profile Strategy), should have been fully integrated.

■ Messages should have been adapted to the various audiences.

■ Promotional strategies should have taken into account financial constraints imposed by the fact that this was funded in the main through public money. Sales were likely to fall short of targets if insufficient money and time was invested in marketing.

Adapted from CIM material

6.2 Almost certainly there will be a different set of communication objectives.

■ Making target customers **aware** of a product, service or social behaviour
■ **Educating** consumers about the offer or changes in the offer
■ **Changing beliefs** about negative and positive consequences of taking a particular action
■ **Changing the relative importance** of particular consequences
■ Enlisting the **support** of a variety of individuals
■ Recruiting, motivating or rewarding **employees or volunteers**
■ Changing **perceptions** about the sponsoring organisation
■ Influencing **government bodies**
■ Preventing the **discontinuity** of support
■ **Proving benefits** over 'competitors'
■ **Combating** injurious rumours
■ **Influencing** funding agencies

6.3 Once the non profit marketer has developed the broad objectives for the communications plan the next step is to decide specific messages. These messages may be developed within one of the three frameworks.

(a) **Rational, emotional and moral framework**

(i) Rational messages pass on information and serve the audience's self interest. For example messages about value, economy or benefits.

(ii) Emotional messages are designed to develop emotion to shape the desired behaviour. For example with fear, guilt, shame appeals to stop doing things like smoking, drinking, taking drugs or overeating.

(iii) Moral messages directed at the audience's sense of right or wrong. For example, to support a cleaner environment or equal rights or help the under-privileged.

(b) **Reward and situation framework**

(i) There may be four types of reward: rational, sensory, social or ego satisfaction rewards.

(ii) Rewards may result directly from use, or indirectly from the products in use, or be incidental to use. For example, think about the various rewards offered by cars with catalytic converters.

(c) **Attitude change framework**

(i) Changes in the importance of one or more outcomes
(ii) Changes in the beliefs about one or more outcomes
(iii) Adding new positive outcomes

6.4 Having decided what messages to transmit it is then necessary to decide the style of promotional execution. The following styles are appropriate for consumer goods advertising but can easily be adopted for non profit organisations.

6.5 Example: health education

Styles	Execution
Slice of life	Family doing healthy activities throughout the day
Life style	Father and daughter off jogging early in morning
Fantasy	Dream of winning a marathon
Mood	Exercises in a field of wild flowers
Musical	Exercises to modern music
Personalities	Using a well known successful sports personality
Technical expertise	Quoting performance capability in exercises
Scientific evidence	Showing the benefits of less illness and greater longevity
Testimonial evidence	Members of the public give views on benefits

6.6 How marketers of non profit organisations can reach target audiences.

Method	Comment
Paid advertising	Non profit organisations may have limited funds but this can still be an effective route even on low budgets, as the Save the Children Fund campaign showed. Alternatively the budget may be boosted by obtaining commercial sponsorship.
Unpaid (public service) advertising	Media owners may provide airtime or press space on a free of charge basis as a public service. However, there is little control over this and the times or spaces may occur at unpopular times or places.

Method	Comment
Sales promotions	Short term incentives to encourage purchases or donations. Market control is strong and promotions are often newsworthy (for example Red Nose day or Poppy day promotions).
Public relations	Many of the stories of non profit organisations are of considerable interest. They may feature in the press or the broadcast media. Control over the message is good and feedback is possible.
Personal selling and communications	Staff at all levels of the non profit organisations should be trained in personal communications. They will often have the opportunity to 'sell' to their supporters and possible benefactors.

6.7 **Categories of non profit communications** include the following.

- Political party communications
- Social cause communications
- Charitable communications
- Government communications
- Religious communications
- Professional body communications
- Other private non profit communications (hospitals, universities, museums and so on)

Direct marketing

6.8 This is a medium increasingly being used by non profit organisations, particularly arts foundations and charities. It has seven important **advantages for non profit marketers**.

(a) It can be very focused for maximum effect on the target market.

(b) It can be private and confidential. This is especially important when dealing with sensitive issues.

(c) There is less direct regulation on direct mail promotions. In the past charitable advertising in the broadcast media has been limited.

(d) Cost per contact and cost per response is low and controllable, which is important where funds have to be used wisely.

(e) Results are clearly measurable and can make the programmers more accountable.

(f) Small scale tests of proposed strategies are feasible.

(g) The effectiveness of direct marketing can be assessed in terms of behaviour (ie orders, donations, requests for membership).

Behaviour channels

6.9 Non profit campaigns often call for **behavioural changes** on the part of the target audience. It is for this reason that it is valuable to monitor the effectiveness of such a campaign using a modification of the hierarchy of effects model. The model shown below has been adapted for a campaign to encourage the use of contraceptives to aid family planning.

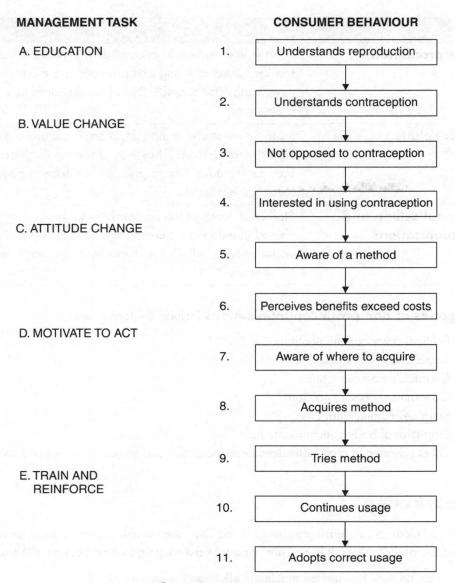

MANAGEMENT TASK

A. EDUCATION

B. VALUE CHANGE

C. ATTITUDE CHANGE

D. MOTIVATE TO ACT

E. TRAIN AND
   REINFORCE

CONSUMER BEHAVIOUR

1. Understands reproduction
2. Understands contraception
3. Not opposed to contraception
4. Interested in using contraception
5. Aware of a method
6. Perceives benefits exceed costs
7. Aware of where to acquire
8. Acquires method
9. Tries method
10. Continues usage
11. Adopts correct usage

*Contraceptive campaign
social behaviour change model*

Source: Kotler and Anderson
Strategic Marketing for Non profit Organisations (Prentice Hall, 1987)

Marketing at Work

Campaign Title: NSPCC - Full Stop

Context

Business

1   The NSPCC set up a five vision programme to tackle the problem of child abuse, head on. This programme sought to:

- Set up an investigative service to run in parallel with the police
- Promote quality parenting
- Work with schools and teacher training colleges
- Develop children-friendly communities
- Work for cultural and legislative change

External

An independent national commission of enquiry (1995) had reported that 'child abuse and neglect can almost always be prevented, provided the will to do so is there'.

Organisational

- The financial resources necessary to implement the five visions were limited.
- There was a strong culture and drive to be successful

Customer

- Giving fatigue, NSPCC fatigue
- Suspicion concerning raising the standard of parenting
- Attitudes - scepticism at the charity's ambition to abolish child abuse/cruelty
- Abuse is universally condemned but people feel helpless ... they don't know what to do and they don't think it goes on near them

Stakeholder

Organisations willing to be associated with cause related issues which equate to sponsorship and assistance with fund raising.

Promotional objectives

The aim was to hit every household in the UK.

- Corporate: to end child abuse
- Marketing: to raise £250 million in 12 months - donated or pledged (normal amount £50m)
- Communication: to raise awareness of child cruelty
  to persuade people to become involved with the cause

Promotional strategy

(a)   Strong pull campaign designed to raise awareness of child cruelty. Campaign to be delivered in two main steps. The first to develop awareness and the second step to be action orientated.

(b)   In parallel there should be a strategy designed to communicate with businesses in order to generate funds, goodwill and support.

(c)   The overall profile of the organisation (NSPCC) shall be raised and communications need to ensure that the integrity of the organisation and those associated with it are maintained. In addition, all communications need to be consistent.

Promotional Mix used to create a dialogue with the Public

- Public Relations
- TV, Posters
- Field Marketing
- Direct Marketing: Direct Mail, Telemarketing
- Website

First phase

Public relations were used at the initial stages of the campaign to help create awareness. Public address systems at railway stations and airports were used as a reminder mechanism.

A national TV campaign, supported by posters, broke soon after the public relations in order to raise awareness and provoke the question within each individual, 'what can I do?'. The message strategy was very emotional and used strong imagery to create shock and attention.

The heavy TV campaign looked to generate 600 TVRs, 85% coverage at 7.1 OTSs.

The supporting poster campaign used 48 sheets on 3,500 sites designed to deliver 55% coverage with 21 OTSs.

Initial enquiries to this wave of communications were heralded by an automated telemarketing bureau.

Second phase

This initial approach was followed up by a 23 million nationwide doordrop campaign. The aim was to provide the public with an answer to the question that the advertising had provoked, namely, to sign the pledge and/or volunteer as a donor or fundraiser.

The envelope picked up the TV creative treatment, repeating as a subdued background motif the image of nursery wallpaper with a teddy bear covering its eyes with its paws. 'Don't close your eyes to cruelty to children'.

It was thought that the doordrop letter addressed as 'Dear Householder' might offend established donors. To avoid this, 160,000 best donors were sent an early warning letter in advance of the campaign breaking in order to get their support. Another million received personal letters just ahead of the doordrop.

It was anticipated that the bulk of enquiries would come from the doordrop action and these were to be handled through personal telemarketing responses (inbound). The web site was also adapted in order that it would be able to accept pledges.

In addition to this the campaign utilised a call-to-action weekend with volunteers staffing 2,000 sites around the country, including most city centres, to remind and raise cash donations.

Promotional mix used to communicate with businesses

- Sponsorship
- Direct Mail/Information Pack
- Internet

Sponsorship deals were made available enabling businesses to align themselves more closely with the campaign. Microsoft have been closely involved with NSPCC for a number of years and they acted as prime movers encouraging other businesses to pledge their support. The advertising for the campaign was sponsored by Microsoft.

Other sponsorship and cause related marketing packages were detailed in a Toolkit distributed to other major organisations.

Direct Mail was also used to encourage businesses to make donations and electronic communications were used to promote pledges on-line.

(Source: Adapted from Goften K (1999) NSPCC aims to convert abuse anger into cash, *Marketing*)

This campaign sought to deal with an issue that most people choose to ignore. The ambitious targets needed an extraordinary marketing communications campaign if it was to be successful. The co-ordinated promotional plan enabled a simple yet hard hitting message to be conveyed to a substantial part of the nation.

It should be remembered that without knowing the budgets made available to fund the campaign and the extent of the contribution made by the business-to-business sector, it is doubtful whether a return on the investment will be made known outside of the charity. However, this should not detract from what is a major contribution to the social and moral welfare of the nation, made possible through astute use of an integrated marketing communications campaign.

7 Marketing communications for small businesses

Action Programme 5

Devise a marketing communications strategy and programme for a small business of your choice. Describe the advantages and disadvantages of such a low budget campaign.

7.1 A glance through the many books on small business management and especially those claiming to reveal the secrets of successful **low budget advertising** will show that readers are given watered down versions of the conventional promotional principles. This again demonstrates that these principles are of uniform application and this is reassuring.

7.2 However, there must be differences between small companies and large companies besides the sizes of the campaign budgets. The overriding differences are of course the **limited resources** in designing and implementing a communications programme and also the matching limitations in the target audience. The implications of these limitations and other aspects are discussed below.

Do-it-yourself

7.3 The key to saving money is to carry out many of the tasks yourself. This will mean learning about the principles and methods of marketing communications. This in itself is a valuable exercise. You can use desk top publishing to design advertising material and local media owners will be only too happy to deal directly with you.

Small agencies

7.4 If you do need professional help there are many one person and small agencies able to offer a package of promotional help on a cost effective basis. Such agencies are keen to help small businesses grow because this is the best way of growing themselves.

Marketing research

7.5 To reduce risks, improve targeting and to get to know your customer's needs and competition better it is important to conduct marketing research yourself. Many small business people rely a great deal on intuition and may be reluctant to conduct research, but it will repay many times the effort devoted to it.

Personal selling

7.6 The owner manager of a small business will also usually be one of the company's main salesmen. This is another way of maintaining a low cost and cost effective marketing budget.

Public relations

7.7 This promotional method does not need substantial sums to get started. Simple press releases can be issued, opening events can be held and even a limited local sponsorship can be done for little expenditure. Again this will often mean doing it yourself or using a small local PR agency.

Direct marketing

7.8 Using direct marketing techniques, either telemarketing or direct mail, can be done cost effectively at local level. The volume of direct marketing activity can be regulated by the amount of time you have available and by the number of customers you are trying to reach.

Door drops

7.9 An alternative method of getting to households is to arrange for door to door leaflet distribution in your chosen target area. This can be considerably cheaper than incurring postal charges. It is also accurate in that particular districts and types of houses can be targeted.

Advertising

7.10 With the expansion of local media including free newspapers and local commercial radio stations, it is possible to tailor your campaign to particular locations. Designing advertising and buying media space or airtime, however, can become quite expensive, especially for frequently repeated advertisements.

Sales promotions

7.11 Using your imagination it is possible to devise a whole range of cost effective sales promotions, which will have the benefit of generating immediate sales and improving your cash flow.

Rapid feedback

7.12 All these methods then can be tried and evaluated at relatively low cost with the added value of a rapid feedback of results that will enable an improved campaign to be developed and implemented.

7.13 The **characteristics specific to low budget campaigns** are summarised below.

Feature	Comment
Do it yourself	Planning, implementation and control
Small agencies	Matching your size
Marketing research	Will reduce risk
Personal selling	Likely to be the main method
Public relations	Can be done at low cost
Direct marketing	Cost effective by telephone and mail
Drop drops	Very low cost targeting
Advertising	Likely to be more expensive
Sales promotion	Immediate benefits to cash flow
Rapid feedback	Allowing for improvements to be made

8 Communications in the 21st century

8.1 Consumers are being overloaded with commercial and non-commercial communications. The growth in marketing communications may not be the worst threat but the sheer **amount** of communication will be. Even now consumers are being supplied with 30 times more information than they process. The difference is still growing with the following far-reaching consequences.

(a) Consumers will be increasingly **selective** in what receives their attention; they will avoid more and more communications which they do not consider interesting or relevant.

(b) They have increasingly **less attention for communication:** they break off contact sooner in order to switch their attention to the next item.

(c) They may process communication at **a shallower, more superficial** level.

(d) They are starting to consume **more pictures at the expense of words**.

8.2 These developments have considerable communication consequences. It is becoming more difficult to reach people and to gain and retain their undivided attention. People are also becoming more cynical about the content of communication.

Action Programme 6

In view of communication overload, what would you recommend as a future marketing communications strategy for your own organisation or for an organisation of your choice?

Chapter Roundup

- This chapter includes case studies of successful campaigns.

- **Industrial marketing communications** strategies can be very different from consumer campaigns. There are differences in such areas as purchase motivation, customer needs, product specifications, level of customer service needed and so on. This calls for different approaches in employing the various promotional tools.

- **The marketing of services** is similar to the marketing of products in many ways, but there can be differences because of such factors as **professional and legal constraints**, the nature of capacity available, and the buying process itself. Personal selling is more important.

- In **non profit marketing communications** there is likely to be less money available, messages are likely to be subjected to greater scrutiny and the objectives of the communication will be quite different from those applying in consumer marketing. The major categories of non profit communicators are political parties, social causes, the government, religious bodies and professional bodies.

- The main feature of marketing communications for **small businesses** is that **resources are limited**. This will mean that more is done in-house and at a local level, though all the usual promotional tools can still be employed.

- In attempting to understand the impact of communications it is important realise that every variable interacts with other variables and cause and effect cannot easily be distinguished. Effective communications are those that increase brand **awareness**, stimulate **trial purchase** and **reinforce** brand loyalty. The amount of communication to which people are now being subjected means that it is becoming increasingly difficult to communicate successfully.

Now try Question 13 at the end of the Study Text

Quick Quiz

1   Describe the principles which are valuable in assessing the effectiveness of communication

2   What is the purpose of the Advertising Effectiveness Awards? (3.1)

3   Name the major differences between industrial and consumer marketing. (4.1)

4   Draw the Gronroos model showing service communications. (5.5)

5   What are the characteristics of the promotion of services? (5.6)

6   What are the differences in selling goods and services? (5.7)

7   Describe some communication objectives of non profit organisations. (6.1)

8   What are the different types of non-profit organisation? (6.7)

9   Why is direct marketing particularly suitable for non-profit organisations? (6.8)

10 What are the features of low budget campaigns? (7.13)

Action Programme Review

1   (i)   Size of business, market sector, FMCG/business-to-business/service/not for profit.

    (ii) These factors and issues should be based on result of context analysis – business, customer, stakeholder, internal and external.

    (iii) Communications objectives should focus on changes in awareness, attitudes and behaviour. These should relate to marketing and business objectives.

    (iv) Pull, push and profile are the main communications strategies available – what communications tools have you identified for each strategy?

    (v)   If you have identified sales or market share, remember the difficulty of direct association with communications due to other marketing factor effects. You should be measuring the effectiveness against the objectives set.

2   The market has changed significantly since BT won this award back in 1996. BT face stiff competition from cable operators for domestic business, but more importantly from the mobile network companies. Most of these companies use heavyweight pull strategies based on advertising and sponsorship. The mobile networks also employ push strategies with handset manufacturers such as Nokia, Motorola and Ericsson. Offers include 'free' handsets for taking out service contracts with the respective network company.

    BT have focused a lot of their efforts on attempts to persuade customers not to switch to alternative suppliers and for those who have switched, to return to BT.

3   Depending on which sector you have chosen to look at, you will have identified a range of different kinds of communications strategies and tactics employed. A lot of emphasis is usually placed on developing brand images via pull activities. However there is a lot of activity at the point of purchase, whether this be a supermarket, off licence, pub, bar or club. The latter outlets have undergone significant changes themselves in recent times with new types of bars being opened in town and city centres based on different themes. They provide different opportunities for drinks companies of all types to promote their brands.

    New drinks sectors have been created and account for a large share of communications activity. Ready to drink, bottled products, such as Bacardi Breezer and Smirnoff Ice have become popular with young – 18-24 – drinkers.

4   You should have identified integrating factors relating to different levels of strategy – business, marketing and communication – all linked via the objectives set. It is not just a question of using the same strapline or visual image on all of the communication, but also as to how the overall communications activities relate to what the business as a whole is attempting to achieve. Remember that internal communications play an important role in achieving integration and the relevance of push and profile strategies.

5   Your answer should have looked at the advantages and disadvantages of different strategic options viz. push, pull and profile. The communications tools should be specific to the strategy or strategies selected.

6   Much more attention is being paid to communications at an individual level via customer relationship marketing programmes. This is evident in all sectors as companies can have millions of customers in a global market. This is being made possible by improvements in technology. Remember however that in many developing countries use of mail, television and telephone is still limited. It will be some time before all individuals have access to the Internet, even in developed markets.

It is not now unusual for consumers to be very selective about those companies with whom they wish to communicate and do business. This concept of 'permission marketing' could provide a platform for future communications strategies.

Part G

Cross Border Communications

Key Issues in Marketing Communications Across Borders

14

Chapter Topic List	
1	Setting the scene
2	Cross border marketing communications
3	Cultural considerations
4	Media considerations
5	Legal considerations
6	Standardisation vs adaptation
7	International communications alternatives
8	Multinational communications agencies

Learning Outcome

☑ Be appreciative and sensitive to issues associated with cross-border marketing communications

Syllabus References

☑ Cultural, social and media influences

☑ Organisational type and communication approaches

☑ The adaptation/standardisation debate

Key Concept Introduced

■ Culture

1 Setting the scene

1.1 In this book we are restricted to one chapter on this topic, and so we are really only scratching the surface of the complexity behind international marketing communications. This chapter begins by addressing the key question posed by the syllabus: to globalise or not to globalise? Then we go on to discuss various aspects of national differences.

Links with other papers

1.2 Your knowledge of the international scene will be supplemented by study for another Diploma subject, *International Marketing Strategy*.

2 Cross border marketing communications

A global village?

2.1 As far back as 1983, Levitt argued that consumers the world over were converging in tastes and that the globalisation of markets was at hand. Levitt saw the emerging global village as presenting a huge opportunity for multinational companies to standardise products and attract large numbers of consumers through low costs brought about by economies of scale.

2.2 **Factors contributing towards the globalisation of markets** include the following.

    (a)   More **sophisticated consumers** who holiday outside their home country and are willing to experiment with non domestic products and services.

    (b)   The trend towards **elimination of political, trade and travel barriers** worldwide.

    (c)   The **internationalisation of broadcast and print media** (for example, cross border satellite transmission means consumers receive common programming).

    (d)   The **saturation of domestic markets**, leading companies to search for growth for their goods and services in new markets.

Vive la difference?

2.3 Levitt's globalisation argument has been criticised for adopting a production rather than a marketing orientation. **Standardisation may suit companies, but may not be what consumers are seeking**. An alternative view is that **consumer markets are fragmenting rather than converging**. Consumers are seeking to express themselves as individuals and do not want to be treated as part of a homogeneous mass. Products and services should therefore be **adapted** to individual country markets.

2.4 These two conflicting opinions provide a starting point for any consideration of international marketing management.

    (a)   It is unlikely that the majority of companies competing outside their own home market will be able to standardise their marketing mix completely.

    (b)   Nor is it likely that they will choose to adapt their marketing mix totally for each country in which they operate.

(c)   The nature of the product or service, consumer buyer behaviour and competitive market environment will all dictate the appropriate strategy to adopt.

Marketing at Work

Consumers in India are acutely price sensitive. They will think nothing of spending an entire morning scouting around to save five rupees. As a result, India has the largest 'used goods' market in the world. Most washing machines in the Punjab are used to churn butter, and the average washing machine (conventionally deployed) is over 19 years old.

"What many foreign investors don't understand is that the Indian consumer is not choosing between one soft drink and another; he's choosing between a soft drink and a packet of biscuits or a disposable razor" says Suhel Seth of Equus Red Cell, an advertising company.

What this means for foreign investors is that they must price cheaply, and therefore source almost everything locally, to keep costs down.

There are other problems. Standard refrigeration becomes pretty useless when acute power shortages occur. Most consumable goods perish pretty quickly in the climate. And the country's fragmented regional culture means advertisers have to focus on common ground (such as music, Bollywood and cricket).

Is it worth the effort? Investors say that overcoming such obstacles has equipped them for success in any market in the world.

Adapted from the *Financial Times*, April 2002

3   Cultural considerations

Key Concept

Culture is a term used to describe the set of values, beliefs, norms and artefacts held in common by a social group.

3.1   Companies operating outside their home markets have to be aware of the implications of **cultural differences** for all aspects of the marketing mix. Marketing communicators need to be particularly sensitive to culture if messages are to work in global markets.

3.2   We absorb the culture of our home society as we grow up. Our family, our religious institutions, and our education system all play a part in passing culture from one generation to the next. Some behaviours and customs learned early in life are likely to remain resistant to the best marketing or promotional efforts. For instance, attitudes and behaviour with respect to particular foodstuffs can be culturally ingrained.

3.3   Culture evolves. Although core cultural precepts are passed from one generation to the next, the values of society do change. Before the second world war, a 'marriage bar' existed in white collar occupations such as clerical work and teaching. When a single working woman married, she was expected to give up her job to look after her husband. This social norm seems inconceivable to us today.

3.4 Various dimensions of culture are relevant to the international marketing communicator

- Verbal and non verbal communications
- Aesthetics
- Dress and appearance
- Family roles and relationships
- Beliefs and values
- Learning
- Work habits

Verbal and non verbal communication

3.5 Common-sense dictates that care must be taken when **translating copy** from one language to another. A catchy phrase in the home market may not work so well elsewhere. A literal translation of an advertising slogan, 'as American as apple pie' would be meaningless in many countries.

3.6 Usually, agencies will aim to interpret and adapt in order to capture the spirit of a communication message, rather than relying on a mechanical word for word translation.

3.7 Most agencies will buy in the services of a translation house when required. This will usually ensure that translation is carried out by someone who speaks the vernacular language of the country in question, an important point given that languages are in constant evolution. If an agency subsidiary or local company office exists in the overseas market, it can also be helpful to incorporate their advice. Back translation, where the copy is translated back into English, can be a final precaution.

3.8 It may be difficult to decide exactly which language to choose for translation purposes. The official language of China is Mandarin, but a large proportion of Chinese living in the south of the country have Cantonese as their native tongue. In Canada, although the majority of the population speak English, packaging must include a French translation.

3.9 An additional consideration is that of the **space required for foreign language text**.

3.10 Brand and product names must be assessed for their suitability in international markets. Mars changed the name of their Marathon chocolate bar to Snickers in 1990 to facilitate their global communications strategy. A different approach is demonstrated by companies who choose to go with different names in different markets. For instance Ford's Mondeo name works well in European markets, where the 'world' association comes across powerfully. In the US market however, the car is called the Contour.

3.11 Sometimes the phonetic sound of names can cause a problem. The French soft drink Pschitt would have obvious disadvantages in the English-speaking world.

3.12 People communicate both by using language and by their use of **non verbal signals**. A shake of the head to British people, means no and a nod yes. This convention is reversed in some cultures.

3.13 Spatial zones can communicate. In Western societies, we give work colleagues or acquaintances a large zone of personal space. Only family and close friends will enter an individual's near zone. If a colleague comes too close, our reaction is to back off, as our personal space is being invaded. This is not so in some Far Eastern countries, where space is at a premium and people have far less privacy. There, it is acceptable to stand far closer to others.

Aesthetics

3.14 Attitudes towards different design and colour aesthetics vary around the world. A fragrance or toiletries carton decorated with chrysanthemum flower graphics would not be a success in France, where the flowers are traditionally associated with funerals. Similarly, the colour white, which carries connotations of freshness, purity and fragility in the UK is the colour of mourning in China.

3.15 Different cultures will have grown up with their own rules about visual representation. The idea of showing a figure partially out of frame is well known in Europe. In much of Africa by contrast, figures that go over the edge of their frame transgress the cultural rule about how pictures should look.

Dress and appearance

3.16 Dress, be it formal or social, is very much constrained by culture. Advertisers need to be aware of cultural dress codes when deciding if an execution prepared in one market will be acceptable in another. In Europe, for instance, adverts for shower and bath products will often depict a semi-nude model. Such executions would be out of the question in the Middle East where women can only appear in advertisements if carefully attired.

Family roles and relationships

3.17 Family has always been the dominant agent for transmitting culture. However, it may be that family influences are on the decline, at least in Westernised societies. It is now the norm to talk about the nuclear family, geographically isolated from grandparents and other relatives. Single parent families are also on the increase. This contrasts with many third world countries, where the extended family lives in a tight knit community.

3.18 Family roles can differ greatly from country to country. Recent television adverts in the UK have shown fathers shopping in the supermarket with their children (Bisto); fathers washing children's clothes while their wives are out (washing powder commercial); and men cooking happily in the kitchen (Sainsbury's). In countries with more rigid gender codes, these executions might be either absurd or offensive.

Beliefs and values

3.19 Beliefs and values evolve from religious teachings, family structures and the pattern and nature of economic development in that society. In our culture, material well being is important, people tend to be defined (and define themselves) by their work roles, individualism and equal opportunities are held dear and time is a precious commodity. Different cultures may put a different emphasis on these values. Any communications imagery designed to be used internationally should therefore be scanned for **underlying values or beliefs that are culture specific**.

Learning

3.20 The level of education within a culture is an important factor for the international marketing communicator. Low **literacy levels** will mean that verbal methods of communication take precedence. Press advertising and direct marketing may have to be ruled out. Packaging may need to be simplified, and point of sale and sales promotion techniques handled with care.

3.21 In some societies, education emphasises the value of rote learning. In others, critical thinking is encouraged. This may affect the way in which information is transmitted within a market.

Work habits

3.22 Not all societies conform to the Monday to Friday, 9.00am till 5.00pm work routine. In Hong Kong, the working week extends until Saturday lunchtime. In some parts of South Europe, it is usual to work from very early in the morning until early afternoon. Workers then go home for a siesta.

Advertising culture

3.23 It has been suggested that in addition to being sensitive to a country's culture in general, **marketers should be aware of the level of a country's advertising literacy**. She argues that advertising in any national culture develops in a predictable way, and according to its position on this development curve, it can be described as having either high or low advertising literacy. Thus, imported advertising can be inappropriate because the advertising of country A is at a different stage of development from that of country B.

3.24 Five levels of advertising development

Level	Comment
Least sophisticated	The emphasis is on the **manufacturer's description** of the product. Messages are factual and rational with much repetition. Product or pack shots take prominence.
Unsophisticated	Consumer choice is acknowledged so emphasis switches to the **product's superiority** over the competition (eg products that wash whiter, feel softer).
Mid point	**Consumer benefits are emphasised**, rather than product attributes. Executional devices may include the use of celebrity endorsements or role models may give demonstrations, for example a dentist endorsing toothpaste products.
More sophisticated	Brands and their attributes are well known, so need only **passing references** (perhaps by way of a brief pack shot or logo). The message is communicated by way of **lifestyle narrative** (eg Gold Blend couple; Bisto family).

Level	Comment
Most sophisticated level	The **focus is on the advertising** itself. The brand is referred to only obliquely, perhaps at a symbolic level (eg Silk Cut; Benson & Hedges). Consumers are believed to have a **mature understanding of advertising**, and are able to think laterally in order to decode messages.

Action Programme 1

Choose a country which is quite dissimilar to your own. You could perhaps choose somewhere that you have visited on holiday, or that a friend, relative or colleague has visited and told you about. Using the headings listed in paragraph 3.4, compile a list of similarities and differences between the culture of the foreign country and that of your own.

Ideally, this should be conducted as a class exercise, so that you can pool your experiences.

4 Media considerations

Exam Tip

Media is a complex, highly specialised area within marketing communications. International media is even more of a minefield and therefore the CIM does not expect Diploma students to have expert knowledge within this field. **What can be expected however, is a grasp of the factors influencing media choice in overseas markets,** and some understanding of the practical problems which may be experienced when planning the use of media.

4.1 The UK is a media rich country which offers a great variety of choice to the advertiser. Press is a well segmented sector with over 6,000 consumer and trade and technical magazines, as well as the national and regional newspaper titles. Commercial television now includes terrestrial and satellite channels. Radio as a sector is strengthening, with both local and national stations. Cinema and outdoor are mature mediums.

4.2 This diversity is not always mirrored in overseas markets. **Media availability can vary greatly from country to country**.

4.3 Trying to gain a perspective on the international media scene is a frustrating task. Different sources give conflicting information because of different definitions and different methods of data collection that have been used. Any facts that are collected tend to become dated very quickly because of the dynamic nature of the media sector. Whatever information is gained from secondary sources will always need to be double checked for accuracy in the home market itself.

Press

4.4   The first point to check when contemplating press as a media option, is the **literacy levels prevailing within the country**. The majority of European nations have literacy rates of 98% or 99%.

4.5   In the UK, there are a large number of **national newspaper** alternatives (24 at the last count). Although some countries are similarly well served with national papers from which to choose (eg Germany, Finland), others have more of a tradition of reading strong daily regional papers.

4.6   The UK has one of the world's largest **trade and technical press sectors**, with business-to-business advertisers being particularly fortunate in the choice available to them. A strong trade press sector however, tends to go hand in hand with a strong economic industrial base. Less developed nations may have few, if any, trade media vehicles.

4.7   It is wise to preview any candidate title before going ahead with a decision to include it on the media schedule. This will help in gaining an understanding of the editorial stance of the publication and give an impression about the calibre of the competitive advertising. It also allows the intending advertiser a chance to gauge the quality of media reproduction.

4.8   There is some debate about whether truly **international press options** exist. Serious business journals such as *Time*, *Newsweek*, and the *Economist* are widely available, as are women's titles with different national editions (eg *Marie Claire*, *Cosmopolitan*, *Elle*). General interest magazines such as *Reader's Digest* and in-flight magazines reach many markets. However, such publications are likely to be read by only a niche business and professional or lifestyle group. To reach the less wealthy, less well travelled wider population, other local media will have to be accessed.

Action Programme 2

In Germany, where more advertising money is spent in magazines than in any country other than in the USA, the main classifications are supplements, 'ad mags', consumer magazines, customer magazines, and trade and technical journals. Supplements are loose inserts in newspapers or periodicals with a magazine format and with many pages printed in four-colour. The principal types are programme, quality, special topic, and trade and technical. Programme supplements, the most widely read, are published once a week and carried in daily newspapers. Editorial content is largely concentrated on previews of radio and television programmes. Quality supplements are found in some of the major newspapers and are largely read by males in managerial and professional positions. Special topic supplements come out at irregular intervals with various carriers. Trade and technical supplements focus on topics of interest to readers of the specialised journals in which the supplements are placed.

Imagine you are a media buyer and have, say, six different products or services that you want to advertise in German magazines. What products/services would you place where?

Television

4.9 Before TV can be included on the media options list, two important questions need to be answered.

- How extensive is television ownership?
- Do commercial stations exist?

4.10 In the UK, 98% of households have a television. In India, by comparison, television ownership is low, as purchase of the cheapest set is beyond the means of the majority. However, television watching may be a group activity and so while **ownership** is low, **reach** might be higher.

4.11 The opportunities for television advertisers seem overwhelming in Italy, where there are 15 licensed national TV channels and several hundred local TV stations. Advertisers face a different sort of problem in Norway. The first terrestrial commercial channel started broadcasting in September 1992. Before that date, the only television advertising seen by Norwegians was on satellite stations.

4.12 Satellite television is perceived to offer good opportunities for reaching wide audiences across national boundaries. MTV, the pan-European music station, targets 16 - 34 year olds and is received in 27 different countries.

Outdoor

4.13 The UK lags behind many European countries in its use of posters as an advertising medium. Outdoor offers a good opportunity to communicate to international target groups, as copy tends to be minimal and visuals are key.

Cinema

4.14 Cinema may not always be experienced in the same way around the world. In some countries, cinema is viewed in outdoor theatres. There can also be dramatic variations in the quality of the films which are screened. Both these factors may affect how advertising is received by cinema goers.

Radio

4.15 While the cost of purchasing a television set is prohibitive in some nations, radio ownership seems to be ubiquitous around the world. In most countries, radio plays the role of support medium.

Media planning and buying

4.16 As well as the usual media planning considerations (campaign objectives, target markets, media availability, budgets), there may be specific factors which need to be taken into account when planning in international markets. For a food product, media scheduling will need to take account of climatic and seasonal characteristics of individual countries.

4.17 Some international print media may be purchased from the home country market via international media representatives. Other media may have to be bought by a local country agent, acting for the advertiser.

4.18 Media buying practices can vary from country to country. In the UK, published ratecard costs tend to be negotiable downwards. Other countries may be less flexible in negotiations.

Marketing at Work

MTV

MTV potentially faces strong competition from the BBC and Virgin since the launch of digital television. It needs to reinforce its position by raising awareness, but this is a problem because audience perceptions of MTV vary widely across Europe.

MTV's Europe Music Awards ceremony was targeted mainly at the Netherlands, Switzerland and the UK, but research indicated that it needed to adopt different approaches in each country.

(a) In the UK its tactic was to highlight how many superstars were coming to the awards and play up the competitive aspect. One poster showed stars like George Michael and Bryan Adams; another featured rival Britpop acts Oasis and Pulp.

(b) In the Netherlands young people like to see MTV as a reassuringly familiar part of their lives. The marketing had a softer more subdued feel, and consists of magazine ads with soft images of domestic situations.

(c) In Sweden MTV's viewers tend to be more politically disaffected and an anti-establishment image is more appealing. The campaign focused on newspaper ads consisting of replica newspaper pages with graffiti style slogans such as 'Join Our Party'. MTV also placed Join Our Party toilet rolls in the toilets of bars and nightclubs, to achieve the desired subversive effect.

5 Legal considerations

5.1 Laws and regulations governing marketing communications must obviously be observed. Each country will have its own set of restrictions which apply to advertising, packaging, sales promotion or direct marketing.

5.2 **In the EU alone, there are a number of significant differences regarding the regulation of advertising between member states**. A recent Gossard TV commercial came under scrutiny in the UK for its risqué execution. In France, the problem was not the generous display of cleavage, but the fact that the advert was set in a bar where alcohol was being consumed. There is a ban on TV alcohol adverts and the Gossard ad needed to be re-edited to fall in line with French restrictions.

5.3 In some countries, restrictions apply to the use of non native models and actors. This can mean that advertising has to be reshot for specific countries.

5.4 **Packaging regulations** can vary. In a number of European markets, the push towards environmentally-friendly packaging has resulted in far more stringent rules than apply in the UK. In Denmark, soft drinks may not be sold in cans, only in glass bottles with refundable deposits.

5.5 **Direct marketing** is an area under threat from EU legislation. In the UK, direct marketers must offer consumers the choice of opting out of receiving further mailings. Recent European proposals suggest the idea of allowing consumers the choice of opting into direct mailings. This seems to imply that companies would have to write to consumers in advance of a direct mail campaign, asking consumers if they wanted to receive mail.

Cross border advertising

5.6 The European Commission issued a green paper in May 1996 on *Commercial Communications in the Internal Market*. This covered all forms of advertising, direct marketing, sponsorship, sales promotions and public relations. The paper explained the savings that could be made if advertisers could benefit from economies of scale within the EU by standardising campaigns, as far as cultural differences allow. It anticipated that, without action, the problem would get worse with the advent of the Internet.

5.7 The current position is that there must be overriding reasons relating to the **public interest** for imposing additional national rules on communications, and these rules must be 'proportionate' to the public interest objectives. However, to test the validity of current national restrictions on commercial communications through the courts takes several years for each case. Many regard national advertising restrictions as thinly veiled protectionism.

5.8 The green paper proposed that a new body be set up as an alternative to the courts. It would be chaired by the European Commission and made up of representatives of each member state, with a brief to assess whether national rules meet the public interest and proportionality tests. There would also be a new central contact, enquiry and information point on commercial communications.

Marketing at Work

National restrictions

'Sweden forbids all advertising aimed at children under 10; Greece bans TV toy advertising between 7am and 10pm; some countries require ads for sweets to carry a toothbrush symbol; others have rules intended to curb advertisers from encouraging children to exercise 'pester power'.

The same maze of national rules exists when it comes to promoting alcohol, tobacco, pharmaceuticals and financial services.'

There are proposals to set up a new body to deal with these issues, which are felt to be significant barriers to cross border trade.

'Early meetings of the new body would examine national differences in sales promotions and sponsorship regulations ... On sponsorship, for example, the Netherlands was singled out as having particularly restrictive curbs on events sponsorship, while the UK and Denmark were seen to impose strict rules on broadcasting.

Price advertising and discounting is another area likely to get early attention. Measures are so disparate that cross-border campaigns using discounts are all but impossible ... In Germany, cash discounts are limited to 3% and the advertising of special offers is also restricted. Austria, Belgium and Italy also have strict regimes. In contrast, in Scandinavia, where the advertising law is more closely linked to consumer protection rather than unfair competition considerations, price advertising is encouraged – Swedish law, for example, promotes comparative price advertising between traders '

Source: Financial Times

6 Standardisation vs adaptation 6/02

6.1 Strategies appropriate for companies operating in international markets

(a) **Standardise** product/standardise communication (for example, Coca-Cola).

(b) **Standardise product/adapt communication** (Horlicks is promoted as a relaxing bedtime drink in the UK and as a high protein energy booster in India).

(c) **Adapt product/standardise communication** (washing powder ingredients may vary from country to country depending on water conditions and washing machine technology. However, the communication message of clean clothes is the same).

(d) **Adapt product/adapt communication**.

(e) **Invent a new product** to meet the needs of the market.

Action Programme 3

Over the next few months as you work towards the *Integrated Marketing Communications* exam, scan the marketing and advertising trade press alongside the quality papers for examples of products and services which adopt the different strategies listed above. You will be able to generate your own list of current examples to illustrate points you make in the examination. Examiners welcome up to date relevant examples which demonstrate that you keep abreast of current practice.

6.2 **Advantages of standardising communications** include the following.

(a) **Economies of scale** can be generated. A single worldwide advertising, packaging or direct mail execution will save time and money.

(b) A **consistent and strong brand image** will be presented to the consumer. Wherever users see the brand, they will be reassured because the messages received will be the same.

(c) A **standardised communications policy** allows for **easier implementation** and control by management.

(d) Good **communications ideas are rare** and should be exploited creatively across markets.

Marketing at Work

Pirelli

A Pirelli ad featured Marie-Jo Perec, a double Olympic gold medal winner, outrunning an avalanche, a tidal wave and a river of volcanic lava. The ad is thought to have cost over £1m to make, but it ran in up to 40 countries from China to South Africa. This needs to be compared with the cost of making multiple commercials, a different one for each country: it is thought to cost at least £250,000 to make a decent 30-second ad.

'There are certain clues which showed that this ad was designed to run internationally. There was no dialogue, as that would mean expensive and potentially difficult translation. And the images were universally recognisable - human against nature. The only potential problem was that Perec's sprinting costume could be considered too skimpy for some Islamic countries'.

Source: Financial Times

6.3 **Arguments against standardising communications** include the following.

(a) Any standardisation policy **assumes consumer needs and wants are identical** across markets. This may be a false assumption, as the example below illustrates.

(b) Centrally-generated communications concepts may prove to be **inappropriate for the specific culture** of the local market.

(c) **Media channel availability and infrastructure varies** widely from country to country.

(d) A country's level of **educational development** may prevent a standardised approach. For instance, a press campaign featuring detailed copy would be a non starter if literacy levels were low.

(e) **Legal restrictions** may prove to be a stumbling block. For example, France does not allow any advertising of alcohol on television; cashback sales promotion offers are not allowed in Italy or Luxembourg.

(f) Standardisation may encourage the **'not invented here' syndrome**, so that local management become lacklustre about creative ideas and communications policies imposed from above.

(g) Different countries have economies which may be much more or much less **developed** than others. Factors that need to be considered are as follows.

- ■ What is the level and trend in per capita income?
- ■ Is the balance of payments favourable or unfavourable?
- ■ Is inflation under control?
- ■ Are the exchange rates stable?
- ■ Is the currency easily convertible?
- ■ Is the country politically stable?
- ■ How protectionist is the country?
- ■ Who controls distribution channels?

7 International communications alternatives

7.1 It is all too easy to focus on advertising and packaging as the prime communicators in international campaigns. However, sales promotion, public relations, sponsorship, exhibitions, direct marketing and personal selling can all play a part.

Sales promotion

7.2 Sales promotion encompasses a range of techniques appropriate for targeting consumers, for instance via price reductions, free gifts, or competitions. Trade and salesforce promotions are also implied under the general heading of sales promotion.

7.3 Different countries have their own **local restrictions** concerning different sales promotional devices. For instance, collector devices are a well used method of encouraging repeat purchase in the UK. However, they are not allowed in West Germany, Luxembourg, Austria, Norway, Sweden and Switzerland. Petrol forecourt promotions are very familiar to drivers in the UK, but following a vicious sales promotions battle between petrol companies in 1989, the Malaysian Government banned sales promotion of petrol.

7.4 Sales promotions that are to run across a number of different countries must tap into common tastes, interests and activities. As has been seen from the section on culture, this may not be an easy task.

Public relations

7.5 The UK's Institute of Public Relations describe public relations as, 'the planned and sustained effort to establish and maintain goodwill and mutual understanding between an organisation and its publics'. Publics can include:

- Customers
- Shareholders
- Employees
- Suppliers
- Trade intermediaries
- The local community
- Media
- Government
- Pressure groups

7.6 The importance of any one group will vary from country to country, which will mean that public relations campaigns are **unlikely to be completely standardised** across markets.

7.7 There is some debate as to whether public relations can be standardised at all. There is wide disparity in the sophistication of PR from country to country, as well as the usual list of cultural, language, media and legal barriers. The **political context** of individual countries may also affect the extent to which different public relations techniques can be used.

Sponsorship

7.8 Sponsorship seems a particularly appropriate means of communicating internationally. Internationally televised sporting events have an appeal that crosses borders and cultures, as football, rugby and cricket matches often show.

Exhibitions

7.9 Trade fairs and exhibitions are an effective means of initial **business-to-business contact**, providing an opportunity for producers, distributors, customers and competitors to meet. Where specialist exhibitions take place, rival companies from across the globe are likely to gather under one roof, offering an excellent opportunity for international buyers to compare offerings and place orders.

7.10 Exhibitions allow companies to display goods and mount demonstrations and trials. They can be good as a mechanism for **image building**, especially in new markets. Exhibitions provide a means for supporting local distributors and agents and allow direct contact with customers. There is also the chance to conduct competitor and customer market **research**.

7.11 Detailed evaluation of exhibition results should be carried out in order to fine tune future plans.

Direct marketing

7.12 **International direct marketing** has been growing slowly over the last decade. Factors driving the move to international direct marketing include the following.

    (a)   The growth in sophistication of computer and database **technology**

    (b)   The increasing availability of suitable consumer or business **listings**

    (c)   Growth of **international media**, which can be used for direct response advertising

    (d)   The perceived **accountability** of direct marketing campaigns compared with other communications campaigns

    (e)   The ease with which direct marketing campaigns can be **pre-tested** in order to maximise their effectiveness

    (f)   Improving **skills** of direct marketing agencies

    (g)   Increasing **willingness of the consumer** to purchase items directly

    (h)   Increasing use of **internationally accepted credit cards**

7.13 On the other hand, there are a number of factors **restraining the move to international direct marketing**.

- Lack of telephone and postal **infrastructure**
- Lack of road and rail penetration to facilitate **distribution**
- Lack of **suitable media** to use to target consumers
- Lack of consumer and business **lists** in some countries
- The threat of increasingly **strict legislation** concerning the use of consumer information
- **Consumer backlash** against what is seen as junk mail

Personal selling

7.14 Many of the communications tools described above will rely on integration with the personal selling function. For instance, certain types of consumer sales promotion will require **salesforce support** to gain trade acceptance. Likewise, direct marketing campaigns will create sales leads that require follow up. Personal selling is therefore a likely requirement of most markets.

7.15 Companies may use **agents or distributors** to act in a sales capacity. Alternatively, a company may establish its own branch offices abroad with a team of local salespeople.

7.16 Personal selling will be particularly important in industrial markets where products are high value and complex, or in markets where purchasing is controlled by government agencies.

Exam Tip

Students answering exam questions on international aspects of communications tend to focus on advertising and packaging as the prime promotional vehicles. Examiners welcome answers that demonstrate that other options such as sales promotion, public relations, sponsorship, exhibitions, direct marketing and personal selling have been considered.

8 Multinational communications agencies　　6/02

8.1 The factors influencing the choice of communications agencies were discussed in Chapter 12. In broad terms these factors would also influence selection of agencies to handle **communications on an international basis**. Decisions would also take into account the differences in the kinds of approaches to communications discussed elsewhere in this chapter.

8.2 Often the decision making process will be influenced by the structure of the client company and how far they **devolve marketing responsibility** on a regional basis. Some elements of the communications strategy and branding may be handled centrally, whereas **implementation is dealt with locally** where more detailed knowledge with regard to media and other context issues can be applied.

8.3 For many of the larger multinational and global companies such as Coca Cola, Heinz or Procter and Gamble there is a need to deal with **agencies who have sufficient resources** of their own to handle the size of budgets being allocated. As there has been **consolidation** taking place among multinational businesses through acquisition and merger, this has also been happening among communications businesses. Agencies such as WPP have grown partly by success in winning new business but also through the acquisition of other agencies in different parts of the world.

8.4 Other agencies offer multinational services to clients by being part of **networks**. They maintain independence as individual companies but via informal and sometimes formal collaborations, they can provide client services in different geographic markets. Sometimes clients may appoint a **lead agency** who will hold ultimate responsibility for planning and co-ordination of agencies in different markets.

8.5 Advances in new technologies make the process of handling the communications needs of sophisticated multinational clients more straightforward but may not always replace the need for local knowledge.

Chapter Roundup

- Different viewpoints exist concerning the **globalisation of markets**. On the one hand, there

  to market **standardised products** worldwide. An alternative view is that consumer markets are fragmenting and that products and services need to be **adapted** to individual preferences.

- The international marketing communicator needs to decide whether or not it is appropriate to **standardise communications across markets**.

- Companies operating outside their home markets need to be aware of the implications of **cultural differences** for all aspects of the marketing mix. Verbal and non verbal communications, aesthetics, dress and appearance, family roles and relationships, beliefs, learning and work habits are dimensions of culture of particular relevance to communications.

- Planning and buying media across borders can be a complex task. **Media availability** can vary greatly from country to country. **Media conventions** which apply in a home market may not apply elsewhere.

- **Laws and regulations** governing marketing communications must obviously be observed. Each country will have its own set of restrictions which apply to advertising, packaging, sales promotion and direct marketing.

- **Research** should be used to **support decision making** before a campaign is planned. Research can also help **evaluate** whether objectives have been met at the conclusion of a campaign. However, obtaining accurate, unbiased, up to date information can be difficult. Conducting primary research on an international basis requires the help of experts.

Now try Questions 14 and 15 at the end of the Study Text

Quick Quiz

1 Define the term culture, and identify dimensions of culture of particular importance to the

2 What kind of problems can be anticipated when translating copy from one language to another, and how can these problems be overcome? (3.5 - 3.11)

3 Describe the factors which influence choice of press as a medium in international markets. (4.4 - 4.8)

4 List the arguments for and against standardising marketing communications. (6.2 - 6.3)

5 What opportunities are afforded by participating in an international exhibition? (7.9 - 7.11)

6 Explain the reasons why international direct marketing has experienced growth over the last decade. (7.12)

BPP
PROFESSIONAL EDUCATION

Action Programme Review

1   Once you have completed this, consider the implications for differences in approach to marketing communications.

2   What differences would there be if you were promoting these products or services in the UK or another market?

3   Your own research.

Questions and suggested answers

1 Marketing communications strategy

Prepare an outline of a talk you are to give to a group of Marketing Managers on the subject of Marketing Communications Strategy. Describe the key elements of the communications planning process, showing how marketing communications strategy is distinguishable from, though part of, overall marketing strategy. Plan to illustrate your talk with examples of strategy drawn from your experience.

2 Communication process

Explain the standard communication process model using marketing examples to illustrate the various terms and concepts involved.

3 Perceived risk

The level of perceived risk a consumer might experience when purchasing products and services can vary significantly across product categories. Knowledge of these risks can impact on the design and implementation of promotional strategies.

Using examples from both the consumer and business-to-business sectors to illustrate your answer, explain how marketing communications can be used to reduce different types of perceived risk.

4 Retention and loyalty

Examine the growth in customer retention and loyalty based schemes and comment on their effectiveness as a strategic marketing communication instruments. Use any two loyalty schemes of your choice to illustrate your answer.

5 Internal marketing

The increasing awareness and emphasis given to internal marketing communications suggest that an organisation's employees are an important market segment in their own right. Write a report explaining why this group is now perceived as important and suggest how such internal communications might be used to improve communications with other externally based stakeholder groups.

6 Technology and communications policy

Write a short report evaluating the impact that recent technological advances have had on the marketing communications policy of organisations. Illustrate your answer using a minimum of two products or services from a market of your choice.

7 Branding in business-to-business markets

Many organisations in the business-to-business sector have begun to use branding as a significant part of their marketing communications strategy. Write a report explaining this development. Use examples to illustrate your points and comment whether this trend is likely to continue.

8 Branding and marketing communications

Branding is a common strategy adopted by both manufacturers and retailers in consumer markets. Using examples of brands from a country of your choice, evaluate the effectiveness of branding as a marketing communication strategy.

9 The uses of advertising

Advertising has a variety of uses including the stimulation of demand, reminding and reinforcing, counteracting competitors and so on.

Examine and discuss these and other uses of advertising, using relevant examples.

10 Media strategy

Choose any two current national consumer advertising campaigns which use media in significantly different ways. Describe the objectives of the two campaigns. Explain why, in your judgement, the two campaigns have used media differently. Comment on the effectiveness or otherwise of the two campaigns.

11 Expenditure

As a marketing manager write a short article for inclusion in a company magazine suggesting how the amount of money spent on marketing communications might be strategically important. Use examples to illustrate your article.

12 Agency restructuring

It has been noted that many advertising agencies have failed to adapt and restructure themselves in order to keep pace with the increasing demands and international communications strategies of their clients. What are the reasons for this apparent incompatibility and suggest how agencies might adjust to better meet their client needs.

13 Evaluate repositioning

As a journalist working for a marketing magazine, write an outline for an article which evaluates a campaign that was intended to (re)position an industrial or consumer product of your choice. As part of your answer you should evaluate the situation facing the organisation, explain how the campaign was designed to meet the objectives identified and comment on the apparent effectiveness of the programme.

14 With or without?

Choose a country with which you are familiar. Write a short report to a manufacturer of tea and coffee who is considering entering the beverage market in the country of your choice. Outline relevant cultural and social trends, the likely target end user, the retailing structure and the choice or appropriate media in the country through which to promote the company.

15 Netline technologies

The growth of the mobile phone industry has been dramatic over the past decade. The market size has continued to expand as more people have become familiar and comfortable with the technology. Whilst there are a range of different types of users and customer segments, the majority of product packages offered have been based on price and volume of calls made. This may be as a response to the intense competition for new users and the high level of churn (loss of customers to other networks). In this context attempts to find stronger market positions based on the motivations people have for using mobile phones have started to emerge.

However, one of the problems associated with the use of these phones is the annoyance factor. Public irritation with mobile phone users is often provoked by the inconsiderate and loud use of these telephones in public places such as restaurants, theatres, pubs and travel facilities such as train stations and airport termini. For example, a survey by Synergy Brand Values identified at 44% of people agreed that the use of mobile phones should be prohibited in public places.

As if in answer to this issue, Netline Technologies have invested in the development of a device that can deactivate mobile phones. Developed initially for military purposes, the product is now regarded as having many consumer applications. The device, branded as C-Guard, prevents calls being made or received by jamming the airwaves with radio waves. The device is activated the moment it senses that there is an incoming call or when a call is about to be made as a phone searches to open a line. This means that it is now possible to ban the use of these telephones in designated places and can also help people to avoid those embarrassing moments when they forget to switch off their telephones, for example, in places of religious worship.

One potential difficulty concerns people who need to be able to receive calls due to the nature of their work. To overcome this, Netline have adapted the system so that it can recognise particular telephone numbers so that, for example doctors can be reached whilst at dinner when all other diners would be prevented from receiving calls.

C-Guard has the potential to allow for the creation of 'Phone-Free' areas in restaurants and trains, rather similar to non-smoking areas. The system, set to retail at roughly $750, also permits theatres, cinemas and other places of public entertainment for their patrons, whilst airports and airlines can automatically disarm potential safety hazards. Scientists and the medical profession in particular can improve the quality of their work without fear of disruption and costly delays caused by interference to their equipment.

Netline Technologies have patented and protected the C-Guard device although it is anticipated that there will only be a short period of time, of less than a year, before imitation devices are brought to the market by competitors. Netline recognise the urgency associated with the need to establish themselves in the market and have now embarked upon marketing the brand in countries and regions where the mobile phone is well established. Their policy has been to appoint regional (often country specific) distributors under a franchise arrangement. Franchise holders are responsible for the purchase of C-Guard system boxes and for the appointment of sub-dealers or retailers, perhaps their own subsidiary companies, to provide local coverage. They are also responsible for the distribution, training, installation, maintenance and marketing of the C-Guard system in their region.

Distinct and consistent branding is an important part of the marketing strategy and associated communications. Franchisees are contractually required to adhere to strict brand identity policies and are only to use promotional materials developed centrally by Netline.

Franchisees see the potential of being first into the market with a simple to install, easy to maintain product that provides clear user benefits. It is also expected that there will be further facilities that can be offered to up-grade a system and that there will be further advanced products based on the technology developed for C-Guard. End users will be encouraged to see the benefits of being associated with the 'C-Guard' protection system. Meanwhile, Netline will encourage members of the public to look for the 'C-Guard' sign and ask for it by name.

As Marketing Communications Controller for Netline Technologies you are required to prepare a short internal report for the attention of the Marketing Director.

This report should:

(a)   Identify and evaluate the key strategic issues associated with the marketing communications of C-Guard during the first two years of its launch.   **(20 marks)**

(b)   Make appropriate recommendations to address the issues you have identified.

(20 marks)

(40 marks)

You are not required to prepare a marketing communications plan.

1   Marketing communications strategy

REPORT

To: Marketing Managers

From: Marketing Communications Manager

Date: December 20XX

Ref: Presentation on the subject of marketing communication strategy

1   Audience/objectives

The audience consists of marketing managers. We can assume therefore that they are reasonably well versed in the actual marketing planning process.

Although they will be knowledgeable about the planning process their involvement in the detail will vary from person to person. Some will have a close working knowledge, others will only have limited experience of planning directly themselves.

There will also be degrees of scepticism. Some will be committed planners others will not.

The objectives of the talk can therefore be defined as follows.

(a)   To show how marketing communication planning is an integral part of the overall company planning process.

(b)   To demonstrate that without this link communications planning would be less effective.

(c)   Lastly, to illustrate the talk with practical examples of strategy.

2   The total planning process

It is vital that we as marketing managers understand the corporate planning process and the role of marketing planning within it. Furthermore, because marketing communications accounts for a significant share of the marketing mix it is important also to understand the integration of the marketing communications planning process.

Each level of the organisation has a hierarchy of:

- Objectives
- Strategy
- Tactics

The tactics of the upper level then become the objectives of the next level down in the organisation. The levels we can consider usually are:

- Corporate
- Functional (including marketing)
- Activity (including marketing communications)

These relationships are shown in more detail in the diagrams below. The first is Simon Majaro's Planning Hierarchy. The second shows the relationship of corporate, marketing and communications planning in more detail. The third shows the operational planning stages of marketing communications.

Clearly each of these diagrams of the real situation will vary from company to company according to size, nature of business, and experience of planning. In some predominantly marketing organisations the link between corporate and marketing objectives will be a very close one.

In larger companies with separate operating divisions another level of planning will be introduced. These operation divisions are often called 'strategic business units'.

The planning hierarchy

The planning hierarchy
by Simon Majaro

The strategic marketing and tactical communications planning process within the overall strategic marketing planning process

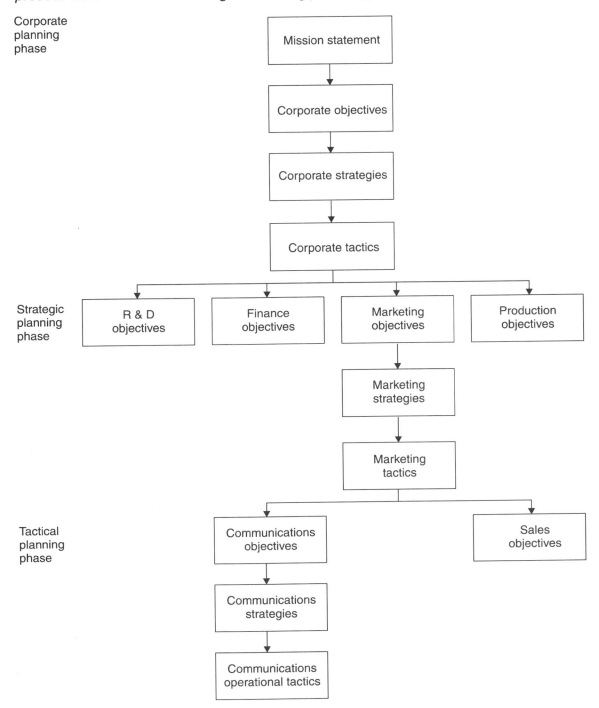

BPP
PROFESSIONAL EDUCATION

The operational planning stages of marketing communications

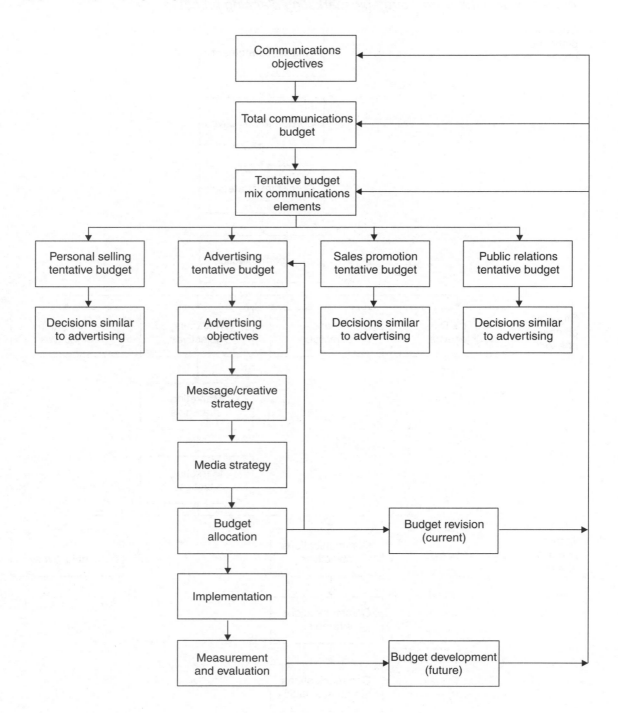

2 Communication process

> *Tutorial note.* Make sure you give examples, as instructed in the question. Examples from the world of promotion are, of course, the best choice, especially references to current campaigns.

Communication has a number of definitions but essentially can be defined as **a sharing of meaning**. In order for the sender and receiver of information to communicate they must share some common ground.

Communication begins with what is known as the **source**. A source can be a person or organisation which has something to say to an audience. For example, a source could be a door-to-door sales representative who wants to communicate the benefits of a wonderful new mop or it could be a charity which wants to communicate the need for donations to assist them in their work.

The **receiver** is the individual or organisation who **decodes** the message. So in the two examples cited above, the receiver of the benefits of the mop could be those concerned with housework, while the receivers of the charity message could be those who have an interest in the work of the charity.

In order to **transmit a meaning**, the source must convert the meaning into a series of signals which represent ideas or concepts. This process is known as **encoding**. This is where confusion can arise and so marketers need to be careful to use signals that the receiver can identify with: they must know their target market. Language is an important factor here and if the organisation is international then translation issues must be taken into consideration.

When sharing a coded meaning with the receiver, the source must select and use a **medium of transmission**. This is responsible for carrying the coded message and can include printed media and air waves, as in radio and television signals. The key factor in transmission is to choose the appropriate media. For example, there would be little point in advertising a revolutionary new mop in the middle of a sports event as the audience would have little interest in it.

In this process of **decoding**, signals are converted into meaningful concepts and ideas. When the result of the decoding is different from what was encoded, **noise** exists. Noise can be both literal and figurative. Noise may originate in receivers. They may be unaware of a coded message because their **perceptual processes** block it out or because the message received is too obscure. Some Guinness ads were criticised by the media industry as being too obscure, but were nonetheless very successful.

The final stage in the communication process is the **feedback to the source**. In the earlier example of the mop, feedback can be immediate. The prospective customer can give both verbal and non-verbal feedback in the form of body language and eye movements. Slamming the door on the salesperson's face is a very clear piece of feedback. In the case of the charity, feedback may be immediate or long term, in the form of legacies in wills, say. Communication feedback is generally judged by a change in sales.

3 Perceived risk

Introduction

Perception relates to how individuals **interpret** the stimuli they receive and how they **organise** the stimuli in order to make sense and understand the world. Of course, people sense and perceive stimuli in many different ways depending upon a number of criteria. For example, each person's experiences, culture, education, income and social and psychological make-up frame their perceptive abilities.

Perceived risk stems from perception and is associated with the risk an individual experiences when purchasing products and services. Six main types of risk have been identified as follows.

Perceived risks

> Performance
> Physical
> Financial
> Social
> Ego
> Time

The degree to which these **risks** impact on individuals varies through **time**, across **product categories** and by **particular circumstances**. Invariably, one or two of these risks dominate a single purchase decision with the other risks subsumed and/or under control. One of the tasks of marketing communications is to help reduce these **dominant risks** or lower them in such a way that they become manageable and do not threaten or deter a potential purchase.

For example, **finance is very often a dominant risk** with expensive purchases, associated with **high involvement** purchase decisions. To overcome this type of risk, promotional messages might emphasise value for money, announce a winter sale, confer status, suggest high quality or association with an aspirational group or lifestyle. Volkswagen ran a successful campaign that stressed the low (and less than expected) cost of the Polo.

Product performance risks can be countered with guarantees, money back, size, extended warranties and associations with tradition, experience and in some cases craftsmanship. Safety became a position adopted by many in the tyre market, for example, Goodyear, (which was endorsed by a police officer) and Continental, braking on the flat roof of a building.

Fashion and clothing items often employ **social and ego risks** as the dominant factors. These are addressed by images and messages that either deflect attention to other attributes such as the material, the cut of the item, price, or attempt to appeal to an individual's perceived self image. A further approach is to suggest rewards such as admiring glances from significant others or association with an admired celebrity.

Branding is an important means by which perceived risk can be reduced across a number of areas. Used extensively in the consumer sector, branding enables customers to understand and recognise a product/organisation's values quickly and communicates an entire **bundle of intangible benefits and satisfactions** that appeal to prospective buyers. Consistency in communication is therefore important in order that these values be easily observed and maintained to facilitate easier shopping/buying experiences.

Source credibility is also an important means by which perceived risk can be minimised or managed. Enabling buyers to not only **recognise** a brand or source of a message is one thing but in order that they **believe** in the source there must be an element of **trust** and perceived **expertise** associated with the source of the message. Therefore, whether the message is transmitted through sales personnel, sales promotion devices, direct marketing or through advertising and public relations instruments it is the credibility attributed to the source that is of major importance.

Perceived risk is not only a factor in the consumer market but is present in the business-to-business sector as well. The use of more **factual information** and **rational benefit** appeals predominates, reflecting reduced emotional content and social and ego risks. Performance, financial and time risks tend to be more prevalent. These are addressed through warranties, delivery promises and quality guarantees.

XYZ sell **cables and wires** to the telecommunication sector. Buyers undertake exhaustive research in order to specify the correct cable configuration and their **decision making units** apply rigorous criteria to ensure that product performance risk is minimised. XYZ use the cable specification information to communicate **quality** and to explicitly communicate professionalism and cable technology leadership. To do this, personal selling and sales literature combined with demonstrations and third party references constitute the main thrust of the marketing communication activities. Whilst parts of the consumer sector have recently started to lay greater emphasis on **customer retention** activities, the business-to-business sector has for a long time tried to build lasting **relationships** through courtesy, prompt attention and the reduction of performance risk through product quality.

The development of technology has assisted both sectors, partly through the **Internet** and through management of large amounts of **information**. The business-to-business sector has fostered the development of relationships through **E-commerce**, which also serves to reduce **time risks**.

Conclusion

There is no doubt that perceived risk is an active and important element in the decision making process of both individuals and organisations. Marketing communications can be used to reduce these risks and to stress other benefits associated with product purchase.

4 Retention and loyalty

Introduction

The growth of *customer* **retention and loyalty schemes** has been quite marked in recent years. There is a difference between the two although it is apparent that many commentators see these and **relationship marketing** as one and the same. This can be misleading as there are substantial differences between them.

The idea that consumers can display loyalty towards a brand or product in the same sense that they are loyal to partners and sports teams is questionable. However, this has not prevented the explosive increase in card based loyalty schemes, and especially those developed by the UK supermarkets, most notably Tesco and Sainsbury's.

Growth of customer loyalty schemes

The reasons for this growth are many and varied although it has to be said that none of the schemes would have been possible without the increase in **computing power** and the huge reduction in computing costs that have occurred since the end of the 1980s. **Database technology** and the ability to fuse different types of customer related information has helped transform marketing communications. Channel power has moved from manufacturers to retailers who are now able to collect and store information at the point of sale about their customers and their product purchases.

A major influence on the development of these schemes has been the realisation that the costs associated with searching for new customers far exceeds the costs associated with keeping current customers. This may seem obvious, but it is only recently that many markets have become **mature** and stationary. Many new markets such as that for mobile phones have experienced such high levels of **customer loss or churn**, that it is important for the organisations in these markets to hold on to as many customers as possible, **cross sell** more products and so improve levels of profitability.

A further reason for the growth of these schemes has been the general strategic shift in communication spend from **above- to below-the-line**. Advertising is still an important part of the communication mix but rising media costs and **media and audience fragmentation** have driven organisations to shift increasing proportions of their spend below-the-line. Customer retention initiatives represent a form of sales promotion and whilst there are many different variations the central theme of **reward for continued patronage** continues to be a favoured approach.

AirMiles

British Airways developed the AirMiles scheme from the overcapacity identified on certain flights. The scheme allows BA the opportunity to reward their more loyal customers with free air travel, at little cost to themselves. The business travel segment is an important market and by encouraging regular fliers to collect AirMiles, BA were adding benefit to the purchase decision and in doing so added value and competitive advantage to flying with BA. The global alliances that BA has since developed allows travellers the opportunity to collect AirMiles on a number of different carriers and flights. This further protects against overcapacity, provides for customer retention and perhaps contributes to an element of loyalty and the development of a competitive relationship between carriers and travellers.

UK supermarket loyalty schemes

Following the lead of Tesco, Sainsbury's offers its Nectar scheme which awards customers with points when a purchase is made at a number of outlets, including Debenhams. These points can be exchanged for cash off a purchase or accumulated into a voucher which can be used to purchase a variety of different products, one of which is AirMiles.

This scheme along with the others in the sector appear to be effective. What may be happening, of course, is that rather than loyalty being demonstrated it is more a means of added convenience. The schemes provide a reason to return to the same store and so reduce the amount of experimental shopping (visiting rival stores). Indeed the stores actively encourage people to shop more often at their store rather than the once a week/fortnight big shop. The 'thank you' or even incentive is the collection of reward points.

One of the traps that need to be avoided is that these loyalty/retention/reward schemes **should not be relied upon alone** to provide the growth that Sainsbury's and Tesco seek to satisfy their shareholders. In-store ambience, ease of parking/access, display, store layout, range of goods, pricing and the overall shopping experience are significant contributors to customer retention levels and overall levels of customer satisfaction.

Effectiveness

The strategic significance of these loyalty schemes should not be underestimated. Sainsbury's held off for a long time before following Tesco's lead. The implication is that these schemes represent not an advantage necessarily but more of a **competitive requirement**. Once a loyalty or reward scheme is established in a market by one organisation it appears that all other players need to offer a competitive scheme. **Competitive advantage** rests with the first entrant, whereas **competitive parity** becomes the imperative for the others. This can be further evidenced by the proliferation of retention schemes offered by High Street retailers such as Boots and W.H. Smith and the store card schemes offered by the majority of national retailers.

These schemes appear effective and may represent good value for promotional spend. One of the alternatives is to spend the 'reward money' on advertising. The measurement and overall effectiveness of advertising has been questioned for a long time whereas retention schemes are **easily measurable and the impact clearly visible**.

5 Internal marketing

Introduction

The notion that **employees constitute an important market segment** is relatively recent but has been gaining increasing acceptance. Employees are seen as important because they have particular needs and wants, some of which are satisfied by work which they exchange for, both pay and intrinsic benefits such as belonging, self esteem and self identity.

It is only through employees that management are really able to achieve their corporate goals. Therefore, the **direction and philosophy of an organisation**, whether it be in the private or public sector, is an integral part of an organisation's strategy and its communications with externally based stakeholders.

The benefits of internal marketing communications

- Staff **motivation**
- Staff **retention**
- **Resource** utilisation
- Developing **competitive advantage**
- Moving towards **integrated** marketing communications

Staff motivation

Involvement and participation within the organisation and its strategic and operational activities improves motivation and organisational identity improves. By encouraging employees to identify with the mission and values of an organisation, any gap between an organisation's external identity and its internal identity is narrowed.

Staff retention

In a period when staff skills are at a premium it makes good sense to preserve the current work force. Good communications are important in retaining qualified and valued members of the workforce. This in turn can breed experience and contribute to the development of better products and services and improved, credible external communications. B&Q, a DIY warehouse in the UK, feature their own staff in their television advertising. This helps develop employee identification as they are perceived to be valued, and externally it provides a point of differentiation from the other DIY stores in the sector.

Resource utilisation

Good communications can help identify areas where there is duplication of effort and, where possible, improve the level of resource utilisation.

Competitive advantage

The service element of the product offering is important so there must be increased attention given to training and skills. Associated with this is the competitive shift as more and more product offerings become less distinctive in their own right. Differentiation through the service component has provided companies such as KwikFit, TNT Express and British Airways with competitive advantage.

Links with external communications

The development and increased focus on integrated marketing communications means that internal marketing communications cannot be ignored.

Many **external stakeholders** communicate on a regular basis with the employees of an organisation. Customers are obviously a very important group and need to be treated in the right manner in order to build levels of customer satisfaction. Suppliers and distributors, shareholders, financial service providers and members of the local community also communicate. All receive messages from the organisation, interpret them in particular ways and through the images formed develop, maintain or alter the reputation of the focus organisation.

Employees are essentially opinion formers and through 'word of mouth' communications and behaviour they help shape the views external stakeholders have of the organisation. In this sense therefore, internal marketing communications are an integral part of the move toward integrated marketing communications and cannot be ignored. The way an organisation is perceived by employees may differ to the way the organisation is perceived by external stakeholders. The extent of any such gap is said to be reflected in the strength of the organisation's overall identity. It follows that management should assist their employees to understand what is central to the business, what is distinctive about the business and what is enduring.

6 Technology and communications policy

To :   The CIM Examiner
From :   A CIM Student
Title :   The Impact Of Technology on Marketing Communications Policy
Date :   June 20XX

1 Introduction

The context within which marketing communications has been developed by organisations has changed significantly over the last ten years. The prospects for further, even faster, periods of change seem inevitable as technological advances shorten **life cycles**, speed **product development** and facilitate faster and more accurate **communications**.

2 Media fragmentation

In order to cope with the changing conditions in which consumer brands and business-to-business products find themselves, organisations have had to keep pace with changing technology and adapt their promotional strategies accordingly. For example, it used to be possible to use television advertising through ITV, to reach mass audiences and be confident that the message had been seen (if not understood). Today, in the UK, technology has helped spawn two further terrestrial channels and a plethora of cable and satellite channels. The consequence of this is that it is no longer possible to reach the same audience because they have been split up over the new programme offerings. This **media** and **audience fragmentation** means that media planners and their clients must now regularly review their policies regarding media selection in order that they exploit every opportunity to communicate with their target audiences.

This media fragmentation has been accelerated by the decline in the number of newspapers that are read and the increase in consumer and trade magazines. Again, this makes it increasingly difficult to reach audiences. Conversely, **technology** has developed systems that makes it **easier to identify new audiences** and then buy into media that will be read by the target group. Therefore, it can be argued that technology might be splintering audiences but it also enables more effective use of the marketing communication budget, as there is less wastage.

3 Direct marketing

The use of the **database** to generate direct mail and telemarketing has accelerated recently and has also led to an increase in the attention given to integrated marketing communications. Database management allows for **improved targeting** and more effective customer communications. Direct marketing represents one-to-one communications, communications that can be adapted to meet the specific needs of individual customers.

Whilst there are many examples of pure direct marketing, many organisations choose to utilise the direct approach in combination with traditional media. Therefore **direct response television (DRTV)** utilises the normal media but through display of the client's telephone number on the screen, people can be motivated to phone the number to either find out more information or even make a purchase. This level of integrated marketing communications is used by a significant number of organisations in the financial services sector in particular.

From an organisation's perspective this facility would not have been possible without the use of new technology. For example, Direct Line or First Choice Holidays may use DRTV and generate thousands of responses within two minutes of an advertisement being transmitted. In order to handle this volume of enquiries, the industry has seen the development of **call centres** situated all round the country, if not abroad in some cases. Calls are routed to available operators who have been trained to respond to client questions. For this to happen a substantial investment needs to be made by the client into integrating the activity in the communications plan, allocating funds, training people and printing suitable literature.

4 The Internet

The frenetic growth of the **Internet** and **websites** over the past five years has had an important impact on the way organisations have had to review the way they communicate. Websites represent a fundamental change in the way communications are used. Through traditional approaches organisations used promotions to intercept people, either when watching television, reading a paper or driving to work. The Internet reverses this approach, as audiences now deliberately visit websites of their choice, in their own time, in a search for information. The client can only set up a site and hope to attract sufficient numbers.

In the business-to-business sector, in particular, technology now permits the development of **electronic commerce** whereby online enquirers can undertake **full transaction facilities** and have products delivered to specific addresses world wide. Marketing communication policies therefore need to reflect the degree to which the Internet and websites contribute to the whole balance of the communication mix and the degree to which the other parts of the promotional mix are integrated.

5 Other Developments

Examples include notebook computers for use by the sales force, coupon dispensers for sales promotions, name tracking devices for public relations and a whole raft of tools that can be used for segmenting and evaluating audiences. The net impact of these technological advances is that organisations must continually review their communication opportunities and be more flexible and proactive in their search for truly integrated marketing communications.

6   Conclusions

The outcomes from utilising these technological developments can be seen in increased levels of **profitability**, increased **accountability**, more effective **brand management**, greater levels of **customer satisfaction**, faster new **product development** and ultimately improved **customer retention levels**.

7   Branding in business-to-business markets

To :   The Marketing Director
From :   A CIM Diploma Student
Date :   8 December 20XX
Ref :   Branding within The Business-to-Business Sector

1.0   Introduction

This report seeks to identify what **branding** is, establishes what **business-to-business communications** consist of, and then attempts to consider how branding can assist this form of marketing communications in this sector.

2.0   What is a brand?

A **brand** is a design, name, sign, symbol or logo that **differentiates** one product from another and which is valued by customers. A brand is a composite of tangible and intangible elements mixed together in such a way that the resultant mix is not only meaningful but possesses values that are relevant and pertinent to customers.

Brands have many advantages for both the manufacturer and the buyer. Essentially, a brand enables the brand owner to maintain some control over how the products are sold through retailers and other distributors. It prevents the onset of **commodification**, allows for premium pricing, **speeds purchase decisions**, generates familiarity, reassurance and most importantly **trust**. It is through trust that **loyalty** can be developed, which in turn can bring increased profits and competitive advantage for the brand owner.

3.0   The business-to-business sector (B2B)

Branding has been an integral part of the consumer market for a long time. However, the BtB market is characterised by **longer decision-making times**, generally **high involvement decision processes**, the involvement of many people in the **decision (DMU)**, large sums of **money** and **potential risk**.

In the past, **rational informative benefit** based communications were regarded as important. However, the merits of using **emotional imagery** in the messages communicated to organisational buyers, and bringing together a number of identity cues under a brand umbrella, has been seen to be attractive to many BtB organisations. In many of the markets in the BtB sector, competition is **priced based** and only through **communication of the augmented product** can the totality of the services and the value that a particular supplier can provide start to be established.

Businesses buy benefits just as consumers do, but they also willingly buy **relationships**. Branding provides for the establishment of a long-term relationship. Personal selling, sales support and packaging are part of the overall 'product' that organisations buy.

In addition to the business benefits of branding, organisations have witnessed the **value** that some brands in the consumer sector have attained. The value of some brands far exceeds the total tangible asset value and adds to the appeal to create strong business-to-business brands. The battle by VW and BMW to buy Rolls Royce and the value placed by Nestlé on Rowntree all testify to the value and strength of the brand.

4.0 Examples of business-to-business brands

The Intel brand has received a high level of promotional support and represents an attempt to develop a brand that has value for both the BtB and consumer sectors. Hewlett Packard has developed brand strength in the different markets in which it operates. IBM, Dell and Compaq have realised the benefits of brand strength when dealing with trade customers and the leverage it can bring in getting high distributor visibility or shelf-space.

Dexion is a strong brand in the partitioning and shelving market. Little known in the consumer world, Dexion enjoys a very strong position in the BtB market. Branding in the BtB sector has to be market specific otherwise funds are wasted. Therefore the identity cues used need to be managed tightly and focused upon the principal stakeholders.

5.0 The future of branding

The use of branding in the BtB sector will probably continue to increase as organisations seek to differentiate themselves, **extend their brands** into new products/markets and seek to find new ways of reach key members of DMUs. Some consumer brands are becoming much more flexible and allow their owners to extend into new markets, for example, Virgin. It is unlikely that this will be possible with BtB brands but opportunities to straddle consumer and BtB markets, as demonstrated by Intel, will be attempted by an increasing number of brands in the future.

8 Branding and marketing communications

> *Tutorial note.* The depth of understanding that students have of the branding concept will be significant indicator when answering this question. Branding as a strategy is central to marketing communications and a rounded understanding is important.

Branding is an important **consumer marketing tool** and companies such as Nike, Cadbury's, Procter & Gamble, Virgin and British Airways have developed sophisticated means of managing and developing their brands. Many business-to-business organisations are starting to recognise the power of branding and are utilising the approach themselves.

A brand is a term, logo, name, symbol or design that identifies the product or service within particular markets. It may be that these elements are combined together in some way to provide a **distinguishing facility** within a competitive environment. Branding therefore, is a primary means of differentiating a product or service. As product content, quality and facilities continue to converge, the importance of distinguishing one product from another becomes more and more important. Branding allows for the development of competitive advantage and **adds value to the core product**. This value may not be understood or appreciated by all members of the population, but what is important is that members of the target audience appreciate and value the brand.

Branding brings many advantages to both consumers and a brand's owners. These are set out in Table 1. However, it is only through **communication** that the essence of a brand is conveyed and maintained. Therefore, marketing and corporate communications are absolutely essential for effective branding to be developed.

British Airways have used branding to help achieve corporate goals. BA use branding at a corporate level by differentiating the airline from all other airlines. They also use product based branding to differentiate particular routes and ancillary services. When British Gas wanted to launch a credit card and move into the financial services market the name (mark, symbol) of British Gas was not appropriate. The wrong values and cultural associations were tied into British Gas, which might have prevented or impeded a successful launch. They selected the name Goldfish and used a variety of different means to distinguish and separate the brand from the parent.

Customer benefits from branding	Supplier benefits derived from branding
■ Assists the **identification** of preferred products ■ Can reduce levels of **perceived risk** and so improve the quality of the shopping experience ■ Easier to gauge the level of **product quality** ■ Can reduce the **time spent** making product based decisions and in turn reduce the time spent shopping. ■ Can provide psychological **reassurance** or **reward** ■ Provides cues about the nature of the **source of the product** and any associated values	■ Permits **premium pricing** ■ Helps **differentiate** the product from competitors ■ Enhances **cross-product promotion** and brand extension opportunities ■ Encourages customer **loyalty/retention** and repeat purchase buyer behaviour ■ Assists the development and use of **integrated** marketing communications ■ Contributes to **corporate identity** programmes ■ Provides for some **legal protection** ■ Provides for greater **thematic consistency** and uniform messages and communications

Table 1

Benefits of Branding
Source : Fill (2002)

Conversely, Virgin have *developed and extended* the Virgin brand into many different markets, mainly because of the strength of the equity associated with Virgin. Marketing communications strategy therefore has been based around maintaining and developing the strength of the Virgin brand.

There *are* different types of brand and numerous listings and topologies of brands.

(a)   There are **manufacturers' brands** such as IBM, Cadbury's and Ford, **retailer** brands such as Marks and Spencer, Tesco and Sainsbury's and **generic brands** as practised in the pharmaceutical industry, where a very low price and the absence of promotional materials is the prime characteristic.

(b)   Brands are a reflection of the relationship between the corporate body, the product itself and the competitive context within which it is positioned. As a result of these variables a number of different brands types can be identified.

(i)   Pirelli, Gillette and Kwik-Fit have a **single product group offering** so that the name of the organisation is the same as the lead name of individual products.

(ii)   Companies such as Lever Brothers have followed a **multi-brand strategy** so that products in the company's portfolio are branded without reference to the parent company. Marketing communications are required to maintain this policy and to build values associated with each product in different ways. Should a single brand experience a crisis then the other brands in the portfolio need not be damaged, unlike the **family brand** approach as followed by Kellogg's and Cadbury's, where the organisation's name is a visible and imperative part of the name of each product in the portfolio.

Marketing communications needs to build the strength of the brand over the long term, and it needs to be flexible in order adapt to changing market conditions. Many of the long-term successful brands such as Shell have been able to **maintain core values** and develop a level of **consistency** in their communications.

Brands carry a measure of **goodwill**, which can be the prime attraction of predators. When Nestlé bought Rowntree, the value of brands such as KitKat led to a price far in excess of the **asset value** of the company. A view of the **future stream of earnings** a brand is likely to generate is a major factor when determining the take-over price. The Rolls Royce brand is extremely attractive with strong equity and future earnings potential. Volkswagen have paid a price premium to snatch the purchase of Rolls-Royce away from fellow German company BMW.

9   The uses of advertising

Advertising can serve a number of uses and each of the major ones will be examined in turn below.

(a)   Promotion of products, organisations and causes

Advertising can be used to promote products, services, politics, religious beliefs, organisations and anything which a promoter wants to advertise. Essentially advertising can be classified into **product** and **institutional**. Product advertising promotes goods and services. Institutional advertising, on the other hand, promotes organisations and is often used by financial services where there are a very wide range of products.

(b)   Demand stimulation

This form of advertising is used when completely new products are first placed on the market. The idea is to stimulate primary demand and to gain **acceptance** of the product. Sony conducted this kind of pioneering advertising when they launched their Walkman range of products in the early 1980s. An advertiser could wish to build what is known as **selective demand** where competitive advantages are emphasised. For example, Volvo advertising places great importance on the safety aspects of their products.

(c)   Offsetting competitors' advertising

Defensive advertising is conducted in order to try to offset the impact of competitive advertising. It is used most often by firms in extremely competitive **consumer product markets** such as the supermarket industry.

(d)   Assisting sales personnel

In a personal selling situation, advertising has a role to play in **preparing consumers** by informing them about the product's features and benefits. This form of advertising assists salespeople in finding good **potential customers**. An example would be where a car manufacturer launches a new model and this is advertised in the press and on TV: interested parties are advised to go to their local dealer for further details.

(e) **Increasing product usage**

The demand for any product will be limited in the sense that there are only a fixed number of consumers. In order to improve sales a number of actions can be taken. The geographic areas in which the product is sold can be enlarged or an organisation can develop and promote a larger number of uses for the product. Johnson's have chosen the latter course of action and this has proved very effective. Among other products, they produce a range of toiletries designed specifically for babies, but with the birth rate in decline, they have realised that the baby market will decrease and so they have emphasised the mildness and sensitivity of their products to an adult market.

(f) **Reminding and reinforcing**

The aim of both reminder and reinforcement advertising is to prevent a **loss of sales or market share**. Reminder advertising is used to let consumers know that brands are still available. The breakfast cereal market is highly competitive with products being sold especially for children, the health-conscious and the weight watcher. Kelloggs cornflakes do not comfortably fit into any of these specialist categories, and so Kelloggs felt the need to reposition the product before it became lost. A series of television adverts where adults who were given the cornflakes complained that they had not eaten them since they were children, and then upon trying them remembered how good they were, was extremely successful. Reinforcement advertising informs current users that they have made the right choice.

(g) **Alleviating sales fluctuations**

Seasonality can have a dramatic impact on an organisation. For example, gardening equipment sells very well but in winter items such as lawnmowers are difficult to find in stores. Advertising is often designed to stimulate business during sales slumps and this can be effective through, for example, price reductions at the end of a season.

10 Media strategy

Introduction

I have chosen to use two very successful advertising campaigns. The first is for Boddingtons Bitter using magazines and posters as its main media. The second is the British Airways 'The Worlds Favourite Airline' campaign which was successfully shown around the world and utilise television as its main medium. Both campaigns won the Institute of Practitioners in Advertising awards.

(a) **Boddingtons Bitter**

(i) **Background**

Boddingtons bitter was an established beer brand in its regional heartland, Manchester. Whilst it was the leading bitter brand in its region, it was not a national brand. In its regional markets, sales were showing signs of decline. Alongside this the UK bitter market was facing increased competition from imported premium bottled beers which were targeting its core drinkers. When Whitbread Brewery bought Boddingtons, they saw the Boddingtons brand as a strategic opportunity to launch a bitter brand nationally. Consumer taste was moving towards unpasteurised conditioned beers such as Boddingtons and away from traditional keg bitters such as Whitbreads own bitters Trophy and Best.

(ii) **Marketing objectives**

(1)   To launch the Boddington bitter, and establish it as a national premium brand, whilst keeping faith with its regional heartlands.

(2)   To develop both pub and take-home markets.

(iii) **Marketing communication objectives**

To position Boddingtons as the ultimate, smooth-drinking pint and do it in an accessible, humorous way.

(iv) **Marketing communications strategy**

The brand was rolled out nationally both as a 'pub pint' and a canned version. The success of the launch would be determined predominantly on the strength of brand image that the advertising campaign could establish.

It was decided that a **slow build-up campaign strategy** should be adopted. For this reason TV was not chosen, as its impact would have been too rapid and the process of slowly educating its target audiences would have been damaged. The agency also felt that TV was too 'mainstream' for the Boddingtons brand. Most other brewers used TV advertising. Instead, a media strategy was developed which concentrated on back covers of magazines and supplements, to the extent that these became the recognised home of the brand. Press advertising was used locally to maintain support for the brand at home. Two years later press and poster advertising were used nationally to ensure the brand's image was maintained.

The creative brief emphasised the smooth creamy pint and the agency developed its advertising around this attribute with the use of ice cream and double cream images.

(v) **Effectiveness**

The campaign was extremely effective. Boddingtons is now the UK's fourth largest bitter brand whilst at the same time it has strengthened its position as market leader in the North West. The canned bitter has attained market leadership with 48% of bitter drinkers saying they 'drink it nowadays'. The sales of Boddingtons bitter showed a direct correlation with the advertising campaign.

(b) **British Airways**

(i) **Background**

In 1981/82 British Airways made a loss of £541 million. Staff morale was low and a MORI opinion poll revealed that the City regarded it as the least attractive investment amongst those the Government planned to sell off. In 1982 Lord King became chairman to prepare it for privatisation. Within 12 years British Airways transformed its performance and image both in the UK and internationally. Whilst improvements in its service played a major part in this transformation the advertising campaign that was developed to support it established British Airways as an international brand leader.

(ii) **Marketing objectives**

(1)   To increase market share on established routes.
(2)   To achieve consistently high load factors on all BA flights.

(3)   To sell as many seats as possible to full fare-paying passengers.

(iii)   **Marketing communications objectives**

(1)   To position British Airways as a global brand.

(2)   To ensure that British Airways is the first choice airline.

(iv)   **Marketing communications strategy**

Whilst improvements in service and quality were important factors in BA's turnaround, competitors were matching them in these areas. It was therefore necessary to position BA as the most prestigious, more 'international', 'ahead of the field' and more friendly than its competitors. This was achieved through an advertising campaign shown throughout the world developed by Saatchi and Saatchi.

Television was the medium chosen for this campaign and over ten years BA spent £400 million. The title of the campaign, which was used consistently throughout, aimed for BA to be perceived as the 'world's favourite airline'. The backdrops and scenes created for the advertising were memorable. The same advertisements were shown in all the key international markets with language being the only modification. BA delivered a **global communication campaign** with high impact, using scenes and images that were appropriate across a range of cultures.

(v)   **Effectiveness**

The advertising achieved worldwide acclaim but more importantly BA achieved all its objectives. A close fit was demonstrated between the shift in BA's image in various countries and the appreciation scores for its advertising. British Airways still had to deliver the appropriate levels of product and service to its customers but without the global advertising campaign the achievement of its key marketing objectives would not have been possible.

11 Expenditure

Using our Money Wisely on Marketing Communications

by

A Marketing Manager

The amount of money any company spends on marketing communications, and advertising in particular, is absolutely crucial. Are the communications **working**, are they **effective**, are we getting **good value**, could we get it more **cost effectively**? These are all good questions, which that all management teams must ask themselves regularly and be able to respond to when challenged.

What I intend to do here is to provide some information about how we decide how much to spend on marketing communications. Before we look at these specific areas it is useful to consider what marketing communications is and what it is supposed to do. Then it will be possible to look at the **different approaches to budgeting**.

If you think about the key areas where, each and every day, we **communicate with various audiences**, it should come as no surprise that marketing communications is important to our success and can cost a great deal. Broadly, we communicate with the following.

- Customers
- Dealers
- Employees
- Shareholders
- Financial advisers

- Suppliers
- Local communities
- Competitors
- Media
- Many other interested parties

Of course the level of interaction will vary in intensity with each of these audiences depending upon a number of variables. However, marketing communications is about creating and sustaining a **dialogue** with each of these **stakeholder** audiences. We need to **inform** audiences about new developments within the company, new products and services and about what we as a company believe and value. We need to **persuade** audiences, especially customers and potential customers, we need to **demonstrate how we are different** and of value to each of them, and we need continually to **remind and reassure** our customers not only who we are but also about our products and services.

BA invested over £60m in their corporate rebranding exercise in order to be identified as a global, not British, airline. Kellogg's, Nestle, Cadbury's, Unilever and the many other fmcg manufacturers invest millions each year on advertising in order to maintain and/or grow their **market shares**. Organisations in the business-to-business sector spend much less on advertising but more on personal selling and sales support. The area where the investment is made is not important to this paper. We are, however, interested in the **effective** and efficient use of **limited resources**.

In order to inform, differentiate, persuade and/or remind (DRIP), we need to invest and allocate some of our finances to marketing communications. Choosing the right level of investment is important but it is not a science. We have learnt over the years and we have a good idea about what the right level of investment might be. Some companies allocate a **percentage of sales** as the appropriation, whilst others just take **last years' figure** and add a percentage for inflation. Others allocate what they can afford whilst a few just **guess**. All of these methods have flaws in that they are neither customer focused nor designed to do the right job.

Some other techniques involve **investing the same as our competitors**. Which competitor and how can we be sure that we are achieving real competitive **parity**? The **advertising/sales** (A/S) **ratio** provides an **industry benchmark** in order that we can understand whether we are investing above or below the industry average.

This ratio has proved useful but it does not provide the answer we are looking for as it focuses only on advertising. As we also use sales promotion, direct and interactive marketing, public relations, the sales force plus internal marketing communication activities, there are severe limitations to this approach.

It was reported that Procter & Gamble wanted to reduce their amount of advertising from 25% to 20% and use the 'savings' to fund price-offs in order to compete more **effectively** with their own-label competitors. A counter view from the company was that they wanted to use their advertising and media expenditure much more **efficiently** yet maintain their overall visibility. This was a strong strategic approach and it courted much criticism and debate.

By gauging the percentage of our communication spend against the total spent by all others in the market, we are able to determine what is known as **share of voice**. These figures can be compared to our **share of market** and through analysis we can determine how much we should spend to achieve the market share we set ourselves. Whilst this is intuitively appealing there are some real difficulties in making this work and it does not really apply to our growing market.

PIMS (Profit Impact of Marketing Strategy) is a database system that uses actual data from real organisations across a variety of industries and market sectors. Through analysis of the database it is possible to determine what **return on investment** can be achieved based upon a number of variables. Depending upon whether a company is market leader, number 2 or just another player it is possible to make judgements about, for example, the level of above and below-the-line promotional expenditure, or the right amount of trade communications.

We can use a number of these methods and compare the outcomes. We should determine what it is we want to achieve **(goals)** and how we think our various **push (trade)**, **pull (consumer)** and **profile (corporate)** communication strategies will work. We then determine the **actual costs** of putting it all into action, and then make changes as necessary. This **objective and task approach** is perhaps the soundest technique of them all, but it does require a great deal of **time** and accurate prediction in order to make it work.

Pedigree Petfoods said that after the tins and the cost of the meat, the third most important factor to be measured and evaluated was the **cost of the media** and **level of discounts** used to advertise their pet food products. This further serves to demonstrate that the level of communication spend can be a very significant part of an organisation's activities and needs a **strategic perspective**.

In order to grow and thrive it will be even more important for our company not only to make **good use** of marketing communications, but to also **invest** in communications in order that it maintains dialogue with the right audience, using with the right message at the right time.

12 Agency restructuring

Introduction

Advertising agencies have been subjected to a number of significant **external pressures** in the last ten to fifteen years. Their response to these pressures has been mixed, and in many cases cautious, perhaps mindful of the need to monitor and avoid fashion swings and management fads.

Reasons for possible incompatibility

The reasons why some of these organisations have failed to keep pace with their clients needs are as follows.

1   Hierarchical structures
2   Market complexity
3   Reliance on the commission payment scheme
4   Failure to implement integrated marketing communications
5   The plethora of new media and subsequent fragmentation
6   Audience fragmentation
7   The variable quality of overseas support
8   Poor positioning
9   Agency complacency

Many of these points are interrelated and the causality factor often hard to determine. Time does not permit a full examination of all these issues, so I shall select a few and consider some of the points in more detail.

The **structure** adopted by many advertising agencies is **hierarchical** and in many ways the necessary **speed of reaction** required by many clients. These structures have strong historical roots, and in that sense are hard to change. **International operations** demand consideration and preferably experience of **cross cultural issues**, **networking** and, in many cases, **delegation to country agencies**, some of whom may require more support and guidance than others. Hierarchies require **authority and control** in order that they function appropriately. Such conditions may not always exist overseas, may be incompatible with client structures and may hinder the decision making process.

Developing international and global brands is a complex activity which requires special skills, from both a client and agency perspective. These may be hard to secure. When looked at in terms of the level of investment associated with international brand support, the issue becomes increasingly complex.

Management consultancies have taken a lot of strategic work away from many advertising agencies. This has had a knock-on effect in terms of international brand support. Poor positioning therefore has been a contributory factor to this problem of incompatibility.

The plethora of **new media** and subsequent **fragmentation** of both audiences and media have proved problematic. Some traditional full service agencies have developed central media buying units in order to provide added value for clients, but the issue of media planning and scheduling has become more complex. When an international dimension is superimposed, the degree of complexity increases.

Complacency and a lack of drive to change is a contributory factor in many cases. A predilection to preserve the status quo regarding their **relationships with clients** suggests that some agencies lack strategic vision and may also not be fully aware of their clients' goals. The fault may, perhaps, lie with clients not communicating their marketing communication strategies effectively. Matters are certainly not helped by the willingness of many clients to change agencies mid term, or as a result of merger and acquisition activity.

How might agencies adjust?

There are therefore, many potential **gaps** between the **expectation** of clients and their respective agencies. One of the choices agencies need to make is whether to anticipate client needs internationally or whether to remain orientated to the domestic arena and make ad hoc arrangements to support any client who develops an overseas requirement.

How integrated does the agency need to be? Full integration for all agencies is obviously not practical, or strategically viable. However, in terms of meeting client needs, restructuring and adaptation to the new environment with a view to establishing differing levels of integration, and in this case international support, may be useful. Agencies need to establish the right balance of expertise and integration to suit client needs.

At the heart of this problem about incompatibility there seem to lie three main issues. These are about **structure**, **strategy** and **relationships**. Agencies and clients need direction and knowledge in order that they can manage these three variables, and in doing so reduce or at least minimise any gap in expectations and support.

13 Evaluate repositioning

Proposal for Article

To :   The ABC Marketing Journal
From :   CIM Diploma Student
Title :   The Repositioning of X
Date :   9 June 20XX

Rather than just present a standard answer, I have chosen to set out the structure of a suitable response to this question and interlace it with possible brand orientated comments.

A good response lies with the key words in the question. These key words are 'evaluates' and 'reposition' and these constitute the framework for the answer. The actual structure for the answer is given in the last sentence.

The answer should commence with a simple descriptive scene setting. For example:

For a long time Lucozade was seen as a restorative health drink which was only administered to sick children and nursing mothers. Indeed the messages transmitted during the early phase of the brand's life conditioned its audience to perceive the drink in exactly this way. It was positioned such that the only legitimate way to consume the product was if you were sick.

The problem associated with this was that the positioning restricted the number of people who could consume it. As a result the brand began to lose market share as competitor products took advantage of the niche (or hole) that Lucozade had forged for itself.

This then sets the scene and provides the context for the answer.

The next section is needed to confirm what positioning is. A formal definition would have been sufficient.

According to Kotler, **positioning** is the 'act of designing the company's offering and image so that they occupy a meaningful and distinct competitive position in the target customers' minds.'

Such comments clearly suggest that the positioning of products is a **communication based activity**, one that relies on the relative impact of a number of similar products and how they are perceived. Lucozade was positioned very clearly and to a defined audience, but the illness market was not large enough to sustain profitability and the well being of the brand.

Having set out what positioning is, it is then necessary to consider what the owners did in order to correct the falling market share and how repositioning the brand was to be a successful remedy.

Market research was undertaken to try to understand the attitudes people had towards the brand and to other soft drinks in the market. Results indicated that attitudes towards the brand and the taste were largely positive but the most interesting result was that people never made it their first choice purchase and never bought it for their own consumption. It was always a brand that was bought for others, and those others were normally sick. The brand strengths revolved around the drink's taste and restorative and energising powers. The research also revealed that there was a gap in the market for a high energy sports drink.

The only sensible course of action was to communicate a new set of parameters so that the new (desired) target audience could frame the brand, understand its benefits and values and perceive it in a new way.

It is at this point that the second requirement concerning the objectives and the campaign design should have been considered.

This repositioning exercise therefore required a new creative approach in order that the brand be perceived in a totally new way, one which capitalised on the strengths of taste and restorative powers. To appeal to the new sports drink market required an entirely different set of messages, a new communication paradigm to use the current vernacular.

It was decided to use a sports personality to endorse the brand. Daley Thompson was selected partly because of his successful career and partly because he was recognised and liked by a huge cross section of the population. To utilise his impact both television and magazine advertising were selected as the primary media. The advantages of this combination were:

(a)   They reached **mass audience**

(b)   It permitted the use of **colour** which allowed the strong orange colour of the bottle contrast with the label colours which are red and yellow

(c)   The **sports orientation** could be reflected in the **action and motion** that television presented.

Having explained, reasonably briefly the objectives and the campaign the concluding section needs to deal with the third requirement, the apparent effectiveness.

The success of the Lucozade repositioning can not be underestimated. Market share was restored, profits increased and the average age of the consumer was reduced by nearly 50%. In addition to this, retailers were pleased with the campaign, many of whom stock the drink in their refrigerators next to other soft drinks. **Brand extensions** are both a compliment and a testimony to the strength of brand. Needless to say, the Lucozade brand has experienced a number of subsequent successful extensions, all of which contribute to **brand equity**.

14 With or without?

REPORT

To: F W Smith - Managing Director of Super Beverages Ltd
From: T Leaf
Date: 4 June 20XX
Ref: UK tea and coffee market conditions

1   **Executive summary**

This report suggests that the tea and coffee *market* in the UK is large but competitive. There are a range of target markets, depending upon convenience or real product preference.

Cultural and social trends are considered: the indications are that the market is unlikely to decline but consumption may be static.

Growth within the market is dependent upon **brand switching**, which is difficult and can be expensive to achieve.

The **retail structure** reflects concentration in five main supermarkets for the convenience market. The independent sector deals with specialist beverages and each sector requires an entirely different marketing communications strategy.

The availability of a wide range of sophisticated *media* allows many opportunities to reach target audiences.

The report concludes by recommending that entry will depend upon **positioning** and **brand development**.

2   Situation analysis

This report has been prepared in order to assist you with your decision about whether or not to enter the UK market for tea and coffee. Various aspects of the market are considered, in particular the social and cultural trends, the retail structure and media opportunities.

3   Target end users

There are a number of segments that could be investigated further to determine the depth of potential.

- Convenience coffee users
- Real coffee users
- Tea bag users
- Real tea users
- Specialist tea users

The majority of tea is consumed by users spread across the socio-economic profile with coffee users skewed more to the ABC1 profile. Real coffee has become more popular in recent years, particularly in the 30 to 45 age range.

Opportunities may exist to **position** a new instant coffee or tea product by real **differentiation**. The market is currently dominated by a number of key brands, who use taste and smell (rich aroma), lifestyle (up-market and affluent) and usage (tea bag shape) as the principal means of differentiation. However, the market is relatively static and experiencing little real growth.

4   Cultural trends

Traditionally tea is drunk at the end of the afternoon and first thing in the morning and coffee is drunk at the end of a lunchtime or evening meal. These traditions are giving way as new products such as decaffeinated coffee and specialist teas become more popular. There are no significant regional differences to the consumption of either drink although more tea is drunk than coffee.

Consumption of tea in the UK is probably high in comparison to other European markets and from that point of view the UK market is attractive to new entrants. However, margins are tight and profitability is only likely to be generated by developing niche markets or by finding a new market segment.

5   Social trends

The number of cups of tea consumed may well continue to rise as the population ages. Tea is a relatively low-involvement product decision and it is important to establish **brand loyalty**, as taste deters switching.

The traditional family unit continues to be eroded as divorce rates continue to climb and the number of single parent families also increases. At the same time there is an increasing awareness of the need to eat a healthy diet and take more exercise. Because of this decaffeinated coffee products have taken a substantial foothold in the UK market.

Associated with this point about **lifestyle** is the increased attention being given to **green and ethical issues**. In particular the exploitation of third world workers has been highlighted by a number of pressure groups and in this sector there has been negative publicity directed at tea producers in India.

6 **Retail structure**

The retail structure has changed dramatically over the past 10 years. Five major supermarkets dominate 65% of food purchases. Manufacturer and own-label branded tea and coffee products are bought from these outlets, in packages that suggest a purchase cycle of 2 to 3 weeks. Tea bags are packaged in card based cartons; instant coffee is distributed in glass jars, which adds to weight and cost. To secure sufficient market coverage it will be necessary to gain a listing with at least one of these main supermarkets. A strong **promotional support package** will be expected, incorporating trade allowances, joint promotions and price deals to remain competitive and provide strategic leverage.

There are a number of specialist retailers who deal with high quality teas and coffees for those segments who prefer high grade, unbranded products. Depending upon the target market, attention will need to be paid to negotiations with central buyers for the supermarket sector or a variety of individual buyers in the independent sector.

7 **Media factors**

The UK is a media rich country, and the choice of media opportunities is expanding. With 98% of the population having access to at least a single television, it is possible to reach a **mass market** to develop a branded product.

There are numerous newspapers and consumer magazines in which advertising is possible. The development of a branded tea or coffee will be based partly around suitable print formats to reach different target audiences.

In addition to this, billboards, transport and cinema media will be an integral part of mass market campaigns.

With a purchase cycle of 2 to 3 weeks it will be necessary to generate and maintain top-of-mind **awareness**. Whilst this will incur high absolute costs the relative costs associated with reaching each member (or 1,000 members) of the target market will be quite small.

To promote tea and coffee in this market it will be necessary to use peripheral cues, as consumers are not particularly interested or **involved**. The use of long copy formats is not a requirement and so the media used to prompt **awareness and preference** will favour television and billboards rather than print.

The are a number of **trade magazines**, such as *The Grocer*, in which it will be necessary to communicate with the central **supermarket buyers** and, more importantly, the independent specialist buyers who run their own retail outlets. Unlike the consumer market, these **buyers are highly involved** and it will be necessary to provide detail about the product and its constituents and origins if **credibility** is to be established.

8 **Conclusion and recommendations**

The UK consumes huge quantities of tea and increasing quantities of coffee. The instant beverage market is driven by a number of major brands so successful entry will be dependent upon **accurate positioning and communication** with the target segments.

15 Netline technologies

To :   Marketing Director
From :   Marketing Communications Controller
Date :   8 Dec 20XX
Ref :   Key strategic marketing communication issues facing Netline Communications

1   Introduction

C-Guard represents a new product and it is likely to be copied within twelve months. Actions taken now will lay the foundation for the success of the product and for its ability to withstand future competition.

This report is in two sections. The first seeks to highlight the **key strategic issues** that impact on the marketing communications of C-Guard and the second sets out some **recommendations** in order that Netline successfully addresses these issues.

2   Key strategic issues

One of the problems associated with this part of the report is establishing the key strategic issues. General communication issues can be identified, but for the purposes of this report it is necessary to focus on the key strategic marketing communications issues. They are not presented in any particular order or priority.

1   The public's **perception** of the product and the values they place on the benefits of C-Guard

2   **Marketing channel**/franchisee related communications

3   The overall level of communication **effectiveness and efficiency** associated with the campaign

These three primary issues will now be explored.

2.1   The public's perception of the product and the values they place on the benefits of C-Guard

Public demand for C-Guard protection will be important in building the market and will be a significant factor in encouraging businesses to install the C-Guard system. In order that **business-to-business clients** be willing to install C-Guard, they should be persuaded that public opinion favours such facilities and that the annoyance factor of mobile phones needs to be addressed. Acceptance of the product concept is important, so it is crucial that initial communications convey appropriate messages (including the benefits of C-Guard).

The **attitudes and perceptions** of mobile phone users and non-users will be researched so that appropriate messages be conveyed and a dialogue established. Whilst further research is necessary to establish which of the many public 'areas' (or vertical market segments) have the greatest need/potential, it is important to develop C-Guard as the market leader and maintain its number one position.

2.2   Marketing channel/franchisee communications

A key strategic communication issue has already been resolved. Control over **brand identity** is not to be devolved to franchisees and responsibility will remain with Netline. However, the franchisees appointed to distribute C-Guard require support not only with training and installation issues but also with brand support and their communications with their employees and customers.

Communications in the marketing channel are potentially confusing. On the one hand, communications between Netline and franchisees might be generally **informative and motivational**, whilst communications between the franchisee and their clients will probably be more **emotive and persuasive** in nature. This issue needs to be appreciated and suitable strategies put in position.

2.3 The overall level of communication effectiveness and efficiency associated with the campaign

In order that the marketing communications for C-Guard are effective and efficient the total communication process should be highly professional. A number of areas need to be addressed if the effectiveness and efficiency is to be maximised, for example, the **international dimension** of C-Guard's distribution, the **financial resources** to be appropriated, the **agencies** to be appointed, the **goals** to be achieved, the **messages** to be sent to different stakeholders and the **media** to be used to convey them.

3.0 Recommendations

In the light of the key strategic communication issues established earlier it is necessary to make some recommendations about how the issues can be overcome.

3.1 The public's perception of the product and the values they place on the benefits of C-Guard

Public perception, whether mobile phone users or not, is crucial to the success of the product. To help influence perceptions the development of a **strong brand** for C-Guard is imperative. Associated with branding is the **position** C-Guard is seen to occupy in the market.

A **pull communication strategy** is necessary, and the essential aspect of the strategy should be the **development of a brand**. Through branding, Netline will have the opportunity to communicate a **consistent and relevant identity** so that the public can recognise quickly and easily understand the values associated with the product. Branding will also enable the development of public **attitudes and awareness**, important in the first six months of the launch. A decision about the degree to which C-Guard and/or Netline is branded (**product** and **corporate brand** respectively) needs further consideration.

Associated with branding is the way in which C-Guard is **perceived and positioned** in the mind of the public and business customers. **Positioning** is important as once established it is a lengthy and difficult to reposition. Care must be taken to associate the brand with **relevant values** and substitute products. Is the no smoking similarity and association a viable long term position for C-Guard?

3.2 Marketing channel/franchisee communications

A **push communication strategy** will need to be established. This strategy, aimed at communicating with members of the marketing channel, should seek to provide **message consistency** and reflect the desired level of quality in order that the overall values of C-Guard be reinforced. This will also assist the motivation of franchisees to work on the C-Guard brand, but it will also be communicated to their business-to-business customers.

The development of **strong franchise relationships** will be important in order to establish market credentials and to withstand strong competitive activity in the future.

3.3 **The overall level of communication effectiveness and efficiency associated with the campaign**

The effectiveness and impact that the campaign has will be a reflection of the degree to which the marketing communication activities are integrated. Management are responsible for these decisions and it is imperative that they make these decisions on a holistic basis and that the CEO is seen to lead and endorse the integrated approach.

It may not be possible to achieve full scale integration at the outset, but that should not deter from **setting targets** for the establishment of an integrated approach. This may be achieved on an incremental basis by first aiming to **co-ordinate the messages conveyed** through the promotional tools and then moving to a co-ordinated marketing mix.

To assist this process, it is necessary to ensure that the **business philosophy**, **marketing strategy** and **promotional objectives** be consistent with each other. Management play an important role co-ordinating, advising and controlling this aspect of the communication process. **Internal communications** will be important in creating internal identity with the C-Guard brand and the values associated with Netline's overall business development.

Marketing communication agencies need to be appointed who can not only provide and identify with the integration requirements but who have the necessary networks, experience and potential to assist the international development and distribution of C-Guard. Decisions about whether messages should be **adapted or standardised** in fresh international markets can be assisted by the contacts and experience of these important outsourced providers.

The **financial resources** will need to be allocated such that the **push, pull and profile** strategy investment requirements are met. Use of the **PIMS database** may be of assistance in order to generate the best possible **return on investment**.

The campaign will require a substantial amount of advertising in order to **create awareness** and **establish brand values**. Management need to ensure that the media time/space purchased is bought at the best possible rate. It is probable that Netline need to appoint a **media buying house** in order to derive the best deal.

In addition to the advertising, all the **promotional tools** will be used at some time in the campaign. Public relations will be important, especially at the launch, to carry public opinion. Sales promotions will be required at certain times in the financial year to encourage businesses to install the system, direct marketing will be used to create associations and identity with C-Guard and personal selling will be required to set up franchises and for selling into business accounts.

To assist the goal for **effectiveness and efficiency** a marketing communications plan will need to be generated. A degree of **flexibility** will be beneficial, but the use of the planning approach will serve to **focus** thoughts, help **co-ordinate activities** in line with the promotional goals and will act as a **communication device** so that all involved with the marketing communication activities are aware of what is happening and when.

4   **Conclusion**

C-Guard represents an important commercial opportunity and a chance to meet a real customer need. Marketing communications are important in order that these opportunities and needs are satisfied, and the development of an integrated approach represents a step in the right direction.

List of Key Concepts and Index

BPP
PROFESSIONAL EDUCATION

See overleaf for information on other
BPP products and how to order

CIM Order

To BPP Publishing Ltd, Aldine Place, London W12 8AA

Tel: 020 8740 2211. Fax: 020 8740 1184
email: publishing@bpp.com
online: www.bpp.com

Mr/Mrs/Ms (Full name) _____

Daytime delivery address _____

_____ Postcode _____

Daytime Tel _____ Date of exam (month/year) _____

	6/03 Texts	9/03 Kits	Success Tapes	Passcards
CERTIFICATE (STAGE 1) NEW SYLLABUS				
1 Marketing Fundamentals	£19.95 ☐	£9.95 ☐	£12.95 ☐	£5.95 ☐
2 Marketing Environment	£19.95 ☐	£9.95 ☐	£12.95 ☐	£5.95 ☐
3 Customer Communications	£19.95 ☐	£9.95 ☐	£12.95 ☐	£5.95 ☐
4 Marketing in Practice	£19.95 ☐	£9.95 ☐	£12.95 ☐	£5.95 ☐
ADVANCED CERTIFICATE (STAGE 2) NEW SYLLABUS				
5 The Marketing Customer Interface	£19.95 ☐	£9.95 ☐	N/A	£5.95 ☐
6 Management Information for Marketing Decisions	£19.95 ☐	£9.95 ☐	N/A	£5.95 ☐
7 Effective Management for Marketing	£19.95 ☐	£9.95 ☐	N/A	£5.95 ☐
8 Marketing Operations	£19.95 ☐	£9.95 ☐	N/A	£5.95 ☐
DIPLOMA OLD SYLLABUS *				
9 Integrated Marketing Communications	£19.95 ☐	£9.95 ☐	£12.95 ☐	N/A
10 International Marketing Strategy	£19.95 ☐	£9.95 ☐	£12.95 ☐	N/A
11 Strategic Marketing Management: Planning and Control	£19.95 ☐	£9.95 ☐	£12.95 ☐	N/A
12 Strategic Marketing Management: Analysis and Decision (9/03)	£25.95 ☐	N/A	N/A	N/A

* Texts and kits for remaining new syllabus items will be available in the spring and summer of 2004.

SUBTOTAL £ ☐

POSTAGE & PACKING

Study Texts and Kits

	First	Each extra
UK	£5.00	£2.00	£ ☐
Europe**	£6.00	£4.00	£ ☐
Rest of world	£20.00	£10.00	£ ☐

Success Tapes/Passcards

	First	Each extra
UK	£2.00	£1.00	£ ☐
Europe**	£3.00	£2.00	£ ☐
Rest of world	£8.00	£8.00	£ ☐

Reduced postage rates apply if you **order online** at www.bpp.com

Grand Total (Cheques to *BPP Publishing*) I enclose a cheque for (incl. Postage) £ ☐

Or charge to Access/Visa/Switch

Card Number ☐☐☐☐

Expiry date ☐☐ Start Date ☐☐

Issue Number (Switch Only) ☐☐

Signature _____

We aim to deliver to all UK addresses inside 5 working days. A signature will be required. Orders to all EU addresses should be delivered within 6 working days.

All other orders to overseas addresses should be delivered within 8 working days.

** Europe includes the Republic of Ireland and the Channel Islands.

REVIEW FORM & FREE PRIZE DRAW

All original review forms from the entire BPP range, completed with genuine comments, will be entered into one of two draws on 31 January 2003 and 31 July 2003. The names on the first four forms picked out on each occasion will be sent a cheque for £50.

Name: _____   **Address**: _____

_____

_____

How have you used this Text? *(Tick one box only)*	**During the past six months do you recall seeing/receiving any of the following?** *(Tick as many boxes as are relevant)*
☐ Home study (book only)	☐ Our advertisement in the *Marketing Success*
☐ On a course: college _____	☐ Our advertisement in *Marketing Business*
☐ With 'correspondence' package	☐ Our brochure with a letter through the post
☐ Other _____	☐ Our brochure with *Marketing Business*

Why did you decide to purchase this Text? *(Tick one box only)*	**Which (if any) aspects of our advertising do you find useful?** *(Tick as many boxes as are relevant)*
☐ Have used companion Kit	☐ Prices and publication dates of new editions
☐ Have used BPP Texts in the past	☐ Information on Text content
☐ Recommendation by friend/colleague	☐ Facility to order books off-the-page
☐ Recommendation by a lecturer at college	☐ None of the above
☐ Saw advertising	
☐ Other _____	

Have you used the companion Practice & Revision Kit for this subject?   ☐ Yes   ☐ No

Your ratings, comments and suggestions would be appreciated on the following areas.

	Very useful	Useful	Not useful
Introductory section (How to use this text, study checklist, etc)	☐	☐	☐
Setting the Scene	☐	☐	☐
Syllabus coverage	☐	☐	☐
Action Programmes and Marketing at Work examples	☐	☐	☐
Chapter roundups	☐	☐	☐
Quick quizzes	☐	☐	☐
Illustrative questions	☐	☐	☐
Content of suggested answers	☐	☐	☐
Index	☐	☐	☐
Structure and presentation	☐	☐	☐

	Excellent	Good	Adequate	Poor
Overall opinion of this Text	☐	☐	☐	☐

Do you intend to continue using BPP Study Texts/Kits?   ☐ Yes   ☐ No

Please note any further comments and suggestions/errors on the reverse of this page.

Please return to: Kate Machattie, BPP Publishing Ltd, FREEPOST, London, W12 8BR

REVIEW FORM & FREE PRIZE DRAW (continued)

Please note any further comments and suggestions/errors below.

FREE PRIZE DRAW RULES

1 Closing date for 31 January 2003 draw is 31 December 2002. Closing date for 31 July 2003 draw is 30 June 2003.

2 Restricted to entries with UK and Eire addresses only. BPP employees, their families and business associates are excluded.

3 No purchase necessary. Entry forms are available upon request from BPP Publishing. No more than one entry per title, per person. Draw restricted to persons aged 16 and over.

4 Winners will be notified by post and receive their cheques not later than 6 weeks after the relevant draw date. Lists of winners will be published in BPP's *focus* newsletter following the relevant draw.

5 The decision of the promoter in all matters is final and binding. No correspondence will be entered into.